THIS PRECARIOUS MOMENT

For more resources please go to www.ThisPrecariousMoment.com

- Links to videos
- Study questions for all chapters for small groups and Sunday School classes

THIS PRECARIOUS MOMENT

SIX URGENT STEPS THAT WILL SAVE YOU, YOUR FAMILY, AND OUR COUNTRY

JAMES L. GARLOW AND DAVID BARTON

ASSISTED BY
TIM BARTON & KERRY TEPLINSKY

SALEMBOOKS
an imprint of Regnery Publishing

Salem Books™ is a trademark of Salem Communications Holding Corporation
Regnery® is a registered trademark of Salem Communications Holding Corporation

Cataloging-in-Publication data on file with the Library of Congress

ISBN 978-1-62157-790-4
e-book ISBN 978-1-62157-845-1

Published in the United States by
Salem Books, an imprint of
Regnery Publishing
A Division of Salem Media Group
300 New Jersey Ave NW
Washington, DC 20001
www.Regnery.com

Manufactured in the United States of America

10 9 8 7 6 5 4 3 2

Books are available in quantity for promotional or premium use. For information on discounts and terms, please visit our website: www.Regnery.com.

Jim dedicates this book to
Rosemary

David dedicates this book to
Cheryl

SPECIAL THANKS

Jim and David are indebted to many people for helping this book become a reality.

We say thank you to the entire Regnery Publishing team, but especially to president Marji Ross, who believed in us, and to Gary Terashita, editor-in-chief of Salem Books, who proved to be such a patient and understanding acquisitions and text editor.

Other people helped along the way including:

- Researchers Sarah Freeman, Kristina Smith, Katie Schonhoff, and Jonathan Richie
- Audrea and JP Decker who, as brilliant cultural observers and political leaders, brought a fresh millennial perspective on many issues.

Jim and David are deeply indebted to a stellar immigration attorney:

- Esther Valdes who spent hours with us, helping identify and define key issues in the debate.

We are profoundly grateful for two writers and researchers who labored many hours alongside us:

- Tim Barton, son of David, carried the load on the Millennials section. As a millennial and a critical thinker, he added a dimension Jim and David could not have brought
- Dr. Kerry Teplinsky, a cardiologist who along with his lawyer wife gave up their occupations to live in Israel. Although, wife Sandy Teplinsky is known for her numerous published works on Israel, it was Kerry who researched and contributed much to the section on Israel.

We were so dependent upon these superb thinkers and writers who assisted us in such profound ways. Their "fingerprints" are on those two sections.

We say thank you to understanding family members who were so supportive and understanding of all the extended hours (and even key events we missed) as we labored on this book.

CONTENTS

THE TIME IS NOW

(David and Jim are co-authors of this book, but this first chapter is written by Jim.)

I n late December 2016, and early January 2017, the nation was still spinning from the contentious election between Hillary Clinton and Donald Trump. As the inauguration of Mr. Trump was approaching, the same thought kept coming to my mind.

I believe it was something God was telling me. After all, the Bible says, "Commit your works to the Lord, and he will establish your *thoughts*" (Proverbs 16:3, KJV). The recurrent thought I just couldn't get away from was we are at a tipping point as a nation. Four major issues have to be promptly and directly addressed if we are to survive as the same strong country we have been in previous generations.

Those four topics are:

- Racial healing
- The immigration disaster
- A spiritual revival among Millennials
- The relationship between the United States and Israel.

Of course, there are many issues that need to be addressed, but these four dominated my thinking, and I believe they were impressed on me by the Lord.

The first time I verbalized this impression was on January 19, 2017. At twelve noon on that day (and exactly twenty-four hours before the swearing in of the new president), I was leading an Inaugural Prayer Event a few blocks from the US Capitol. It was at this meeting I first publicly laid out these four issues, telling the crowd, "*We have to see racial healing, the immigration challenges fixed, a spiritual and intellectual revival among Millennials, and the restoration of a proper relationship between the US and Israel.*" In my thinking, a clock started ticking that day.

ADDRESSING THE FOUR

Of those four issues, we have seen a great beginning toward restoring the proper relationship between the United States and Israel. Trump, during his presidential campaign, outlined changes he would make, and he has begun to follow through. For example, he announced the US embassy in Israel would be moved to Jerusalem,[1] became the first sitting president to visit the Western Wall in Jerusalem (one of the holiest Jewish sites in Israel),[2] decertified the Iran nuclear deal[3] that directly threatened the security of Israel,[4] and appointed a strong and unequivocal defender of Israel as US Ambassador to the United Nations[5] who has unilaterally vetoed UN resolutions hostile to Israel.[6] The Israeli Ambassador to the United States has affirmed that current political relations between the two countries are the best they have been in modern history[7] (but there still remains a vast disconnect in many churches and among many people of faith that must be confronted and solved).

But although we are beginning to restore the relationship between the United States and Israel in some areas, little progress has been made in addressing the ethnic strife in our nation. Immigration issues also have remained largely unresolved, and we have not yet seen a desperately needed spiritual renewal among Millennials resulting in Biblical thinking and living.

THIS BOOK

While on a trip to Washington, DC, in early 2017, I met with Marji Ross, president and publisher of Regnery Publishing. We were discussing a book I would write for them, and I casually shared I felt we had to resolve four national issues. She stopped, looked up at me, and pointedly said, "Write on that!" I paused for a moment and then said, "Okay, I will!"

I asked to co-author the book with David Barton, and the idea was quickly embraced (a great decision on their part). David is nationally known and needs no introduction anywhere he goes. He wrote the lion's share of this book—he did the heavy lifting.

DAVID BARTON

Many are unaware David owns what has been described as the world's largest privately owned collection of early-American writings and artifacts (more than 120,000 originals or copies of originals from before 1812), including handwritten writings from our Founding Fathers. Most authors document their writings about history by relying on secondary or tertiary sources. Not David. He actually owns the primary sources—the eyewitness records—and he documents from them.

I have been in his impressive library and museum. In fact, I was there when a vocal critic and noted academic came to try to prove David was wrong (at least from his viewpoint) on historical matters. David didn't argue. He merely motioned for a staff member to produce the original writings that backed up each of his points. He not only grasps the issues, he owns the sources.

In real life, David and I have essentially swapped roles. I have a Ph.D. in historical theology. David has a bachelor's degree in Religious Education. However, in life, I became the pastor of a local congregation and have been my entire adult life. David, on the other hand, has become a brilliant historian, recognized as an historical expert not only by textbook publishers but also by state legislatures and government agencies, as well as state and federal courts. He is the perfect person with whom to partner on this project.

FOUR THINGS—OR SIX THINGS?

You may wonder why the subtitle of this book has "six things" rather than "four things."

As we began our work on the four things, we quickly saw two more things were inseparable from the other four and that lasting solutions for the four would not be achieved without addressing these two as well, so we included them:

- The need for the Christian church to actually act like the church, once again operating by Biblical teachings and standards and addressing issues from that viewpoint
- Rekindling our understanding of America's founding on a distinctly Biblical foundation, openly operating (until recent years) under Christian principles.

PROVISO

We recognize each of these six topics is loaded with landmines.

For example, if anyone today makes a comment about racial issues, someone will immediately decry him or her as a "racist." This label has become a sledgehammer to discredit persons willing to engage the issue as well as to intimidate others from speaking out. But we can't remain silent and on the sidelines. It is because we long to see the sin of racism obliterated and its effects on our nation reduced that we will directly confront this issue.

Equally volatile is the topic of immigration. Verbal grenades are launched by one side or the other whenever this topic is addressed. But if we want to see a solution, it will be rooted in Scriptural and historical understandings rather than on the misinterpretation of Scriptural passages so commonplace in much of the religious and political communities today.

As with the other issues, the word "Israel" can hardly be uttered without evoking some reaction. But we must have an honest Biblical and historical understanding of Israel and know why our relationship with Israel matters so much more than with any other nation.

And Millennials are our future—they are the next leaders in everything. Medicine. Military. Politics. Religion. You name it. Everything. But statistics show they currently are the most secular and history-illiterate generation since America's founding. As the present generation steps aside and the new one begins to lead, we long to see them grounded in Biblical and historical truth.

Also, statistics show that much of the Christian church is weaker than at any time in our history. It has lost both its backbone and its voice and is no longer recognized as a significant influence on any issue. This is not conjecture; it is documented fact. A primary reason people are dropping out of church is it is irrelevant to practical daily living,[8] and as a result, church attendance has been plummeting.[9]

Finally, Americans·no longer follow Jesus's admonition to judge a tree by its fruits (Matthew 7:16)—we can no longer point to history to show what works and what doesn't, whether in government, law, public policy, religion, or anything else. We have developed national amnesia.

America is more polarized today than at any time since the years leading up to the Civil War. If there are to be solutions reached and a national healing achieved, we must openly address these issues and begin a dialogue on them.

THE PRAYER

Regardless of which side of these issues you come down on, we pray what is in this book will create a conversation and help bridge the rift separating Americans on these important topics.

SECTION ONE

RACIAL HEALING

*There is neither Jew nor Greek, there is neither
slave nor free man, there is neither male nor
female; for you are all one in Christ Jesus.*

GALATIANS 3:28, NASB

The goal of this section is to enhance understanding regarding the sin
of racism and its causes and examine what we can do to encourage
racial healing.

CHAPTER 1

ESTABLISHING A FOUNDATION

What can two white guys (Garlow and Barton) say about the topic of racism? A lot. Why? Because racism is a human problem directly addressed by both the Bible and history. Admittedly, there are areas where two white guys cannot make a difference. Regardless, we care deeply and personally about the racial divide in America. Along with most Americans, we long for racial unity and racial healing.

Although racism exists with all ethnic groups, our focus here will be primarily on black–white relations, which is what usually dominates public discussions. But there are definite truths regarding racism (and the solutions for it) that apply to every race. We will cover those in this section.

PROCEED WITH CAUTION

It seems almost impossible today to discuss racial issues without setting off emotional responses or outbursts. The issue has become so super-charged and often involves such hypersensitivity many simply won't touch it. Sadly, most discussions of racial themes have become loaded with figurative land mines, and there is so much polarization on this issue that regardless of your race, you are likely to be criticized for your views:

- WHITES accuse BLACKS of whining when they bring up inequities in life or hearken back to past historic injustices
- WHITES accuse other WHITES of pandering when they try to reach out and understand blacks on difficult racial issues
- BLACKS accuse WHITES of being racists when they speak against the practices, policies, or beliefs of black leaders
- BLACKS accuse other BLACKS of being "Uncle Toms" when they agree with whites or believe differently from the vocal black leaders in the culture.

In such a climate, what progress can be made?

Being aware that whatever we write may be vigorously criticized by someone caused us to wonder whether to even address this subject. But we can't ignore this topic for the simple reason God doesn't.

SIN REQUIRES REPENTANCE

At its core, racism is a heart problem—a problem of sin. Although some view it as a political problem with political solutions or as an economic problem with economic solutions, foundationally, it is a spiritual problem. Although government support can be useful on some issues regarding racism, its funds, programs, and laws will not change the human heart. Because racism is a violation of Biblical truth, genuine racial healing will require repentance before God for resentment against those with a different skin color or ethnic culture.

CHAPTER 2

DEFINITIONS ACCORDING TO THE BIBLE AND OTHER LEADERS

There is no shortage of headlines telling Americans of their deep racial dislike for one another. Are these banners right? Is America racist?

WHAT IS RACISM?

First, let's define the terms.

Interestingly, racism is a modern word, being used first in the early twentieth century.[10] (Of course, racism existed long before the word came into use, for racism has been a problem with humans throughout their 5,500 years of recorded history.)

By definition, racism involves *"the idea that one's own race is superior and has the right to dominate others, or that a particular racial group is inferior to the others."*[11] Racism can thus be expressed in two ways: one can be a racist by favoring their own race above others, or one can be a racist by opposing another race (or races).

In America today, the term *racism* is generally considered to be whites against blacks,[12] but in reality, racism exists whenever *any* race has an over-affection for itself or is against the race of another. So it is just as possible to be a black racist who elevates his own race as it is to be a white racist who denigrates the black race. (Some contend blacks cannot be racists because they are inherently the underclass to the whites who have the power, thus the term "white privilege." We will examine this issue later.) When historic segregation occurred at the hands of whites, it was wrong; sadly, however, there are places where it is occurring again—but this time from within the black community,[13] and it is just as racist and just as wrong.

Traditionally there were only four overarching categories of race: Caucasian, Mongoloid, Negroid, and Australoid.[14] However, a term closely associated with race and very familiar to Americans is *ethnicity*,[15] and there are as many as 24,000 ethnicities subdivided under these four races.[16] Since the 1950s, the United Nations no longer acknowledges races but rather ethnicities.[17]

As will be seen shortly, from a Biblical viewpoint there is only one race: the *human race*. But in this section, we will use the term "race" according to contemporary usage; that is, the "black race," "white race," and so forth.

THE BIBLE

So what does the Bible say about ethnicity and race?

In the New Testament, ethnos (ἔθνη) is the Greek word forming the basis of our word *ethnicity* (there are also similar Greek words, including φυλή, λαός, γλωσσα, γένος, etc.). In the Old Testament (that is, the Hebrew Scriptures), there is a Hebrew equivalent for ethnos: מִזְּוֹג. Each of these Bible words is a descriptive used to help inform the narrative—like saying someone is from Florida, is tall, is right-handed, lives in Minneapolis, has blue eyes, and so forth. However, the Bible generally divides humans into only two significant groups: (1) those who know and follow Jehovah God and (2) those who don't.

That's as simple as it gets for the reason that God is not concerned with race. For example, a Jew is one who follows God and obeys the Torah and can be Semitic, Anglo, Asian, Hispanic, Black, Indian, Slavic, or any other race or ethnicity. So, too, with Christians. It is the relationship with God that matters.

Race, ethnicity, and skin color are superficial; they will pass away. (As science acknowledges, *"All races share 99.99+% of the same genetic materials, which means that division of race is largely subjective."*[18]) God simply does not focus on the 00.01% that makes us different. As the Bible affirms:

The LORD sees not as man sees: man looks on the outward appearance, but the LORD looks on the heart. 1 SAMUEL 16:7, ESV

Racism is the result of looking on the outside rather than the inside. The Bible openly rejects the notion of racism and its outward distinctions:

From one man He made every nation of humanity to live all over the earth. ACTS 17:26, ISV

If you show partiality, you are committing sin and are convicted by the law as transgressors. JAMES 2:9, ESV

There is neither Jew nor Greek, there is neither slave nor free, there is no male and female, for you are all one in Christ Jesus. GALATIANS 3:28, ESV (By the way, even though our focus in this section is on racism, it is noteworthy that this verse also addresses elitism, i.e., "slave or free," along with sexism, i.e., "male and female.")

God doesn't value an individual based on his or her race. This was a lesson learned by Vietnam veteran Dave Roever (www.daveroever.org), who related:

I left my tear ducts on a river bank in Vietnam decades ago when I was horrendously injured by a white phosphorus hand grenade exploding in my hand, resulting in massive blast damage to the upper trunk of my body—back, chest, arms, hands, and face. A white hot chemical coated over 37 percent of my body causing severe third degree burns.

As a result of his horrific injuries, Roever became bitter, depressed, and empty, hating not only himself but everyone, regardless of their race—in fact, he hated the entire human race. It all changed one day when a woman visited him:

That day I sat there on Ward 14A, Brooke Army Medical Center, San Antonio, Texas, facing the ward entrance. I saw everyone who came in . . . and they saw me: one eye, one nostril, one ear; no hair; scarred and burned. They couldn't miss me! . . . She entered unannounced and walked straight to me. She was robed in hospital garb, which indicated that she was a patient. But why was this woman on an all-male ward? She was a black woman with pink hands which were void of the ebony color of her race—an indication that she recently had been burned. *"Hi there,"* she said, but my intense pain and self-pity maintained a steady, passive glare, not allowing me to be conversational. I was not prejudicially rude. I hated everyone and everything equally! She passed on by—or so I thought. A moment later, she placed her pink, burned hands that were once black, on my pink, burned shoulder that was once white. I have seen us with the cover pulled back and we are all the same color. Pink! Pink is not a movement, a political rallying point, or a rock group. It's more than a color. It's the common denominator of the human race. After all the race-baiting and hatred between religions and politics, after the prejudice and cultural clashes, pink is the color of mankind—the unanimous likeness of all humanity, created in the likeness of God. God is pink. Forever I will be grateful for that black woman who courageously crawled over the barrier of race to reach out to this hurting white boy who could not fend for himself. As she touched my shoulder, she began to pray and two people of the same color—the color of pain, the color of hurt, the color of loss—bonded together.[19]

God's view of ethnicity does not involve race, but only whether individuals know Him. This should be our view as well. In fact, God tells us to help everyone come to know Him, so the result will be what was reported by the Apostle John:

I looked, and behold, a great multitude that no one could number, from every nation, from all tribes and peoples and languages, standing before the throne and before the Lamb, clothed in white robes, with palm branches in their hands. REVELATION 7:9, ESV

From God's perspective, there is only one race: the human race. There definitely are different cultures, and sometimes there is ethnic strife between them, which breaks the heart of God. The cry of our hearts is for the human race to become one great family, as God intended. That is why we are directly addressing this issue.

CHAPTER 3

PROGRESSIVISM'S DESTRUCTIVE "IDENTITY POLITICS"

One result of secular thinking and Progressivism (on a rapid rise in America today) is that it turns the focus away from the Biblical emphasis on the general human race and individuals within it and instead places the focus on specific races and ethnicities. The result is what is known as "identity politics," whereby individual Americans matter only as part of some larger group, such as Latinos, African Americans, homosexuals, feminists, Muslims, union members, seniors, and so forth. Consequently, Congress now enacts hate crime laws determining which *groups* will receive extra protection (such as homosexuals and lesbians) and which will not (such as veterans and seniors).[20] Under such misguided policies, no longer is every individual equal, and some groups are definitely favored over others.

One way this approach manifests itself is by dedicating months to emphasize specific groups. Thus there is an official month for Black History, Irish American Heritage, Women's History, Asian Pacific American Heritage, Haitian Heritage, Jewish American Heritage, LGBT Pride/History (actually, this group has two months officially dedicated to its study),

Hispanic Heritage, Filipino American History, Polish American Heritage, Native American Heritage, Alaskan Native Heritage, and so forth.

In today's world, if there is not a month for your particular group, you are being discriminated against. Therefore, to combat any and all racism, we should set aside a month to honor left-handed redheads, a month for those who weigh more than 135 pounds, another for those under the age of fourteen or over eighty-six, one for blue-eyed Hispanics, and one for dark-eyed Anglos (or for that matter, any month to honor Anglos at all, or even men in general).

But this is not God's approach. The best way to achieve an inclusive society is His practice of recognizing individuals as part of the human race rather than groups within the human race.

RACE, NATIONS, CULTURES

However, the fact that God focuses on the individual rather than the race does not mean He sees all nations as being one. He doesn't. The concept of race is very different from the concept of nations. It is God Who draws the lines and boundaries of the various nations:

> And He made from one man every *nation* of mankind to live on all the face of the earth, having determined allotted periods and the *boundaries of their dwelling place.* ACTS 17:26, ESV

Not being race conscious does not mean nations and national borders are irrelevant. Moreover, although there is equality in the worth of all individuals regardless of race, this does not mean all their corresponding cultures are the same. Each race and ethnicity adopts its own distinct culture, and they vary widely. The Apostle Paul recognized this, acknowledging:

> To the Jews I became like a Jew, to win the Jews. To those under the law I became like one under the law (though I myself am not under the law), so as to win those under the law. To those not having the law I became like one not having the law (though I am not free from God's law but am under Christ's law), so as to win those not having the law. To the weak I became weak, to win the weak. 1 CORINTHIANS 9:20–22, NIV

RACISM VERSUS CULTURE PREFERENCES

Paul understood that certain customs come to be associated with specific groups of people. It remains that way today. Some cultures (even within the same race or ethnicity) have distinctive styles of music, prefer certain types of cars, use unique jargon, or wear a particular style of clothing. And if individuals from one group do not connect with those who have different cultural practices, it does not necessarily mean they are racist.

For example, individuals who are immersed in rap music will likely be uncomfortable hanging with those who always listen to country-western music, regardless of whether the hearer and listener are both black, both white, one of each, or neither. Similarly, those into fine arts and delicate living are probably put off by the NASCAR world. This is simply a discomfort with certain aspects of the culture associated with a particular group or race rather than a manifestation of racism.

After all, if we were all in agreement on the same cultural practices, there would only be one color of paint on houses, one brand of peanut butter on the shelves, and one style of car in the auto mall. Culture is not race or ethnicity; the two are different and should not be confused.

CHAPTER 4

AMERICAN SLAVERY

Slavery was part of the American landscape for 240 years. It officially ended in 1865, but the racism that produced it remained long afterward, re-manifesting itself throughout subsequent generations in ways ranging from lynchings and Black Codes to harsh discrimination and denial of basic civil rights. The wounds from slavery are old, and its after-effects are countless and deep, and for many today, these wounds are still gaping.

For example, one of David's dear friends was the famous black leader Rev. C. L. Jackson. He was the first pastor in America to be televised nationally from the pulpit on a weekly basis. He built a successful mega-church (Pleasant Grove Missionary Baptist Church) with more than 5,000 families, preached across the world, started hundreds of churches in America and abroad, penned a dozen books, traveled to foreign nations in company with a US president, and was the first black man in the modern era to be invited to attend a service in a major white church in South Africa and to be invited before the South African parliament.

Despite his renown, the Rev. Jackson's beginnings were humble. He was raised in deep east Texas, eight miles from the nearest city. His family personally experienced racism and racial attacks in ways no one should. His aunt was taken by a mob, raped, and murdered, and the crowd would not allow the family to reclaim the body. Other blacks fleeing lynchings came to their home for safety but were still caught and lynched on a nearby railway bridge.

When Pastor Jackson's mother became pregnant with him, her daily prayer over her unborn child was, "Lord, if this baby be a boy, don't let him hang from a bridge!" This is quite a sobering prayer, and frankly, it is unthinkable for many Americans today. But not for Pastor Jackson. In fact, one of his own staff members was lynched in 1973. Another of Barton's friends, Bishop Jim Lowe, bears on his body the scars of a church bombing he survived—a church bombed simply because it was a church attended by blacks. Hundreds of thousands alive in America today have personally experienced what most Americans believe is only ancient history.

Sadly, for generations, many pastors and political leaders invoked the Bible to justify slavery and racism.[21] It is true slavery existed in Bible times, but never in the way it was practiced in America. To the contrary, slavery was inflicted on national enemies as a lesser punishment than the death usually given them (Joshua 9:24–27, Deuteronomy 20:10–11). And slavery in the Bible was not on the basis of race, nor was it a domestic practice. In fact, the Hebrew Scriptures (what Christians call the Old Testament) decree the death penalty for slave trafficking (Exodus 21:16), and the Christian Scriptures (the New Testament) affirm that God ordained civil law to be used, among other purposes, against *"slave-traders"* (1 Timothy 1:8–10, WEB). And Jesus Himself said part of His mission on earth was to loose *"them that are bound"* (Isaiah 61:1, KJV) and to proclaim *"liberty to the captives"* (Luke 4:18, ESV).

Because slavery touched so many American families and inflicted such deep and lasting wounds in a way nothing else has, it is helpful to know some of the horrors historically associated with it in order to understand the various types of deep injury handed down across the generations.

Let's go back to the 1850s. At that time, the nation was fully polarized—both the pro- and antislavery sides were fully developed and at peak strengths.

The proslavery US Supreme Court seemed to capture the essence of the racist beliefs of the slavery side with its declaration in the infamous *Dred Scott* decision

> They [black Americans] had . . . been regarded as beings of an
> inferior order and altogether unfit to associate with the white
> race, either in social or political relations; and so far inferior
> that they had no rights which the white man was bound to

respect; and that the negro might justly and lawfully be reduced to slavery for his benefit.[22]

This racial contempt was also apparent in public policy, such as the infamous Fugitive Slave Law, which allowed southern slave-owners and slave-hunters to kidnap blacks from the north on the spurious claim they were runaway slaves. Under this law, if any black was accused of being a runaway slave (even if he had been free his entire life), federal law required he/she be denied constitutionally guaranteed rights to habeas corpus, trial by jury, and representation by an attorney. It further stipulated that if a federal magistrate ruled the accused was to be sent to slavery in the south, the judge was paid ten dollars; but if he ruled the accused was free to remain in the north, the judge was paid only five dollars.[23]

As the antislavery side slowly began to gain the upper hand, all southern senators and representatives in Congress resigned their seats to start the Confederate States of America. Typical of their farewell speeches was that of US Senator Robert Toombs of Georgia, who complained that he could no longer be part of the United States because *"you seek to bring an inferior race* [black Americans] *into a condition of equality, socially and politically, with our own people."*[24] And at the state level, Texas, like other southern states, announced it was joining the Confederacy because the United States did not believe

> that the servitude of the African race, as existing in these [Southern] states, is mutually beneficial to both bond and free and is abundantly authorized and justified by the experience of mankind, and the revealed will of the Almighty Creator, as recognized by all Christian nations.[25]

So Texas and other states joined the Confederacy because the Union did not believe racial slavery was good for slaves—they believed slavery was what God wanted and what truly Christian nations practiced.

With this deplorable spiritual deception, is it not surprising the behavior of proslavery advocates was often brutal and reprehensible. An excellent chronicle of their treatment of slaves is seen in what is called the Slave Narratives.

During the Great Depression of the 1930s, the federal government created numerous federal programs to provide jobs for unemployed

Americans, including the Federal Writers' Project. One of its ventures was to interview 2,300 former slaves, transcribing their accounts of life as slaves. Among the numerous records, these are representative:

> When I was three or four years old, my mother was whipped to death by the mistress with a cowhide whip.[26] (former slave HENRY WALTON)

> If a woman was a good breeder, she brought a good price on the auction block. The slave buyers would come around and jab them in the stomach and look them over, and if they thought they would have children fast, they brought a good price.[27] (former slave HATTIE ROGERS)

The personal stories of noted early civil rights leaders were no less affecting. For example, Frederick Douglass testified there seemed to be a sadistic pleasure many slave-owners took in whipping their slaves—and they would whip them for anything—and for nothing. Douglass explained:

> A mere look, word, or motion—a mistake, accident, or want of power—are all matters for which a slave may be whipped at any time. Does a slave look dissatisfied? It is said he has the devil in him, and it must be whipped out. Does he speak loudly when spoken to by his master? Then he is getting high-minded, and should be taken down a button-hole lower. Does he forget to pull off his hat at the approach of a white person? Then he is wanting in reverence, and should be whipped for it. Does he ever venture to vindicate his conduct, when censured for it? Then he is guilty of impudence—one of the greatest crimes of which a slave can be guilty. Does he ever venture to suggest a different mode of doing things from that pointed out by his master? He is indeed presumptuous, and getting above himself; and nothing less than a flogging will do for him. Does he, while ploughing, break a plough—or, while hoeing, break a hoe? It is owing to his carelessness, and for it a slave must always be whipped.[28]

And the writer of the autobiography of Sojourner Truth reported what happened to her:

> They gave her [Sojourner] . . . plenty of whippings. One Sunday morning in particular she was told to go to the barn; on going there, she found her master with a bundle of rods, prepared in the embers, and bound together with cords. When he had tied her hands together before her, he gave her the most cruel whipping she was ever tortured with. He whipped her till the flesh was deeply lacerated, and the blood streamed from her wounds; and the scars remain to the present day to testify to the fact.[29]

And famous slave Harriet Jacobs testified:

> [T]he feeling was that the master had a right to do what he pleased with his own property. . . . He entered every cabin to see that the men and their wives had gone to bed together. . . . Women are considered no value unless they continually increase their owner's stock. They are put on par with animals. The same master shot a woman through the head, who had run away and been brought back to him. . . . The master who did these things was highly educated, and styled a perfect gentleman. He also boasted the name and standing of a Christian, though satan never had a truer follower.[30]

These accounts (and thousands more) occurred over a century ago, and the spirit that produced them is not completely dead today; it just manifests itself in more "civilized" ways. But the reality is the wounds of racism are still very real for many Americans.

CHAPTER 5

RACISM IS WITHOUT A PRIMARY COLOR

However, the modern view that racism is only white on black defies human experience in general and Bible history, world history, and American history in particular. To fully understand the truth about racism in America, there are six important things that every citizen should know about slavery and racism that are largely unreported today.

First, permanent slavery in America was the result of a lawsuit filed by Anthony Johnson, who arrived in America in 1621. He was a prominent landholder, farming hundreds of acres. Johnson was a black man who went to court to be able to hold his black slaves in lifetime bondage, and he won that case.[31] A black man was America's first slaveholder. Repeatedly throughout world history, racism is not confined to a single color.

Second, Carter Woodson (1875–1950) was a famous black historian known as "The Father of Black History." He conducted extensive research in US census data from the 1800s to document the demography of slavery in America. He discovered that among free blacks in the South, a significant percentage were slave-owners[32] (even though they were a small percentage of total slaveholders). Based on Woodson's information, 43 percent of free black households in South Carolina owned slaves, as did 40 percent of free black households in Louisiana, 26 percent in

Mississippi, 25 percent in Alabama, and 20 percent in Georgia.[33] So black-on-black slavery was not uncommon and existed in both the North and the South.[34]

Third, many Native American tribes actively participated as black slave-owners. In fact, according to the census of 1860, in the Choctaw, Cherokee, Creek, and Chickasaw tribes, one of every eight persons counted in the Indian census was a black slave.[35] And Indian slavery of other Indians was also common.[36]

Fourth, the first slave laws in America addressed the ownership not just of black slaves but also white slaves and Indian slaves as well.[37] In fact, *"[f]rom 1670 to 1720, more Indian [slaves] were shipped out of Charleston, South Carolina, than Africans were imported as slaves."*[38] And Indian slavery actually lasted longer than black slavery: *"After the Civil War, President Andrew Johnson sent federal troops into the West to put an end to Indian slavery, but it continued to proliferate in California."*[39] Concerning white slaves, history professor John Donoghue of Loyola explains that, *"Like their African and Native American counterparts, [white] workers from Britain and Ireland were auctioned, weighed on scales, and bought and sold. . . . They were also whipped, branded, beaten, and starved."*[40]

Fifth, in the sixteenth through eighteenth centuries, Muslims took some 1.25 million slaves, both black and white. Their emphasis was more on enslaving Christians than any particular race and numerous white American Christians were made slaves of Muslims.[41]

Sixth, in the American experience, the majority of black slaves had white owners, but the vast and overwhelming majority of whites did not own slaves—at all. In fact, according to the 1860 census, at the beginning of the Civil War, only 8 percent of Americans owned slaves,[42] and that included white, black, Native American, and other slave-owners, not just whites.

Clearly, slavery and racism are a human problem, not just a white-on-black problem. Truth is key to any helpful healing discussion, and an important truth often unknown or ignored today is whites were not the exclusive slave-owners or blacks the sole victims. It is certainly true in American history that blacks definitely suffered disproportionate mistreatment, but racism is a sin, and no sin is confined solely to one race or ethnicity.

CHAPTER 6

NO BITTERNESS ALLOWED

Richard Allen (1760–1831) is a famous black leader from the American Founding. Born into slavery in Maryland, he later purchased his freedom and became a minister. In Philadelphia, he worked hand-in-hand with Founding Father Benjamin Rush (a signer of the Declaration of Independence) on numerous endeavors, including the founding of the first black denomination: the AME (African Methodist Episcopal). Allen also assisted fugitive slaves and operated one of the stations on the famous Underground Railroad.

Allen lived at a difficult time in American history. He personally experienced not only the oppression of slavery but also much racial rejection, prejudice, and discrimination. Yet regardless of those many racial hardships, his message to his own people was clear:

> [L]et no rancor or ill-will lodge in your breast for any bad treatment you may have received from any. If you do, you transgress against God, who will not hold you guiltless. He would not suffer it even in His beloved people Israel; and you think He will allow it unto us? Many of the white people have been instruments in the hands of God for our good . . . And I am sorry to say that too many think more of the evil than of the good they have received.[43]

Notice two clear points made by Allen: First, no rancor, ill-will, or brooding over the evils of slavery, discrimination, and prejudice was to be allowed, regardless of the level of mistreatment. Second, many whites were strong allies and *"instruments in the hands of God for our good."* Concerning the first point, Allen was echoing words from the Bible:

> Watch out that no poisonous root of bitterness grows up to trouble you, corrupting many. (HEBREWS 12:15, NLT)

God's directive is *"No bitterness allowed!"* regardless what anyone else may have done. Bitterness is a poison that infects not only the one who is offended but also those to whom they spew their bitterness. Bitterness comes when, as Allen described it, we *"think more of the evil than of the good."* God's message of *"Don't!"* is what Allen repeated to his people, and that message is no less applicable today than in any previous generation.

(By the way, a current example of this forgiveness is black Bishop George McKinney, Jim's close friend and a prominent and highly respected pastor in San Diego. Although his story is one of painful racial suffering, his father taught him he and his siblings could not live in bitterness—they must always forgive. And they did. Today, Bishop McKinney is a prominent leader in racial healing and a model of how to walk in forgiveness.)

Second, Allen reminded his people, *"Many of the white people have been instruments in the hands of God for our good."* The story of the major sacrifices made by millions of whites for the benefit of blacks is rarely told today.

Consider the new National Museum of African American History and Culture that recently opened in Washington, DC. The way it presents history, no whites fought racism or stood for the rights of blacks until the 1820s. This is patently false and it further fuels modern tensions between races. Consider some simple facts.

Simultaneous with the birth of slavery in America was the rise of the antislavery movement in the 1600s, led by whites who opposed slavery and fought racial oppression. The civil rights movement was largely centered in the most Biblically knowledgeable part of the early American colonies: New England. In fact, famous New England minister John Wise preached in the early 1700s, *"every man must be acknowledged equal to every man"*[44] almost a century before the similar line *"all men are created equal"* appeared in the Declaration of Independence.

In the mid-1700s, Quaker leader John Woolman witnessed slavery for the first time and began advocating vigorously for emancipation,[45] resulting in the Quakers becoming a leading national voice against slavery throughout the 1700s and 1800s. Unitarians were also extremely active in opposing racial oppression.[46] So, too, were the Wesleyans (Jim's denomination)—the only denomination formed solely for the immediate abolition of slavery.

And among the signers of the Declaration of Independence, the antislavery Founding Fathers who freed slaves, called for abolition, or founded or became part of abolition societies outnumbered the proslavery Founders by a margin of three to one. This fact seems dubious to most today, for they have been told that up to forty-one of the fifty-six signers of the Declaration of Independence owned slaves.[47] Yes; many of the Founding Fathers did own slaves—*as British citizens*.

Significantly, King George III vetoed the American antislavery laws passed before the American War for Independence.[48] However, after we separated from Great Britain, many American colonies began to successfully abolish slavery,[49] and many Founding Fathers freed their slaves and became leading voices against slavery.[50] So the important fact bears repeating that generally three of four Founders freed their slaves, spoke against slavery, or led or founded antislavery societies.

Yet today, Americans can name slave-holding signers of the Declaration but virtually none of the many-times-more antislavery signers, such as Benjamin Rush (a founder of America's first abolition society and a leader of the national abolition movement), Francis Hopkinson (who founded schools to teach academics and the Bible to blacks, in contradiction of British policy), Stephen Hopkins (who signed America's first antislavery law), James Wilson (who spoke openly against slavery in his law school), William Ellery (who introduced a national antislavery law), as well as Roger Sherman, John Adams, Robert Treat Paine, Benjamin Franklin, Elbridge Gerry, Sam Adams, Richard Stockton, Samuel Huntington, and many others.

All of these efforts by white pastors and political leaders (and so many more) occurred prior to the 1820s—an important fact conveniently ignored by the National Museum of African American History and Culture.

Furthermore, America is the only nation in the world where whites, on behalf of blacks, went to war against other whites in order to end slavery, resulting in the loss of well over half-a-million white lives. And after the Civil War, the Thirteenth, Fourteenth, and Fifteenth Amendments were added to the Constitution, by whites, in order to secure civil rights and voting rights for black Americans. At the time, whites were the legal voters, and significantly, two thirds of the whites in Congress, and a majority of whites in three fourths of the states, voted, by the passage and ratification of those Amendments, to voluntarily limit their own political power in order to extend equal rights to black Americans.

There are many additional examples illustrating excellent relations between most whites and blacks, but to repeat this aspect of history would not comport with the current secular Progressive narrative about perpetual racial injustice.

So the two lessons from Richard Allen are still very applicable today: God allows no bitterness to be held by His people, regardless of what has happened to them, and many whites sacrificed much for blacks in the fight against racism and should be remembered and honored.

CHAPTER 7

TELL THE WHOLE STORY

The Bible is a book of theology, morality, and literature as well as history. In it, God set the precedent for all historians: He tells the whole story—the good, the bad, and the ugly.

As an example, consider King David. In the Bible, we learn the exciting story of him facing Goliath, along with having earlier defeated the lion and the bear, all of which is very good (1 Samuel 17). But we also learn of his failure with his sons Absalom and Adonijah, which is bad (2 Samuel 13–18). And God does not gloss over David's adultery with Bathsheba or his murder of her husband Uriah, which is definitely ugly (2 Samuel 11). From the Bible, we thus have the historical model for telling the full story; but in America today, the bad and the ugly from American history are heavily emphasized, whereas the good is routinely omitted.

Americans therefore get a steady diet of the southern perspective concerning the history of slavery and racism (which generally involves the bad and the ugly), but nearly nothing of the northern view (which presents much good). For example, who is told that, in early America, blacks in New England regularly voted,[51] and that blacks in Massachusetts were never restricted from voting?[52]

And who today has heard of these people:

- Wentworth Cheswill (1746–1817), the first black elected to office (1768 in New Hampshire)—reelected for the next forty-nine years, holding several different political offices

- Thomas Hercules, elected to public office in 1793 (Pennsylvania)
- Lemuel Haynes (1753–1833), a soldier in the War for American Independence and the first black to have a sermon published and to receive an advanced postgraduate degree. He started multiple churches, often pastoring white congregations, and on George Washington's birthday, in his churches he preached a sermon about his former Commander-in-Chief
- Harry Hoosier (1750–1806), a Founding Era preacher from whom Indiana takes its nickname. (How many in Indiana know the name "Hoosiers" comes from a black evangelist?)
- Black military heroes from the American War for Independence, such as Peter Salem, Prince Estabrook, James Armistead, Prince Sisson, Prince Whipple, and many others
- John Marrant (1755–1791), a child prodigy musician and the first black American successfully to evangelize Native Americans
- Benjamin Banneker (1731–1806), appointed by President Thomas Jefferson as a surveyor to lay out Washington, DC, and a mathematician who produced the first American scientific almanac by a black
- William Nell (1816–1874), a noted historian and author, was the first black to hold a civil position in the federal government (1861)
- Robert Smalls (1839–1915), a former slave who became a Union naval ship captain in the Civil War, a military Major General in South Carolina, and a US Congressman
- John Rock (1825–1866), the first black admitted to the US Supreme Court Bar (1865), being not only a lawyer but also a teacher, doctor, and dentist
- Henry Highland Garnett (1815–1882), the first black to speak in the US House of Representatives (1865).

And there are scores of other similarly uplifting stories of early black heroes of whom Americans hear virtually nothing today. These are not inconsequential names, but they are largely unknown today. Consequently, we can usually recite more of what's wrong with America on racial issues than early heroes or positive moments. The story of oppression is frequently told, as well it should be. But we should also tell the stories of victory, achievement, and cooperation.

CHAPTER 8

THE NO. 1 PREDICTOR OF MAJOR CULTURAL PROBLEMS

God is not race-conscious and neither should we be; yet as noted earlier, there are indeed differences in the customs and practices of the cultures found in every race and ethnicity. The Bible is silent about many cultural habits, saying nothing, for example, about preferences in transportation (whether an affinity for a pickup, motorcycle, minivan, lowrider, or luxury sedan) or about many hobbies (whether baseball, hunting, or electronic gaming).

But there are definitely things the Bible does address, such as sexual practices and family structure, as well as the content of a child's education and the means by which it is to occur. Whenever the Bible speaks, the guidance it gives applies equally to every ethnicity.

THE FAMILY

A direct message given from God in the Bible is He wants children raised in a home with a mother *and* a father, not just one or the other. (God never designed children to be raised by two daddies or two mommies. In fact, if two daddies are good, then why wouldn't three, four, or five be better? And if two mommies are good, then why not a dozen? No, God designed children to come from one sperm and one egg—to have one daddy and one mommy.)

Statistics show when cultures do not follow God's directive for the family, certain predictable problems occur across all ethnic lines. For example, in education, the academic scores of children from single-parent homes (that is, homes without a father and a mother present) are significantly lower than those of children from traditional two-parent families,[53] and those children are almost twice as likely to repeat a grade in school and more than twice as likely to be suspended or expelled from school.[54]

Additionally, young men from homes without a father present are:

- Twice as likely to end up in jail[55]
- Twice as likely to pull a knife or a gun on someone[56]
- Twice as likely to be involved in gangs[57]
- Seven times more likely to be delinquent.[58]

Furthermore, 90 percent of the increase in violent crime between 1973 and 1995 was committed by those raised in single-parent homes,[59] and excessively high murder rates continue to be associated with those born out of wedlock.[60] Children of every race and ethnicity pay a high price when the God-mandated family structure is neglected or rejected.

Yet of all the various cultures in America today, statistics show these specific problems occur at markedly higher levels in the black culture. For example:

- Schools with a majority population of black students have far more violence than other schools[61]
- One in four blacks is illiterate[62]
- Blacks have one of the highest illegal-drug-use rates in the country both for hard drugs (such as cocaine, heroin, and hallucinogens) and for marijuana[63]
- Black teenage girls, by a wide margin, have the highest teen-pregnancy rate,[64] and 71 percent of births in the black community are to unmarried women[65]—one of the primary causes of the feminization of poverty[66]

- Black women make up 15 percent of the female population but have 28 percent of the abortions[67]
- Blacks represent 13.3 percent of the nation[68] but account for 44 percent of HIV diagnoses[69] and 52 percent of HIV/AIDS deaths.[70]

And black Americans are the victims of violence at a rate much higher than any other race or ethnicity.[71] However, the greatest threat of physical danger to black Americans today is not from any outside force (including police) but from other blacks: 90 percent of blacks who die by murder or homicide lose their lives at the hands of other blacks—a percentage much higher than other cultures.[72] In fact, 2010 and 2011, 1,461 more blacks were murdered by other blacks than were murdered by whites in the eighty-six years of lynching from 1882 to 1968.[73] Black-on-black violence is far and away the greatest source of physical danger in the black culture—violence largely the result of a lack of two-parent homes.

Strikingly, for generations, most black Americans were likely to be married, but that reversed in 1960 and is now just the opposite.[74] Although 50 percent of all Americans today are married, only 31 percent of black Americans are,[75] and whereas only 20 percent of Americans over the age of twenty-five have never been married, among blacks that number is much higher: 36 percent.[76] Currently, 64 percent of black families are single-parent, compared with 40 percent of Hispanic families, 30 percent of white families, and 17 percent of Asian families.[77]

One more direct consequence of the breakdown of the traditional family is an increase in poverty—another problem that disproportionately plagues the black culture. Significantly, 37 percent of black families headed by a single woman live below the poverty level, but only 8 percent of married black families do so.[78] And children from single-parent households are more likely to be poorer than children from married-parent households,[79] and two-thirds of children from single-parent homes will end up on welfare.[80]

So how much economic difference does traditional marriage make? The annual average income of a two-parent family is $81,455, but that of a single-mother family is only $25,493.[81] A big difference!

The serious problems plaguing the black community (and that appear in varying degrees in other communities) are not the result of being black. This happens to every community, culture, and ethnicity that rejects God's directives for marriage and sexuality. One's race is inherent and involuntary and cannot be changed, but one's culture and behavior are voluntary and definitely can be changed.

The Bible is clear that sexual activity for every culture and ethnicity is to be confined to a lifelong marriage between a man and a woman, and *any* sexual activity outside of that arrangement is wrong, whether premarital sex, extramarital sex, or homosexual sex. Government won't fix marriage, reduce single-parent homes, end black-on-black violence, raise educational scores, halt gang violence, or end poverty. But personal behavioral decisions, especially those related to strong marriages and Biblical sexuality, will.

As two white authors, we may not be considered qualified to speak to what blacks need to do within their culture. But we do care deeply about the pain experienced by blacks (and those in any culture who face similar problems and heartaches). Although these statistics may sound a bit clinical when reading them, we totally understand they reflect real people with real pain.

These statistics represent the cry of black mothers whose sons never reached their twentieth birthday and of little girls who had no daddies to protect them from pedophiles as they walked home alone from school. They represent little boys who never had enough parental support to play Little League Baseball, and if they did play, there were no daddies to watch them. They represent the tears of elementary-age siblings who had to attend the funeral of their big brother killed by gang violence. Statistics are cold, but the stories behind them are not.

We refuse to be divided by racial lines. We are all part of God's human race—and specifically, with other Christians, we are part of His "one body" in Christ. God reminds us (1 Corinthians 12:15–27) that when one part of His body is suffering, every other part suffers with it. So we—each of us—should do whatever we can to help any other of His children, regardless of the culture or ethnicity from which they come.

CHAPTER 9

THE KEY ISSUE

BENEFITS OF A BIBLICAL FAMILY STRUCTURE

Many positive societal benefits of a man-woman marriage followed by childbearing have already been presented. But there are others.

For example, the family headed by a father <u>and</u> a mother is the finest *educational unit* ever created. It is the great relay in which the baton of truth and values is successfully passed down from generation to generation.

It is also the greatest *social unit* in existence, taking a child from birth onward, molding and modeling him or her on how to appropriately relate to others.

The family is also a remarkable *economic unit.* In fact, debt-relief experts tell us when a family is drowning in consumer debt, if the entire family—the dad, mom, and the children—are united with a financial game plan, the family can move to fiscal health in a much shorter time than otherwise expected.[82]

It is also a superb *recreational unit.* The home was designed by God to be the place of joy, not pain. Fun happens in the family, and there can be laughter in the homes of such families.

And the family is the primary *spiritual unit.* The family, not the church, is the primary means for establishing a deep and lasting love for Jesus and the Bible in the heart of your child. This does not mean the church is unimportant, but God designed it to be secondary to the family in this area.

SOLUTION

Whenever we see a large and complicated problem (such as how to restore the traditional family), there often tends to be a sense of powerlessness—a paralysis seems to grip us. Where can I start? What can I do? I'm only one person. To overcome that sense of helplessness, adopt the approach of the little boy in the oft-told starfish story:

> Once there was an old man who used to go to the ocean to do his writing. He had a habit of walking on the beach every morning before he began his work. One morning after a big storm had passed, he found the beach littered with starfish as far as the eye could see in both directions. Off in the distance, the old man noticed a small boy approaching who occasionally bent down to pick up an object and throw it into the sea. As the boy came closer, the man asked what he was doing. The boy answered, "Throwing starfish into the ocean. The tide has washed them up onto the beach and they can't return to the sea by themselves. When the sun gets high, they will die unless I throw them back into the water." The old man replied, "There are tens of thousands of starfish on this beach! You won't be able to make much of a difference." The boy bent down, picked up another starfish and threw it as far as he could into the ocean. Then he turned, smiled, and said, "It made a difference to that one!"[83]

So determine to make a difference, even if it is just for one person or one family.

For example, volunteer to be an academic tutor of a young child who does not have a daddy, or you could also become a mentor and spend time with young people, taking them out for wholesome fun and activities. And there is the option of becoming foster parents and many more.

Can you change the whole world? No. But you can help one person (or several) understand, embrace, and follow God's pattern for the family. Like the little boy throwing the starfish back into the ocean, you will have made a difference for that person and all whom he or she will subsequently touch in his or her own life.

CHAPTER 10

FROM STATS TO THE STREETS

Improved relations between cultures and races require trust, and trust is achieved when there is understanding. Several steps can be undertaken to improve understanding between races.

SOLUTION SUNDAY

A starting point has been suggested by two US Senators, James Lankford (a white senator from Oklahoma) and Tim Scott (a black senator from South Carolina). They recommend what they call "Solution Sundays":

> Americans do not really get to know their neighbors and fellow citizens at a rally or a big event; we get to know each other typically over a meal, especially in our home. What if Americans intentionally chose to put our prejudice and broken trust on the table by putting our feet under the same table? If it seems too simple and obvious, let me ask you this question: Have you ever had dinner in your home with a person of another race? Many Americans have not. Sunday is a slower, yet significant day, for most Americans. So we challenge each family to give one Sunday lunch or dinner for building relationships across

race, to literally be part of the solution in America. Obviously any day of the week works since the goal is to engage on the personal level of your own home to break down walls and build trust across our communities. It is harder to stereotype when you know people first-hand.[84]

This simple act might not wipe out all racism and tension between races, but it will surely help decrease it. By the way, if you are not used to entertaining people in your home, then how about a restaurant? But regardless of the location, building trust relationships is the key.

What else can be done to improve relationships?

THOUGHTFULNESS IN SPEAKING

Every day, millions of blacks and whites work side by side. Millions live side by side. Millions worship side by side. Millions of their children attend school side by side. It seems Americans get along quite well with each other.

But when generational hurts are raised by blacks, they should not be dismissed with patronizing statements such as, *"Those complaining about racism today were never slaves. It's been over 150 years. They need to get over it!"* Such comments demonstrate a lack of awareness of the phenomenon the Bible identifies as generational forces that can pass down trauma from one generation to the next (see passages such as Exodus 34:7 and Lamentations 5:7).

LISTENING

Controlling our words and responses is a key to change, as is sincere listening. Give serious time to asking questions and taking note of the answers. For example, for whites, seek out black friends and acquaintances and say to them, *"I do not understand the depth of the feelings regarding racism. Can you teach me? Can you help me understand?"* (And blacks should also do the same with those of other ethnicities—learn their perspective as well. A genuine conversation is not one-sided.)

When you ask others to share their experiences (and to coach you in understanding those experiences), what often pours out of people is astonishing. We have discovered many blacks who appeared to have it so together—to be functioning well in life and to exhibit many evidences of "the good life"—begin to share at profoundly deep levels. And the depth of wounding they have experienced is often far beyond what is apparent on the outside. (Jim has sometimes described what comes forth as *"a torrent of pain."*)

Even though what you may hear from them can be discouraging, don't allow it to stop you from listening and reaching out. Admittedly, complete healing does not come merely by talking and listening, but it is certainly a great starting point for building a relationship of trust.

KEEPING A BALANCED VIEWPOINT

We are not talking about spending time with those who perpetually carry the proverbial chip on their shoulder—those who stay in a continually seething and belligerent mode toward all other races. Such persons have developed strident and whiney voices, and there is no reason to be subjected to that shrillness. Genuine racial healing is rarely the objective of such persons.

Furthermore, engaging in sincere conversation does not mean becoming whipping boys for angry blacks (or angry whites). Jim learned this one day in a conversation about racism he was having with several blacks. The view they were giving him (and the view commonly expressed by Progressives in media and academia today) is racism can only be exercised by people who have "the upper hand" with power or privilege—that racism can only be perpetrated by whites and never a black person because blacks are without power.

As the discussion began, a black man pulled Jim aside and said, *"Don't let them manipulate you with the 'power' phrase."* *"Why are you saying that?"* Jim asked. He responded, *"Because if you are a white person with $10,000 in your pocket and you are walking down the street and a black man comes up behind you with a gun and demands you give him all you have, who has the power? Is it the white man with the $10,000, or is it the black man with the gun? Obviously, the man with the gun has the power at that moment."* This illustration came from a black man who had a balanced view.

So in approaching the issues of racism, don't fall in the proverbial ditch on either side of the road. On the one side, avoid the inclination to be dismissive (*"It's been 150 years since slavery!"*), and on the other side, avoid being manipulated or enabling flawed thinking (*"Only whites can be racists"* because of their inherent *"white privilege"* or because they are the so-called *"dominant race"*).

Racism is not a new issue; it has occurred in all nations and races; but the Bible and history provide clear guidance on solutions. There are other specific steps to be taken as well. The most important is repentance. All of us have experienced racism. At some time in our lives, we have likely all had racist thoughts or said racist words not pleasing to the Lord. We must repent. (To "repent" means to turn 180 degrees and go in the opposite direction.)

CHAPTER 11

COMPLEX YET SOLVABLE PROBLEMS

Currently, at least two major issues intensify the problems resulting from fatherlessness in the home. Both of these items often are most closely associated with the black community (but also apply to all others) and can and should be addressed.

1. *Educational conditions in urban schools.* The quality and condition of education in urban schools is markedly inferior to that across the rest of the educational spectrum.

Part of the problem is certainly a result of weakened family structure, but an additional problem with urban schools (and all government schools) is they perpetuate academic mediocrity—they operate at the lowest common denominator. In any class, some students do not want to be there and so will be deliberately disruptive; others want to learn but are underperforming; and some are high-performing and want to be challenged at an even higher level. The teacher cannot meet all these needs and therefore has to aim at the middle, pulling along the under-achiever but dragging down the over-achiever, while losing far too much instructional time trying to control problem-causing students. And the intentional trouble-makers who do not want to be in school frequently pollute others, infecting them with bad and often violent attitudes and behavior.

Education that works best is individualized, and the best way to have such an education is through educational choice: allow parents to choose the schools (and school environments) that best address the needs, skills, and abilities of their children. Sadly, however, there is probably no issue on which professional educrats more promptly close ranks today than in opposing educational choice—and probably no group has suffered more as a result than urban students, especially black urban students.

Ironically, in 1954, when the Supreme Court delivered its *Brown v. Board of Education* decision ordering a desegregation of public schools, professional educrats stood outside the doorways of schools and told black students, *"No! We want you to stay in your inferior schools! We won't let you in here!"* Today, professional educrats stand inside the doorways of failing inner city schools and tell black students, *"No! We want you to stay in inferior schools! We won't let you out of here!"*

Educational choice allows students a chance to escape a failing system, giving them an opportunity not only for a better education, but also for a safer environment. This is why so many parents who can afford it, even non-Christians parents, place their children in some form of Christian education. They want a good academic education for their children in a safe atmosphere with wholesome values. Parents should be able to choose this without paying extra for it.

2. *Criminal justice reform.* The second area directly affecting the black community is the need for judicial and prison reform. Some today complain the justice system is racist, pointing out that only 13 percent of the American population is black[85] but 38 percent of prison inmates are black.[86] This does not prove racism. Blacks have a higher percentage of single-parent families, which results in a higher percentage of children who engage in criminal behavior, so it is likely the higher percentage of black prison population is not the result of race but of family condition.

This does not mean there are no serious issues touching the black community that should be reformed within the justice system. There are.

David is a member of the national criminal justice reform movement known as Right on Crime, which focuses on issues such as overcriminalization, juvenile justice, substance abuse, adult probation, parole and re-entry, law enforcement, prisons, and victims.[87] This group seeks systemic structural reform in each of those areas.

When looking at criminal justice reforms, there are always two competing concerns: how to balance justice for victims and society with appropriate punishments for offenders. Both are important, and the Bible directly addresses both.

A major problem in today's justice system is overcriminalization— the offender, no matter the offense, must be locked up and the key thrown away. But this is not Biblical. You don't take those who commit nonviolent crimes and lock them away with murderers and rapists.

In fact, notice that, in the Bible, God did not establish a prison system. If someone committed a heinous crime (such as murder, rape, infanticide, and so forth), justice was dispensed promptly. (It was not like today's policy of waiting an average of sixteen years in a jail cell before a capital sentence is executed.[88])

For nonviolent crimes, God's objective was justice for the victim and restoration for the offender. Thus, a thief had to repay the victim for what was stolen, along with a substantial penalty (cf. Proverbs 6:30–31, Exodus 22:4, 2 Samuel 12:6). This provided justice to the victim and a punishment to the thief, along with an economic deterrent great enough to make it likely he would not want to steal again in the future. The Bible does not authorize locking away a nonviolent offender for years and decades.

One means that balances the need of justice for the victim and society with rehabilitation and restoration of the offender is faith-based programs.

Currently, 77 percent of former prisoners are re-arrested and re-incarcerated within five years of their release from prison.[89] In recent years, however, many states have added faith-based prisons to their justice system. Prisoners still complete their full sentence, but while in prison, they are given the opportunity to participate in voluntary faith-based programs. The prisoners who go through these programs have a recidivism (that is, a return to prison) rate as low as 8 percent[90]—a rate 85 percent lower than the government rate.

And the positive effects do not stop merely with rehabilitating the offender; there are additional benefits. Currently, 2.7 million young people in America have a parent in prison,[91] and statistics show 70 percent of these children will end up in prison themselves.[92] But if these parents can be rehabilitated and get home to their kids, the family cycle of crime may be broken, which also means fewer crimes in the future.

Educational choice and criminal justice reform are two specific areas that can have a direct positive impact on the black community. Achieving these reforms is something in which all Americans should be involved.

SUMMARY

All the ideas mentioned throughout this section on racism can play a part in lessening racial tensions in America. There are things everyone can do to make a difference: listen, engage in serious conversations, invite those outside your normal spheres into your home (i.e., "Solution Sundays"), work with groups such as Right on Crime to reform criminal justice, contact your legislators about enacting educational choice in urban communities, mentor young people, tutor students, and become involved as foster parents, and your church can become a center to assist former prisoners in learning and transitioning[1] and a variety of other activities. Allow the Spirit of God to break your heart for the sin of racism in our culture. The Bible says some difficult things change ". . . *only by prayer and fasting*" (Mark 9:29, ISV), so fast and pray for racial healing across the land.

Prayer: Lord, our nation is hurting. We cry out for racial healing. We refuse to be in denial of the sin of racism that can impact us in ways we do not always recognize. Help us recognize those ways. If we have been victims of racism, we refuse to live in bitterness. If we have harbored racism, we repent. Help us all become catalysts for racial healing. Amen.

---

1. *See* James. L. Garlow. Well Versed: *Biblical Answers to Today's Tough Issues* (Regnery, 2016), pp. 193–196.

SECTION TWO

IMMIGRATION

*But the stranger that dwelleth with you shall be
unto you as one born among you, and thou shalt
love him as thyself; for ye were strangers in the
land of Egypt: I am the Lord your God.*

LEVITICUS 19:34, KJV

The goal of this section is to understand the Biblical and historical
principles for immigration and apply them in a way that brings resolution to the current dysfunctional immigration system.

CHAPTER 12

CAN WE ALL JUST TAKE A DEEP BREATH?

With such a divisive issue, is it possible to have a calm, fact-based conversation about immigration? Can it be discussed without throwing verbal grenades?

It's likely what you are about to read will challenge you, no matter which side of this debate you are on. And if you believe the Biblical proverb *"iron sharpens iron"* (Proverbs 27:17)—having your thinking tested with sound ideas and reasoning can make you a stronger and better person—then you will probably find this section useful.

TERMS

The issue of immigration has become so polarized today the nomenclature used here may be offensive for some. For example, many are profoundly disturbed at the use of the phrase "illegal aliens" or "illegal immigrants" and see it as condescending and degrading. They hold that the proper phrase is "undocumented persons." But we will use the terms "undocumented" and "illegal" interchangeably because they have the same meaning.

By the way, we do not believe the term "illegal" is dehumanizing. It is a term of accuracy, referring to a person who entered the country illegally or came legally then violated the law by overstaying visa provisions. But as we already made clear in the section on racism, we recognize the inherent worth of every human being and affirm all persons were created in the image of God, regardless of their country of origin or the language they speak. We believe this whether the person is an illegal immigrant, an undocumented person, a legal immigrant, or a natural-born citizen.

HYPOCRISY CONFRONTED

Also, although it is not our goal to offend any reader, we will certainly not hold back from pointing out duplicity wherever it appears.

For example, some rant and rave about illegal immigrants in the country but don't complain about the lower prices of freshly picked produce, reduced construction costs, or cheaper labor for gardening, housekeeping, hotel help, nursing home assistance, and a host of other tasks often performed by illegals at less-than-appropriate wages. Hypocrisy.

Others demand open borders, strenuously object to extreme vetting, and support the availability of generous government services for all who enter. But they usually have locks on their own doors and security systems in their homes and cars, and they strongly object if someone enters their home or uses their possessions without first securing their permission. Also hypocrisy.

GOAL

If you want to hear us say, "Just open all borders to anyone who wants to come in, for it's the Christian thing to do," you won't. And if you want to hear, "Round up the eleven million identified illegals and throw them out of the county, for following the law is the Christian thing to do," you won't. We don't care about political hyperbole (that is, what's "Right" or "Left"); rather, we care what the Bible says and history confirms. The Bible and history provide helpful solutions that work.

CHAPTER 13

A BROKEN SYSTEM

Our immigration system is broken. Americans know it, polling affirms it, and its problems are obvious:

- Our borders are open and unprotected. (If you doubt that, explain how eleven million got here illegally and why there is so much drug and sex trafficking across our borders.)
- The government is unable to track down immigrants who overstay their visas, and too many immigrants with criminal backgrounds are admitted
- Tens of thousands of immigrants are welcomed who have a sworn allegiance to philosophies that require an overthrow of our constitutional system (such as Sharia Law)
- Enforcement of existing immigration laws is indefinitive, and many states and cities simply pick and choose which immigration laws they like and will enforce
- To get here legally takes years, but illegally only days
- When you have something broken in your home, you either fix it or get it fixed. But you don't leave it broken for thirty years.

2016 ELECTION

In the 2016 election between Hillary Clinton and Donald Trump, an amazing 70 percent of registered voters saw the immigration issue as *very important* to their vote,[93] and those voters chose Trump over Clinton by a margin of two to one (64 to 36 percent).[94] The margin was even wider in the so-called "blue" states Trump unexpectedly won.[95]

Few Americans know the immigration issue was so important or the voting differential so large. This is due in large part to the media. They have ensured that those who support open borders and increased immigration are the most publicized voices, but by a wide margin, that position has the *least* public support.[96]

MEDIA

The media have taken every opportunity to attack Trump's immigration policies (a bias which is understandable because media contributions to the presidential candidates favored Clinton over Trump by a margin of twenty-seven to one[97]). The media are happy to publicize Trump immigration critics, especially when they come from within the religious community. For example:

- "Thousands Of Religious Leaders Speak Out Against Trump's 'Extreme Vetting' Proposal"[98]
- "Christian Leaders Denounce Trump's Plan to Favor Christian Refugees"[99]
- "Religious leaders condemn Trump's immigration order".[100]

CHAPTER 14

IMMIGRATION AND THE BIBLE

Many religious critics point to one specific Bible verse as the basis for their opposition to various Trump immigration policies:

> But the stranger that dwelleth with you shall be unto you as one born among you, and thou shalt love him as thyself; for ye were strangers in the land of Egypt: I am the LORD your God. (Leviticus 19:34, KJV)

For example, this was theologian Diana Butler Bass's tweet on her reasons for opposing immigration restrictions

> The foreigner residing among you must be treated as your native-born. Love them as yourself. Lev 19:34[101]

Jim Wallis, the head of Sojourners, a "Christian" social justice organization, similarly noted:

> Evangelicals finally realize that how we treat the stranger [Leviticus 19:34]—these 11 million undocumented people—is how we treat Christ Himself.[102]

Russell Moore, a national Southern Baptist leader, objected because Baptists have a long history of *"welcoming the stranger"*—another reference to Leviticus 19:34.[103] And the Rev. Jerald Stinson of the United Church of Christ pointed to that verse as the reason for his support of open borders.[104]

But there is a big problem with their use of this verse: Leviticus 19:34 in the Hebrew Scriptures (which Christians call the Old Testament) does *not* say what these people claim it says. Let's explain this with a parallel example from the New Testament.

THE MEANING OF A WORD

The word *"love"* appears some 200 times in the New Testament.[105] But that one English word is used for four different words in the original Greek language in which the New Testament was written. The four Greek words all translated as the one English word *"love"* follow:[106]

1. AGAPE: The unconditional love God bestows on His Son and on us all as His children.
2. PHILEO: Love between friends. (Hence, the city of Philadelphia, named from the Greek phileo, is called "The City of Brotherly Love.")
3. STORGE: The relational love of natural affection between family members—of parents to children and children to parents, among siblings, cousins, and so forth.
4. EROS: The sense of being in love; romantic, physical, or sexual love.

So the single English word *"love"* does not convey the full scope of the four different meanings, and if you don't understand which one is being used, you can completely misapply it, thus producing ridiculous results. It would be like seeing the verse, *"Love your neighbor"* (Mark 12:31) and interpreting it as *"Have sex with your neighbor"* (which is indeed one meaning of *"love,"* but definitely not the one used in that verse). So, too, the word *"stranger"* has multiple definitions that vary widely from our one English meaning.

But before getting into the actual meaning, one other point should be made about the use of Leviticus 19:34 by critics of immigration restrictions.

TO WHOM WAS THE COMMAND GIVEN?

In the Bible, God established four separate realms of authority, each having its own distinct responsibilities: (1) the individual, (2) the family, (3) the church, and (4) civil government. So whenever the Bible gives a command, it is important to identify to which sphere that command is directed.

For example, the command to bring up children in the nurture and admonition of the Lord (Ephesians 6:4) was not given to the church or government but solely and explicitly to the family. Similarly, the command to train saints for the work of the ministry (Ephesians 4:11–13) was not delivered to the government or the family but explicitly to the church. And the command to use the sword (the power and force of government) to punish lawbreakers (Romans 13:4) is not a command for the family or the church but solely the government.

Similarly, Jesus's commands to show mercy, forgive, and turn the other cheek were given directly to His followers, not to the government. In fact, if the government turned the other cheek and ignored crime, it would be doing exactly the opposite of what the Bible says it should do. The Bible explicitly warns "When a crime is not punished quickly, people feel it is safe to do wrong" (Ecclesiastes 8:11, TLB), so whenever the government does not promptly uphold a law and execute justice (as it is told to do in Romans 13:4), crime will increase, which is definitely against God's plan. So it is always important to identify to which of the four jurisdictions a verse or command is directed.

Having established the Biblical importance of separate jurisdictions, consider some objections Christian leaders raise against immigration laws. For example, the Rev. William T. Barber, with Repairers of the Breach, complains of President Trump's immigration actions:

> These acts smell of racism and reek of xenophobia. They are the antithesis of the Bible, which declares, "Love the Lord your God with all your heart and with all your soul and with all your mind and with all your strength. The second is this: 'Love your neighbor as yourself.' There is no commandment greater than these." (Mark 12:30–31, NIV)[107]

Were these commands of Jesus as cited by Barber directed to the institution of government, or were they given to the individual followers of Jesus? Read the passage and look at its context. Clearly, the command is to individual followers, not the government.

Similarly, the Rev. James Martin of the Society of Jesus, editor of *America Magazine,* quotes from Matthew 25:

> At the Last Judgment, [Jesus] "will say to people, 'I was a stranger and you did not welcome Me.' And people will say, 'When were you a stranger and we did not take care of you?' And he will say, 'Truly I tell you, just as you did not do it to one of the least of these, you did not do it to Me.' [Matthew 25:43-45]" . . . It is Christ Whom we turn away when we build walls. It is Christ Whom we reject when we slash quotas for refugees. It is Christ Whom we are killing by letting them die in poverty and war rather than opening our doors.[108]

But read the passage he cites. These words are specifically spoken to His individual disciples, not the government.

When good-meaning Christians misapply Scriptures, even if their desire is well-intentioned, the results will be no more effective than trying to use a screwdriver as a shovel or a hammer as a sponge. There are things God designed to be done in certain ways, and to try to do them otherwise will be ineffective at best and disastrous at worst.

THE STRANGER AMONG US

So let's return to the verse so often used (actually misused) by Christians today. The assumption (as seen in the quotes above) is that the word *"stranger"* in Leviticus 19:34 refers to the immigrant, whether legal or illegal. But that word *"stranger"* (just like the word *"love"* in Greek) has multiple meanings in Hebrew largely unknown to English-speakers today.

Perhaps the English word closest to *"stranger"* appears in the Septuagint (a third-century BC translation of the Hebrew Bible into Greek for the use of Jews who no longer spoke Hebrew). There the word *"stranger"* is correctly translated as *"a proselyte"*—that is, *"a convert."* Thus, the *"stranger"* of Leviticus 19 is not just a foreigner who enters the land but is a foreigner who enters with the intent of becoming a Jew—someone who wants to fully follow their customs, laws, culture, morality, religious beliefs, practices, and language. And when a foreign-born citizen finally becomes a Jew, he then gets the same rights and privileges as the native-born Jew (which is the other part of Leviticus 19:34).

Perhaps the simplest illustration of what it means to be a "*stranger*" is seen in the relationship between Naomi and Ruth in the Bible. Naomi was a natural-born Jewish citizen of Israel; Ruth was from Moab but wanted to become a Jew. She therefore pledged to Naomi: "*Where you go I will go, and where you stay I will stay. Your people will be my people, and your God my God. Where you die I will die, and there I will be buried*" (Ruth 1:16–17, NIV). Ruth wanted to lose her former identity and fully assimilate into her new adopted nation, thus making her a "stranger."

In the Bible, there are actually three classifications for Israel's inhabitants (and so, too, in America):

1. The native-born citizen (in Hebrew, called *Ezrach*).
2. The foreign-born immigrant who wants to convert and become a Jew, called a "*stranger*" or "*Stranger of Righteousness*" (*Ger-tzedek*—this is what is referred to in Leviticus 19:34).
3. The foreigner who comes into the land and lives by its laws but does not want to convert, called the "*Stranger of the Gate*" (also called a "*Sojourning Stranger*" —*Gertoshav*).

The first group is natural-born Jews. In America, this is the native-born American citizen.

The second group, the "*stranger*," is a foreigner who renounces his old country and fully commits to becoming a Jew, living by and conforming to the Hebrew Scriptures, who then has the same rights and privileges as other Jewish citizens. In America, this means the foreigner who wants to become an American citizen and renounces all former allegiances, committing to abide by the Constitution and the laws, which are often God-centric and generally based on the Judeo-Christian ethic and morality. And when the foreigner becomes a naturalized American citizen, he then has the same general rights and privileges as native-born American citizens.

The third group is someone who wants to come into the land and is willing to live by the laws of the land but is unwilling to renounce allegiance to his former country and fully assimilate into the new country. (By the way, assimilation is not a dirty word but merely means to fully conform to and become part of.) The Bible describes this person as a *"foreigner"* rather than a *"stranger."* In America, this would be those on temporary worker visas.

CHAPTER 15

THE MELTING POT— A DREAM WORTH KEEPING

An excellent synopsis of the American understanding of a Biblical *"stranger"* comes from, of all places, Broadway. In 1908, during the heyday of American immigration after the dedication of the Statue of Liberty and the opening of Ellis Island, Israel Zangwill, a Jewish immigrant to America, penned a play titled *The Melting Pot*. What he expressed about America in that play was the essence of the Biblical view of assimilation:

> [A]merica is God's Crucible—the great Melting-Pot where all the races of Europe are melting and re-forming! Here you stand, good folk, think I, when I see them at Ellis Island—here you stand in your fifty groups, with your fifty languages and histories, and your fifty blood hatreds and rivalries. But you won't be long like that, brothers, for these are the fires of God you've come to—these are the fires of God! ... Germans and Frenchmen, Irishmen and Englishmen, Jews and Russians— into the Crucible with you all! God is making the American![109]

In 1915, Teddy Roosevelt delivered a similar message:

> There is no room in this country for hyphenated Americanism. When I refer to hyphenated Americans, I do not refer to naturalized Americans. Some of the very best Americans I have ever known were naturalized Americans—Americans born abroad. But a hyphenated American is not an American at all. . . . The one absolutely certain way of bringing this nation to ruin—of preventing all possibility of its continuing to be a nation at all—would be to permit it to become a tangle of squabbling nationalities—an intricate knot of German-Americans, Irish-Americans, English-Americans, French-Americans, Scandinavian-Americans or Italian-Americans, each preserving its separate nationality, each at heart feeling more sympathy with Europeans of that nationality than with the other citizens of the American Republic.[110]

TO BE AMERICAN

Then in 1919, an American Chief of Naturalization penned a work for arriving immigrants (reprinted in 1941), telling them what it meant to become an American:

> An American is a man who is greater in his soul than his class, creed, political party, or in the section in which he lives. To be an American a man must have an American soul, and believe in the spiritual realities upon which America rests, and out of which it was born. America was created to unite mankind by those passions which lift, and not by the passions which separate and debase. We came to America . . . to get rid of the things that divide and to make sure of the things that unite. . . . The man who seeks to divide men from men, group from group, interest from interest in this great Union is striking at its very heart.[111]

Assimilation was always the objective, both in Biblical and American immigration. So any *"stranger"* coming to America must be committed to becoming an American in beliefs, habits, and practices. For example, if they come committed to Sharia courts rather than constitutional courts, or to preserving their own separate financial systems, or their own educational systems, language, customs, and so forth, then they are *not* the *"stranger"* God instructed was to be welcomed into the land.

This should be very easy for a Christian to understand. If we want to live in Heaven—if we want to become a citizen in that new land—we must fully embrace the standards, values, beliefs, and practices God has established for His Kingdom. We cannot just show up at Heaven and be welcomed, but we must renounce our former way of life and conform to and assimilate into God's system. When we do that, then *"our citizenship is in Heaven"* (Philippians 3:20, NIV), and we get the rights and privileges that go with being a citizen in God's kingdom.

So any notion that the Leviticus 19 command to *"love the stranger"* translates into a mandate for an open border and unrestricted immigration is clearly ridiculous.

EUROPEAN LESSONS

Europe currently demonstrates the folly of immigration without assimilation. The policy of the European Union is open borders. They experienced a flood of refugees from the Syrian Civil War. (We recognize "refugees" and "immigrants" are technically two very different groups, but that becomes a distinction without a difference when there are open borders.) Europe has painfully discovered that many came not to assimilate but to take the free stuff, for European nations actually pay immigrants a fixed salary—simply for arriving![112]—no work or contribution of effort or labor is required in return.[113] The Bible pointedly commands *"if any would not work, neither should he eat"* (2 Thessalonians 3:10, KJV), but Europe ignores this command.

CONSEQUENCES FOR WRONG MANAGEMENT OF IMMIGRATION

As a result of the massive influx, Europe is now experiencing skyrocketing crime and terrorism.[114] And immigrant riots are occurring from the many trouble makers among the refugees. The looting, rape, murder, and assault is so high in some immigrant areas they have become "no-go" zones for police,[115] and 80 percent of law enforcement officials in Sweden are looking for new careers.[116] Similar accounts exist in others of the open-border nations. And adding insult to injury, all of this is causing government expenses to soar, requiring citizens to pay even higher taxes.

Understandably, the high price of experience over theory is causing some nations (such as Denmark, Poland, Hungary, Slovenia, Czechoslovakia, and others) to turn in a different direction, taking steps to reduce the free benefits and better regulate their borders.[117] For example, Poland is flatly refusing to accept Syrian immigrants and refugees, so European Union officials are declaring Poland racist and anti-immigrant and are threatening legal action,[118] but Poland is not backing down. They already learned their lesson—the hard way; and it is the same lesson so many other European nations are now beginning to learn.

THE FAILURE TO CULTURALLY ASSIMILATE

During the Chechen Civil War (1999–2009), Poland took in some 80,000 Chechen refugees (nearly all Muslim), but those refugees did not assimilate; they formed their own separate communities, producing high crime rates[119] in a nation well known for its extremely low crime rates.[120] So Poland closed its borders to hard-core Muslim refugees, and it is one of the few nations in Europe that has not experienced a major terrorist attack.[121]

IMMIGRATION THAT WORKS

But although Poland has refused to take hard-core Muslim immigrants, it definitely is not anti-immigrant. In fact, with a population of only thirty-eight million, Poland has accepted some 1.3 million Ukrainian immigrants since Russia's Vladimir Putin invaded Crimea in 2014. But the Ukrainians came to Poland to be part of the country and contribute to it—they wanted to assimilate and become good Polish citizens.[122] So despite the huge influx of immigrants, the jobless rate in Poland is the lowest in twenty-five years, and wages are increasing.[123] This is immigration done correctly.

THE BIBLICAL MODEL

Significantly, when God's people went from Israel to Babylon some 2,600 years ago, the Lord told them concerning that new land: *"Seek the peace and prosperity of the city to which I have carried you into exile. Pray to the Lord for it, because if it prospers, you too will prosper"* (Jeremiah 29:7, NIV). This should be the attitude of every immigrant coming into any new nation: work to help that country prosper and improve— become a blessing to it.

Assimilation is the key word in immigration policy, and any *"stranger"* (Leviticus 19) coming to any nation, whether Poland or America, must be fully committed to becoming a contributor to the good of that nation. It is again worth mentioning: If they don't come committed to the "melting pot" but want their own separate communities, they are not the *"stranger"* God instructed be welcomed into the land.

YEARNING

Americans have extended a welcoming hand to countless immigrants but are perplexed with those who not only fail to appreciate but even attempt to undermine the principles of the country that welcomed them. A major factor in successful immigration is *"the yearning to breathe free"* expressed by Emma Lazarus in "The New Colossus," an 1883 poem written about the Statue of Liberty. People who come to a nation longing for freedom (political, economic, and religious) generally have honorable motivations. For generations, this yearning is what caused assimilation into the American "melting pot."

CHAPTER 16

THE FOUNDERS ON IMMIGRATION

America's Founding Fathers built the most successful constitutional republic in the history of the world. As part of that, they articulated (and implemented) a number of time-tested immigration principles to strengthen and benefit the nation at large.

Significantly, America's early views on immigration closely reflected Biblical ones. This was evident in both the writings of the Founding Fathers and then in the subsequent immigration laws they passed afterward. We would do well to listen to their recommendations.

THE APPROPRIATE PRO-IMMIGRATION STRATEGY

The Founders were definitely pro-immigration. In fact, among the Declaration of Independence's "causes which impelled them to the separation" from Great Britain, King George III's anti-immigration policy was specifically singled out:

He has endeavored to prevent the population of these states; for that purpose obstructing the laws for naturalization of foreigners; refusing to pass others to encourage their migrations hither.[124]

It is logical the Founders were pro-immigration, for as one author has documented:

> Seven of the 39 men who signed the Constitution were immi-grants. In fact, two of the three men most associated with its passage, Alexander Hamilton and James Wilson, were foreign-born. One of the three men who wrote the *Federalist Papers* explaining the Constitution was born abroad. When George Washington chose Justices of the Supreme Court to interpret the Constitution, three of his choices were immigrants . . . Four of the first six Secretaries of the Treasury were immigrants, one each from Switzerland and Scotland, and two from the West Indies. President Washington appointed an Irish immigrant, James McHenry, as Secretary of War in 1796.[125]

COMMON LANGUAGE

Benjamin Franklin was one of the many Founders who spoke openly about immigration policy and his views stressed the Biblical principle of assimilation. For example, when his state of Pennsylvania experienced a high influx of German immigrants, his concern was this

> Few of their children in the country know English. They import many books from Germany . . . The signs in our streets have inscriptions . . . in some places only German. They begin of late to make all their bonds and other legal instruments in their own language.[126]

The goal was not for them to have a parallel culture of their own but to become part of the American culture:

> All that seems to me necessary is to distribute them more equally, mix them with the English, establish English schools where they are now too thick settled. . . . I am not against the admission of Germans in general, for they have their virtues.

Their industry and frugality are exemplary. They are excellent husbandmen [farmers], and contribute greatly to the improvement of a country.[127]

ASSIMILATION

Thomas Jefferson, another pro-immigration Founder, also warned against the dangers of non-assimilation. He began by pointing out the remarkable uniqueness of the American system to which immigrants would be coming,[128] and they would be arriving from nations with a very different type of government (usually monarchies, with class distinction and an elite class of nobility) and with national practices almost exactly the opposite of what they would find here. He therefore warned:

> They will bring with them the principles of the governments they leave, imbibed in their early youth. . . . These [old] principles, with their language, they will transmit to their children. In proportion to their numbers, they will share with us the legislation. They will infuse into it their [old] spirit, warp and bias its directions, and render it a heterogeneous, incoherent, distracted mass.[129]

For Jefferson, the solution was avoiding a parallel culture and ensuring assimilation into the uniquely American culture:

> [I]t is thought better to discourage their settling together in large masses . . . and that they should distribute themselves sparsely among the native for quicker amalgamation.[130]

Alexander Hamilton (an immigrant from the West Indies) echoed the same concerns[131] and identified the same solution:

> Some reasonable term ought to be allowed to enable aliens to get rid of foreign and acquire American attachments; to learn the principles and imbibe the spirit of our government; and to admit of a probability at least of their feeling a real interest in our affairs. A residence of not less than five years ought to be required.[132]

Immigrants needed to spend time in America becoming familiar with its unique Constitution, culture, faith, morality, and practices before becoming citizens. Pierce Butler—an Irish immigrant who signed the US Constitution—agreed. According to James Madison, Butler

> acknowledged that if he himself had been called into public life within a short time after his coming to America, his foreign habits, opinions, and attachments would have rendered him an improper agent in public affairs.[133]

> Butler, *was decidedly opposed to the admission of foreigners without a long residence in the country.*[134]

The Founders therefore established a residency requirement for becoming a citizen. Assimilation was always the objective, and it took time.

SOME IMMIGRANTS SHOULD NOT BE ALLOWED

The Founders also recognized some immigrants should be excluded. As affirmed by Founding Father Fisher Ames:

> The *salus Reipub* [safety of the republic] so plainly requires the power of expelling or refusing admission to aliens.[135]

As Constitution signer Rufus King specifically noted:

> [I] cannot persuade myself that the malcontents of any character or country will ever become useful citizens of ours.[136]

So what was his solution to keep *"malcontents"* from being admitted to America?

> It was the practice of the emigrants from Scotland to bring with them certifications from the religious societies to which they belonged of their honesty, sobriety, and generally of their good character. Why should we not require some such document from all emigrants? And it would be well to add to the testimonial that the person to whom it was granted was not expelled from his country and had not been convicted of any crime.[137]

There needed to be proof of good character and a thorough background check.

CHAPTER 17

EARLY IMMIGRATION

When the Constitution went into effect in 1789, it stipulated Congress could *"establish a uniform rule of naturalization"* (Art. 1, Sec. 8, Par, 4). In the immigration laws they penned (such as those of 1790, 1795, and 1798), many of the principles earlier expressed in their writings became core features of federal immigration policy:

- The immigrant must have good moral character[138]
- The immigrant must not only support the Constitution and our government and laws[139] but also renounce allegiance to any other nation[140] or loyalty to any other system[141]
- The immigrant must believe in the equality of all Americans and renounce any title of nobility[142]
- There must be a residency requirement of five years in the United States before citizenship[143]
- The children of a naturalized citizen also become citizens at the same time[144]
- No anchor babies—citizenship goes from parents to child, not child to parent[145]
- Security risks can be deported and permanently banned from the United States[146]
- The government must protect the borders during times of war[147]
- States would have a definite role in immigration.[148]

CANNOT SERVE TWO MASTERS

Notice several provisions requiring unwavering fidelity to the United States (such as renouncing former loyalties, governments, and systems and then pledging allegiance to America). The reason was long ago explained in the Bible, when Jesus noted, "*No one can serve two masters. Either you will hate the one and love the other, or you will be devoted to the one and despise the other*" (Matthew 6:24 NIV). An immigrant needed to serve one country or the other, one system or the other, but not both.

In fact, let's be clear: Sharia Law is incompatible and often in direct conflict with the US Constitution. One cannot be committed to Sharia Law and at the same time fulfill the required oath to support the US Constitution. As President Dwight Eisenhower once noted, you cannot interpret the Constitution (or the First Amendment's freedom of religion) in such a way that would destroy it:

> The Bill of Rights contains no grant of privilege for a group of people to destroy the Bill of Rights. A group . . . dedicated to the ultimate destruction of all civil liberties cannot be allowed to claim civil liberties as its privileged sanctuary from which to carry on subversion of the government.[149]

For this reason, Sharia supremacists, ardent socialists, members of gangs or drug cartels, criminals, and so forth are among those who should be excluded.

STATES' ROLE IN IMMIGRATION

Notice also the Founders gave states a seminal role in the immigration process, but today states are told they have no role. But the earlier policy makes more sense because the immigrant to America did not live in the United States *per se*, but in Maryland, Florida, Oregon, or wherever, so it was logical states should have a voice. Thus, although Congress set the "*uniform rule of naturalization*," states were allowed to determine additional requirements for immigrants to their state. Typical of state requirements in the early years were these

> Pennsylvania allowed any foreigner of "good character" who took an oath of allegiance to the state to acquire property, and after one year's residency become a citizen entitled to "all the

rights of a natural born subject of this state." New York followed Pennsylvania's model and added a requirement for foreigners to renounce all allegiance to any foreign prince. Maryland's naturalization law required a declaration of "belief in the Christian religion" and an oath of allegiance. In South Carolina, full naturalization required at least two years of residency and a special act of the legislature.[150]

States played an important part in immigration policy until the US Supreme Court issued decisions in 1875 and 1876 declaring states would no longer have any significant role[151]—the federal government would assume the sole powers regarding immigration.

Five years later, the federal immigration law of 1891 created the *first* federal "*office of Superintendent of Immigration.*"[152] The following year (1892), the first-ever federal immigration reception center opened: Ellis Island, adjoining the famed Statue of Liberty. Prior to that, states' port authorities and commissions were the processing bodies for immigrants.

So today's policy of largely excluding states from immigration policy is a stark difference from what was successfully practiced in America for so long.

CHAPTER 18

EARLY IMMIGRATION LAWS

A few subsequent federal immigration acts added provisions also worthy of notice. For example, the Page Act of 1875 continued the emphasis on having good morals by forbidding the importation of individuals "*for lewd and immoral purposes*" or "*women for the purposes of prostitution*"[153]—an early law against sex trafficking. It also added a criminal background check and excluded immigrants guilty of criminal activity.[154]

The 1891 law required that:

- Immigrants must pass a health exam and also be able to support themselves and not become a burden on taxpayers or the government[155]
- The immigrant must have the permission of the United States before coming[156]
- Immigrants here illegally or who become a public charge on the government would be deported[157]
- The government must establish border security at all times, not just during war.[158]

PACED IMMIGRATION

Other notable immigration acts included those of 1921 and 1924, which reduced the number of immigrants being accepted. Large numbers arriving in the aftermath of World War I caused the annual admission numbers to be lowered in order to give time to assimilate the earlier arrivals. Interestingly, in the history of Israel, there were also times when similar moratoriums were enacted.

For example, during the reign of King David and King Solomon, the economic situation was so prosperous *"strangers"* were descending on the nation in large numbers, and many were coming for the wrong reasons. Israel did not want to lose its unique national character and wanted to assimilate those already there, so a halt was placed on incoming *"strangers."*[159]

President Calvin Coolidge explained the similar logic behind America's temporary pause following World War I:

> We are all agreed, whether we be Americans of the first or of the seventh generation on this soil, that it is not desirable to receive more immigrants than can reasonably be assured of bettering their condition by coming here. For the sake both of those who would come and more especially of those already here, it has been thought wise to avoid the danger of increasing our numbers too fast. It is not a reflection on any race or creed. We might not be able to support them if their numbers were too great. . . . We want to keep wages and living conditions good for everyone who is now here or who may come here.[160]

ABSENCE OF PRINCIPLED THINKING

For generations, America's immigration policies mirrored and incorporated many of the principles set forth in the Bible. When we abandoned those principles, our immigration system began to fail and now is no longer unified by core principles but rather has become a patchwork of rapidly changing and often contradictory provisions.

The period in which immigration laws definitely began to move in the wrong direction was during the rise of Secular Progressives at the end of the nineteenth century.

FLAWED THINKING ON IMMIGRATION

Four of their beliefs had a direct impact on immigration policy: (1) a focus on groups rather than individuals, with some groups/races being more important than others; (2) man is innately good, possesses good character, and, given the right environment, will always do the right thing; (3) greater government involvement and regulation improves public policy; and (4) immigration should use the "salad bowl" rather than the "melting pot" approach.

Concerning the "melting pot," separate identities meld into one, but in the "salad bowl," each ingredient maintains its own separate identity, not assimilating with the other ingredients.[2] As one commentator noted:

> [T]he common identity shaped by the Constitution, the English language, and the history, mores, and heroes of America gives way to multifarious, increasingly fragmented micro-identities. . . . Many immigrants, legal or otherwise, are now encouraged to celebrate the cultures they have fled and to prefer them to the one that gave them greater freedom and opportunity. Our schools and popular culture reinforce this separatism.[161]

As the influence of Progressives grew in the late 1800s, immigration policies began to reflect these core Progressive beliefs. But President Benjamin Harrison was no Progressive, and upon taking office in 1889, he called for a return to previous principles:

> Our naturalization laws should be so amended as to make the inquiry into the character. . . . and good disposition of persons applying for citizenship more careful and searching. . . . We accept the man as a citizen without any knowledge of his fitness, and he assumes the duties of citizenship without any knowledge as to what they are. . . . We should not cease to be hospitable to immigration, but we should cease to be careless as to the character of it. There are men of all races, even the best, whose coming is necessarily a burden upon our public revenues or a threat to social order. These should be identified and excluded.[162]

2. In the 1960s, this became known as "multiculturalism."

So in review, good immigration policy seeks assimilation, and historically, several specific policies helped achieve this: a residency requirement before citizenship (thus allowing time to become fully accustomed to and familiar with the unique American system); a pledge of undivided loyalty to the nation, its Constitution, laws, culture, faith, and morality; and renouncing allegiance to any other nation or system of laws.

So given these core principles, what can be said about immigration policies today?

CHAPTER 19

A SNAPSHOT OF THE UNITED STATES NOW

One of the most visible indicators of our current broken system is the number of illegal immigrants—an estimated eleven million,[163] or approximately 3.4 percent of the total population.[164]

DISTRIBUTION

Almost 60 percent of known illegal immigrants are located in six states: California, Texas, Florida, New York, New Jersey, and Illinois. Seven states have actually experienced a decrease in illegal immigrants (Alabama, California, Georgia, Illinois, Kansas, Nevada, and South Carolina), primarily because of a drop in Mexican immigrants,[165] and six states (Louisiana, Massachusetts, New Jersey, Pennsylvania, Virginia, and Washington) an increase, primarily from countries other than Mexico.[166] For years, illegal immigration was a problem primarily in border states such as California and Texas, but today the entire nation is impacted.

STAYING LONGER

Two thirds of illegal immigrants have been in the United States at least a decade—a substantial increase over the 40 percent of 2005.[167] Unauthorized persons from Mexico have dropped from 6.4 million in 2009 to 5.6 million in 2016. The number of illegal immigrants from Asia and Central America has increased.[168]

JOBS

It is estimated eight million undocumented persons are in the workforce, representing about 26 percent of farm workers and 15 percent of construction workers.[169]

CHAPTER 20

CHRISTIANS OR
MUSLIMS?

In recent years, the focus on immigration has broadened to include the influx of refugees—those fleeing wars or persecution. During the Syrian Civil War, millions were displaced and sought refuge in Europe or America, and ISIS was simultaneously slaughtering Christians all over the Middle East, including in Syria.

Significantly, Christians worldwide are now being killed in higher numbers than at any time in world history—some 90,000 are martyred for their faith each year.[170] In the Middle East, Christian populations are plummeting. Representative of this, there were 1.5 million Christians in Iraq in 1991; today the number is only 175,000.[171] The rapid decline of Christians in the region caused publications such as *The Economist* to ask *"whether Christianity will vanish from the Middle East, its cradle, after 2,000 years."*[172]

The United States has been very unsympathetic to persecuted Christians. In fact, statistics confirm 99 percent of the 12,587 Syrians granted refugee status in 2016 were Muslims[173]—only 100 of the refugees were Christians.[174]

Muslim refugees were given much higher priority than Christians, but thankfully, President Trump has announced a change in US policy, stating persecuted Christians should be given priority. He explained:

If you were a Muslim you could come in, but if you were a Christian, it was almost impossible. And the reason that was so unfair (everybody was persecuted, in all fairness) [was that] they were chopping off the heads of everybody, but more so the Christians. And I thought it was very, very unfair. So we are going to help them.[175]

Yet despite the institutional bias against Christians, some Christian leaders object to this change, declaring, *"We would resist that strongly."*[176] They are wrong.

WHERE CAN THEY GO?

Why? Three reasons.

First, assimilation must always be the primary focus in immigration. For more than two centuries, Christians have assimilated into America much more readily than Muslims, for Christian values are much closer to America's core values than are the values of Islam.

Second, persecuted Christians in the Middle East essentially have nowhere to go. With the obvious exception of Israel, every nation is Muslim. It is true many Muslims are also suffering severely in the war-torn areas, but the Middle East is composed of numerous Muslim nations that can be places of refuge for fellow Muslims. But where in the Middle East can a Christian safely go, live, work, worship, and openly live the Christian faith?

Third, for those of us who are believers, the Bible instructs: *"As we have opportunity, let us do good to all people, especially to those who belong to the family of believers"* (Galatians 6:10, NIV). We are to provide especially for the *"family of believers."* This needs no additional commentary.

So should priority be given to Christians fleeing the Middle East? Their lives depend on it.

CHAPTER 21

HOW DID THIS HAPPEN?

Countless politicians have claimed they will fix the problem, but our national immigration policy still lies in shambles.

VOTES AND LABOR

Democrats accuse Republicans and Republicans fault Democrats, but both are to blame. As documented by numerous independent sources, they both have incentives for protecting illegal immigration: Democrats, creating a dependent underclass, see the potential for easy votes, and Republicans, often tied to business interests, see cheap labor. But there is abundant evidence the blame is to be shared in a bipartisan way.

For example, border sheriffs are on the frontline of the open border problems, fighting against drug cartels, gangs, terrorist infiltrations, human trafficking, and the massive influx of illegal non-Americans. The problem of a porous border is indisputably a federal issue, but both Republican George W. Bush and Democrat Barack Obama denied the sheriffs the desperately needed assistance to secure and control the border. And both Bush and Obama took actions that made immigration problems bigger.

DESUETUDE

The main facilitator of illegal immigration is a government doing nothing to change the broken system or enforce the existing laws. When laws are on the books but not enforced, the law is in *desuetude* (pronounced DEH-swah-tude)—it is regarded as essentially ceasing to exist.

If we were husbands and dads in Mexico with hungry wives and children and we couldn't get a job in our native country and we heard the United States was no longer enforcing immigration law and considering that law in abeyance, we would cross the border and get a job to feed our families. The government's failure to enforce its own laws is what caused that crossing. (By the way, since Trump became president, border crossings have dropped 36 percent.[177] No new laws have been passed, but existing laws are being enforced.)

In 1986, the problem of illegal immigrants in the country was so great President Ronald Reagan believed the only way to fix it was to start over—to have a system reset. The result was the Immigration Reform and Control Act of 1986, granting amnesty to the five million immigrants in the United States (of which three million applied, and 2.7 million were granted amnesty).[178] Everyone already here could stay, but from that point forward, the border would be made impenetrable so the nation would never again find itself in a similar situation. But so much for the government keeping its promise to maintain a secure border—we now have at least eleven million.

CHAPTER 22

WHY HAVE BORDERS AT ALL?

Maybe there is a more basic question. Do we even need borders? Why shouldn't we all just join hands and become more global, with open borders? Certainly many globalists want this, but God does not. In fact, when people tried to do this at the Tower of Babel (Genesis 11), God stepped in and put a stop to it.

THE BIBLE AND NATIONS

Significantly, the Bible repeatedly speaks with approval of distinct nations:

- . . . and *all nations* **on earth** will be blessed through him. GENESIS 18:18
- . . . that Your ways may be known on earth—Your salvation among *all nations*, PSALM 67:2
- . . . *go and make disciples of all nations* . . . MATTHEW 28:19
- . . . with your blood you purchased for God persons from *every tribe and language and people and nation*. REVELATION 5:9
- . . . and there before me was a great multitude that no one could count, from *every nation, tribe, people and language* . . . REVELATION 7:9 All NIV.

CHAPTER 23

A WAY OUT

Jim pastors a congregation in San Diego called Skyline Church. In addition to its English-speaking congregation, it also has a Spanish-speaking one. Some in that congregation became quite concerned when Trump became president, fearing they or some of their family members might be deported. But the focus of the Trump administration has been on the deportation of the half-million *violent* illegal immigrants in the country, who are an unnecessary danger to all who live here.

THE HARM OF SO-CALLED "SANCTUARY" CITIES

For example, in San Francisco, thirty-two-year-old Kate Steinle, while walking with her father, was shot and killed by Jose Inez Garcia Zarate. Zarate had been previously deported five times and was back in the country illegally for the sixth at the time of the killing.

Before the shooting occurred, ICE (US Immigration and Customs Enforcement) asked San Francisco law enforcement officers to hold Zarate so they could pick him up, but "Sanctuary City" San Francisco said no. (A "Sanctuary City" refuses to uphold federal immigration laws.) So San Francisco released Zarate, and as a result, Kate was shot and died in her father's arms. Countless other tragedies have been and will be allowed by our not enforcing the law.

Not ashamed of the harm "sanctuary cities" have done to citizens, California's Governor Jerry Brown signed a law making the entire state a "sanctuary state." San Francisco and the 300 other self-declared "sanctuary cities" across the nation are "Exhibit A" for how not to handle the immigration problem.

A THREE-STEP SOLUTION

Based on the eleven million number, the immigration situation in America is the worst it has ever been. So how do we get out of this? Let us suggest a three-step process.

FIRST STEP: PROTECT THE BORDERS

How do you protect the borders? Despite the polarized rhetoric on this issue, statistics are indisputable; where sections of wall have been built along the border, those areas have seen a substantial decrease in illegal crossings, including the dangerous elements associated with gangs and cartels. Therefore, building a wall is a crucial way to protect our southern border. This is not a racist or xenophobic statement. Walls should be built for the same reason Nehemiah built walls in the Old Testament. Nowhere in the Bible does God condemn the walls guarding houses, the fences encircling property, or the locks protecting doors. They are all for the purpose of security and protection.

Ironically, Pope Francis decries building a wall,[179] yet he lives behind heavily fortified walls with military guards. If he doesn't like walls, let him begin by tearing down the Vatican walls. Similarly, many wealthy and visible Hollywood socialites are condemning the building of a wall, yet they all have walls and extensive security around their homes. If they don't like walls, let them tear down those they live behind. They won't.

Walls provide safety for those inside them, and because of the lack of a wall, dangerous drugs flood into our nation, and the drug cartels and human traffickers move easily back and forth. Furthermore, Mexico—our southern neighbor—is ranked as the second-most violent nation in the world.[180] Perhaps the Rev. Franklin Graham said it best: "*Why do you lock your doors at night? Not because you hate the people on the outside, but because you love the people on the inside so much.*"[181]

SECOND STEP: A GOVERNMENTAL ADMISSION

The government has the legal responsibility to enforce the law, and it cannot fail to do so for decades and then suddenly say, "*We are going to deport you for something we failed to do!"* The US government needs to openly acknowledge it has been the greatest contributor to the immigration problem.

You might think our government would never acknowledge wrongdoing, but it has happened numerous times before:

- 1948: an apology to Mexico for allowing farm laborers to cross the Texas border illegally[182]
- 1983: an apology to France for helping Nazi War criminal Klaus Barbie escape to South America to avoid prosecution[183]
- 1988: an apology for the detainment of Japanese Americans in World War II[184]
- 1997: an apology for deliberately infecting black men with syphilis to study the effects of the disease[185]
- 2005: an apology for never having passed an anti-lynching law[186]
- 2008 and 2009: an apology for slavery and Jim Crow laws.[187]

There are many additional examples. It has happened before and needs to happen again—the US government needs to acknowledge it helped created the national crisis of eleven million illegal immigrants.

THIRD STEP: ACKNOWLEDGEMENT BY THOSE BREAKING THE LAW

Step three: is those who came illegally must acknowledge they did in fact come here illegally or they illegally overstayed their visas. It would be almost inconceivable any adult who came here illegally did not know they were breaking a law at the time (although it is different for minors). So even though our government failed to enforce the immigration laws (or did so haphazardly), laws were still *knowingly* broken by those who came. There need to be consequences.

So if one was above the age of eighteen when they came illegally, that individual can go through a process to live here legally but can never become a citizen. That process could include things such as:

- Small, manageable fines paid
- Any existing back taxes paid
- Official papers filed

- English language classes attended (This is not done as a penalty but to give the person access to greater economic and educational options.)
- US History and citizenship classes taken and fundamental American values embraced. This includes a knowledge and understanding of the Declaration of Independence (including its God-centered character) and the US Constitution—the keys to American Exceptionalism
- And there are many other possible combinations of requirements.

For example, other possibilities are that those who are illegal immigrants but wish to be here legally cannot have a "Green Card" (which is a step toward citizenship). Instead, using the colors of traffic lights, they would have an "Amber Card," meaning full citizenship is not a possibility. And for those qualifying for a noncitizen "legalized status," they could work in all arenas of employment and be protected by standard US wage laws, and for legal and travel purposes, these persons would keep the citizenship of the country from which they came.

Additionally, for those who were minors when they came to this country, they could complete all the above, with the exception of the Amber Card. If they do this and have a clean record and good character, then they could apply for citizenship. By the way, the government has every right to utilize a merit-based immigration program prioritizing those who can contribute most to the nation. (The proposed law known as RAISE—Reforming American Immigration for Strong Employment Act—does precisely that.)

We are not proposing amnesty but rather a rigorous pathway to legalization.

CHAPTER 24

THE GREATEST OPPORTUNITY

In finishing this section, immigration is a topic that should also be viewed from an eternal perspective.

CHURCH VERSUS CIVIL GOVERNMENT

As noted earlier, the Church and government have different functions, callings, and purposes. The role of the government is to protect its citizens and enforce the border. The role of the Church, in simplest terms, is to get people to God through Jesus Christ.

THE ETERNAL DEMARCATION

The demarcation of whether people are here legally or illegally is not a question to be resolved by the Church. The major demarcation for the Church is whether someone knows Christ or doesn't and then help every immigrant have an opportunity to know Christ.

IT'S ALL ABOUT JESUS

As Christians, we want immigrants to embrace American values and understand the distinctly Biblical foundations of this nation. But we also want them to come to the awareness that their sins can be forgiven by Jesus's death on the cross and that they can experience the fullness of the Holy Spirit God promises to His children.

Virtually every church sends missionaries to other countries. But now the people from those countries are coming to us! This presents us a wonderful opportunity of expressing God's love to them not only through acts of kindness but especially by sharing the Gospel with them. This could be one of the Church's finest hours if it reaches out to the immigrants in our midst not just to help them assimilate into America but specifically to help them assimilate into the family of God through a personal knowledge of His Son Jesus Christ.

Prayer: Lord, we confess that the issue of immigration seems to have become complex, but we believe you are the God of order. There is a principled way to work through the confusion and chaos that has reigned over this issue. We ask for solutions that honor justice, love, righteousness, and order. Show us the solutions You desire. Amen.

ISRAEL

*The Lord had said . . . "I will make you into a
great nation . . . I will bless those who bless you,
and whoever curses you I will curse; and all peoples on earth will be blessed through you."*

GENESIS 12:1-3, NIV

The goal of this section is to understand Israel historically and spiritually, to expose the evil of anti-Semitism, and to grasp the Biblical
rationale for standing with the Jewish people and the State of Israel.

CHAPTER 25

PUBLIC OPINION TOWARD ISRAEL

If . . . :

- you are a college student, you've probably seen signs around campus regarding Israel; what do almost all of these signs have in common?
- you follow the so-called "mainstream media," what do most of their reports about Israel have in common?
- you follow votes at the United Nations, what do the resolutions addressing Israel have in common?
- you attend a liberal, mainline church, what do mentions of Israel generally have in common?
- you attend some of the hipster seminars on Israel and Palestine now being presented on some Christian college campuses and even in some of America's chic mega-churches, what do they have in common?

Answer: In each of these various venues, Israel is consistently presented in a negative light—as an oppressor, human rights violator, abuser of minorities within its boundaries, builder of huge walls to make daily life unbearable for the Arabs within Israel, and so forth. There is only one problem with these claims: they are not true—none of them. As part of this section, we'll unravel these unfounded charges against Israel.

For starters, no nation is perfect. Israel is not, nor does she claim to be—nor does anyone we know claim it for her. But neither is she guilty of the absurd charges heaped upon her—charges sometimes innocently (but often deliberately) repeated, generally devoid of actual factual data, and usually stemming from the sensationalistic rhetoric often used by Israel's opponents.

Additionally, being "pro-Israel" does not mean being anti-Arab, anti-Muslim, or anti-Palestinian. To be pro-Israel simply means having the view of Israel God sets forth in the Bible, which includes Israel today still playing a key role in the plans of God.

(By the way, ethnically speaking, there are no actual Biblical "Palestinian" people today. True Palestinians—that is, the people in the Bible known as the Philistines—were not even Arabs. They were originally from Greece and arrived in the Holy Land about 2000 BC, leaving the region of Israel and the Holy Land by the fifth century BC. The group now called Palestinians is largely an Arabic creation of the 1900s.)

So how do we explain the anti-Israel hysteria so apparent in much of our nation and world today?

For starters, let's state the obvious: Jews have been hated from the beginning. They are the single most abused people group in the history of the world. Why? The answer is simple: the Jews remind people of the God of the Bible, and there has always been (and still is today) strident opposition to thinking about God. If you take seriously the existence of the Jews, it means there is a God of the Bible Who called them into existence. And if there is a God of the Bible, the Bible makes plain He also gave us a clear moral law. This means I need to obey Him and can't do solely what I want.

CHAPTER 26

RAMPANT ANTI-SEMITISM

So returning to the false claims against Israel, what is usually at the root of these claims? Succinctly stated, anti-Semitism—a hatred of the Jews—is a hatred of the group that most reminds people of the God of the Bible, all He represents, and all He has said.

In some circles today, anti-Semitism is properly frowned upon as racism, but this is too rare. There currently exists an acceptable elitist so-called "intellectual" form of Jew-hatred and anti-Semitism manifesting itself as anti-Israelism.

Israel is under daily attack. Often, it is by bullets and rockets, but the new and more common pandemic is slander and lies. Many college students (and recent graduates) now believe what they heard on campus at anti-Israel events. As a result (and at the risk of using too many foreign words), they believe they have found a *cause celebre* that seems to give them a *raison d'être*—that is, a cause worthy of their existence—an apparently noble issue for a modern social justice warrior. And since an increasing number of church attendees no longer have a Biblical worldview,[188] far too much of the so-called Christian church has also embraced these lies.

BDS

The new battlefront against Israel has been reduced to three letters of the alphabet: BDS—*Boycott, Divestment,* and *Sanction.* It is an effective movement *"to end international support for Israel's oppression of Pal-estinians and pressures Israel to comply with international law."*[189] It proceeds on the belief that economic pressure on Israel will force her to change policies toward the Arab group now called Palestinians. This effort thus encourages (1) *B*—the boycotting of Israeli products, (2) *D*—divesting personal holdings from Israeli companies, and (3) *S*—punishing Israel with economic sanctions.

The movement currently has its greatest support among university investments, liberal churches, academic societies, and the entertainment industry. To date, the actual economic impact on Israel has been minis-cule, but the potential for a substantial negative effect is much greater. For example, the UN Human Rights Council voted to approve a "black-list" of companies and international firms doing business in Israeli "settlements." This list is a prelude to international anti-Israel boycotts, attempting to force the already tiny nation of Israel to give up even more of its scarce and precious land to Palestinians, most of whose leaders have sworn to completely annihilate her.

Two significant things should be noted here. *First*, the so-called settlements targeted by the United Nations are often modern and fully up-to-date Israeli cities with skyscrapers and all the high-tech modern conveniences. These cities are built on official Israeli soil, within the borders of Israel, but the Palestinians want these particular pieces of land for themselves as part of what they envision as a future Palestinian state. They demeaningly call these legitimate Israeli cities "settlements," and American media routinely parrots these debasing terms. *Second*, oppo-nents demand that Israel give up more land to the Palestinians, but Israel is already so small it would fit into California twenty times, thirty-three times into Texas, and eighty-two times into Alaska. Israel is surrounded by a score of Arab nations hundreds of times larger who could easily give land to the Palestinians for them to have a nation, but the Palestinians don't want Arab land; they want Israel's land—and they want the Jewish state of Israel gone, completely.

Interestingly, any boycott of Israel could actually backfire on the boycotters. The list of advanced technological, medical, agricultural, and scientific advances coming out of Israel is so long any true boycott of Israeli products could actually take the boycotting countries back to life in the 1970s.[190] But large international firms doing business in Israel could be harmed if nations or coalitions, such as the European Union, were to formally align with the BDS movement.

APARTHEID

An explosive word often used against Israel is *apartheid*. This is an African word that means *separation*, and it describes the system of racial segregation and subjugation of the African and non-white population in South Africa by white settlers from 1948 to 1994. *Apartheid* is an emotionally charged word designed to evoke an immediate negative response, and it is now frequently used to describe Israel and its relations with the Palestinians.

To feel sympathy for any impoverished or oppressed group and to seek righteous and just treatment of everyone should always be the norm. But the greatest oppression of Palestinians today comes not from Israel but from the Palestinian leaders. Despite billions of dollars of economic aid sent to the Palestinian authorities over recent years, there still remains no effective infrastructure in place for the Palestinian people to survive and thrive, but their leaders live in opulent luxury. Israel does not control those funds and should not be blamed for the resulting struggling condition of the Palestinian people.

Few today know some 15 percent of Israeli citizens are Arabs, and they can work and vote and serve in the government and on the Supreme Court; there are Arab soldiers, doctors, lawyers, and Knesset members (that is, members of the official government) openly serving in Israel today. Unknown to most Americans, Arab citizens have the *same rights* as every other Israeli citizen. Let's repeat this: they have the *same rights* as every other Israeli citizen. (If this is the only sentence you remember from this section, you will have a better grasp of reality in Israel than most Americans.)

Moreover, when Arab Israelis are asked whether they would prefer to be governed by Israel or the Palestinians, they overwhelmingly choose Israel.[191] In fact, since 1947 and as recently as 2009, Palestinian leaders have refused every offer to become an autonomous state within Israel.[192] They don't want to be a part of Israel; they want *all* of Israel and have thus maintained a state of perpetual enmity against them. (Strikingly, several well-known Palestinian groups have been officially labeled terrorist organizations and actively engage in terrorist activity,[193] thus expending their resources in destructive endeavors rather than in building a productive Arab Palestinian society.)

In reality, Israelis come in all shapes and colors. Walking down the streets of Jerusalem, one can hear not only Hebrew but Arabic, Chinese, French, German, Spanish, Farsi, English, and many other languages and can also see faces of those from around the world who make their homes in Israel. They are all Israelis. Israel is a veritable "united nations" of people, including Arabs. To refer to it as an apartheid state would be laughable were this false claim not so often repeated (and believed).

SPEAKING OF "UNITED NATIONS"

In 1975 (nearly three decades after the establishment of Israel), the UN General Assembly adopted a resolution (by more than a two-to-one margin) declaring *"Zionism is a form of racism and racial discrimination."*[194] Zionism is the belief that Jews have three rights: (1) the right to a Jewish homeland (a tiny piece of real estate called Israel that is only one-eighth of 1 percent of the Arabic land in the Middle East), (2) the right to exist as an independent nation (they are just one of approximately 200 nations in the world), and (3) the right to defend themselves. You would think this would be a no-brainer for any people, but no. The United Nations has declared this to be racist—if done by Jews. Arab nations all around Israel do the very same thing—that is, they exist as independent Arabic nations with the right to defend themselves, but somehow it is racist for Jews to do the same thing.

The General Assembly of the United Nations has a built-in institutionalized anti-Israel majority. In fact, since the inception of the United Nations in 1945, more resolutions have been passed condemning Israel than any other country in the world. Consider the absurdity of this: China is well known for its brutality and lack of civil rights; barbaric dictatorships throughout South America and Africa have carried out numerous genocides; millions have died in North Korea in recent years under its dictators, who threaten nations across the world with nuclear attacks; Iran is the chief exporter of terrorism around the world; yet Israel—the only free democratic nation in the Middle East—has received more condemnations than any other country!

Subcommittees of the United Nations (such as the Human Rights Council) have repeated condemnation of Israel as a standing item on the agenda. Ironically, this council has among its members such "stalwarts" of human rights (spoken tongue in cheek) as Iraq, Qatar, Venezuela, Cuba, and Saudi Arabia. These nations, notorious for their heavy-handed ruthlessness and flagrant disregard for human life, are permanent members of the UN *Human Rights* Council and routinely sit in judgment of Israel.

Another equally biased UN committee is UNESCO (UN Education, Scientific, and Cultural Organization). In the past two years, it has passed resolutions denying there is any Jewish connection to the Temple Mount and the Western Wall in Jerusalem, to the Tomb of the Patriarchs in Hebron, and to the burial site of Abraham, Sarah, and their children.[195] (Imagine. Each of these sites came into existence because of the Jews and was integral to Jewish history and existence; but the United Nations says Jews have no connection to these sites.)

Thankfully, there has been a recent noticeable change in the language of the United Nations since the arrival of the Trump administration (which went against international outcry and, in accord with a federal law passed in 1995,[196] moved the US embassy to Jerusalem[197]). Trump's Ambassador to the United Nations, Nikki Haley, represents a fresh voice of reason on the Security Council and has repeatedly stood firmly with Israel and against the extremists at the United Nations.

ENTER THE YOUNG

A current objective for Palestinians and their American enablers is to turn the next generation against Israel. These efforts are regularly focused on college campuses. In fact, in a recent year, there were 1,600 anti-Israel events held on campuses across the country.[198] One event common on college campuses is "Israel Apartheid Week," which often features a replica of the security barrier separating Israel from the Palestinians.

For those unfamiliar with the security barrier, Israel identified the Palestinian communities within Israel from which the bulk of the terrorist attacks against her originated and then built security walls around those most dangerous areas, still leaving average Palestinians free to come and go. Israel built the wall to keep its citizens not only from being blown up, stabbed, and injured in countless ways but also to reduce crime. (Carjacking was routine, with stolen cars taken to chop shops to be sold out as parts to finance further terrorist attacks against Israelis.) The wall may be controversial to those who have never lived (like the Israelis have) with the daily threat of violent death, but both crime and terrorist attacks within Israel have dropped over 99 percent as a result of that security wall, thus saving thousands of lives.[199]

Nevertheless, in the minds of young adults, misinformation campaigns launched by radical groups have successfully turned Israel into worse offenders than the Palestinian terror groups that routinely target innocent victims in Israel. What is most troubling about this transformation in thinking is it is also happening on evangelical Christian college campuses, where the next generation of Christian leaders is being trained.

THE BATTLE FOR PUBLIC OPINION

When Palestinian terrorists slaughter innocent families within Israel or blow up buses full of Israelis (Jim had the well-known "Bus No. 19"—or what was left of it—brought to his church in San Diego and put on display for all to see what the Israelis experience each day), the discussion inevitably comes back to the so-called Israeli "occupation" (of their own land) as the justified cause of the violence, as though such acts of terror can ever be justified.

When Israel is bombarded from Gaza with thousands of rockets shot indiscriminately into its most populated cities rather than at military targets, and when Israel returns fire with pinpoint airstrikes aimed at the origin or the originator of the strikes, Israel is then accused in the press of disproportionate response. Of course, the response is disproportionate—it is disproportionately *less*, for had Israel exercised a proportional response (using an equal number of munitions and rockets against Gaza as were fired against Israel), there would be no Gaza left today.

In reality, Israel is not only the most civilized and advanced nation in the Middle East, but unlike its Arab neighbors, it sends humanitarian and medical aid around the world in times of crisis. Israel is literally a global first-responder. Its military humanitarian teams travel the world with the most advanced field hospitals to serve in areas of devastation.[200] In fact, the World Health Organization recognized the Israeli army's field hospital, sent far and wide into natural disaster sites, as "number one in the world."[201] But it makes little difference how much Israel does, for she rarely earns good will in the press or academia.

CHAPTER 27

GENESIS 12:1–3

In Genesis 12, God initiates a plan to redeem mankind. He calls to an elderly man named Abram (later known as Abraham) and says to him: *"Get out of your country, from your family and from your father's house, to a land that I will show you. I will make you a great **nation**; I will bless you and make your name great; and you shall be a blessing. I will bless those who bless you, and I will curse him who curses you; and in you all the families of the earth shall be blessed"* (1-3 NKJV).

The nation of Israel enters the storyline through this incredibly profound covenant God made with Abraham—a covenant He still keeps to this very day. (Psalm 105:8 assures us: *"He remembers His covenant forever—the promise He made—for a thousand generations."* NIV) According to God, those who bless Abraham and the people and nation he founded (the Jews and Israel) will be blessed, and those who curse his people and nation will be cursed. It is fair to say all world history from ancient times to the present continues to be affected by how mankind responds to this particular precept established by God—by how individuals and nations treat the Jews and Israel.

ABRAHAM, ISAAC, AND ISHMAEL

We know from the book of Genesis that Abraham's children Ishmael and Isaac are the principal characters through whom Abraham's history is written. Ishmael was his first child but was not the child of Abraham's wife, Sarah; he was the son of Sarah's Egyptian maidservant, Hagar.

Such animosity developed between Hagar and Sarah the families needed to be separated. So despairing was Abraham over this family feud he pled with God to bless Ishmael (Genesis 17:18–21, ESV): *"And Abraham said to God, 'Oh, that Ishmael might live before You!' But God replied: 'No, Sarah your wife shall bear you a son, and you shall call his name Isaac; I will establish My covenant with him as an everlasting covenant for his offspring after him. And as for Ishmael, I have heard you. Behold, I have blessed him and will make him fruitful, and will multiply him greatly. He shall father twelve princes, and I will make him a great nation. But I will establish My **covenant with Isaac**.'"*

At God's appointed time, Isaac was born to Sarah, but Ishmael (his older half-brother) mocked them. This resulted in Ishmael and Hagar being banished from the tents of Abraham and sent out into the desert with meager supplies. Abraham was unhappy with the arrangement, but God said to him, *"Let it not be displeasing in your sight because of the lad, and because of your bondwoman; in all that Sarah has said unto you, listen unto her voice; for in Isaac shall your descendants be called. And also of the son of the bondwoman will I make a nation, because he is your descendant. "* (Genesis 21:12–13, KJV 2000). Here is the key point related to history today: although God is merciful to Ishmael, His purposes came through Isaac, not Ishmael. (Isaac became the father of the Jews and Ishmael, the father of the Arabs.)

By the way, have you noticed continual conflict seems to characterize the southern and eastern Mediterranean region, where twenty-two separate Arabic nations now exist?[202] (Some dispute whether Iran is an Arabic nation, but for the purpose of this discussion, we will consider Iran Arab.) Arab nations are not just at odds with Israel, but they are at almost perpetual odds with each other. For example, Arab Egypt considers Arab Syria, Turkey, and Qatar its enemies; likewise, Iran and Iraq both consider Saudi Arabia and Turkey their enemies as well as each other; Saudi Arabia sees Turkey, Iraq, Syria, Afghanistan, and Iran as its enemies; and Syria sees Saudi Arabia and Turkey as its enemies;[203] and the list goes on.

Why do these Arab nations (often considered the descendants of Abraham's son Ishmael)—nations so similar in religion and culture—often go to war against each other? The answer is found in Genesis 16:12 (Jubilee, NIV), where the angel of the Lord told Hagar concerning Ishmael: *"He will be a wild man; his hand will be against every man, and every man's hand against him; and he will live in hostility toward all his* <u>*brothers*</u>*."* Since that day, Arabs not only have great dislike for each other but especially for Israel and the Jews—the descendants of their half-brother, Isaac.

Returning to the story of the Jews, God calls upon Abraham to sacrifice Isaac, whom God refers to as Abraham's "only son" (Genesis 22:12), thus again making clear He excludes Ishmael from the covenant He made with Abraham. As the result of Abraham's obedience in the matter of Isaac, God offers this incredible promise to him: *"In blessing I will bless you, and multiplying I will multiply your descendants as the stars of the heaven and as the sand which is on the seashore; and your descendants shall possess the gate of their enemies. In your seed all the nations of the earth shall be blessed"* (Genesis 22:17-18). Eventually, Abraham dies and *"Abraham gave all that he had to Isaac"* (Genesis 25:5, NASB).

ISAAC

Isaac grows and has children of his own, twin boys Esau and Jacob. Esau is the older and should inherit the birthright but sells it to his younger brother Jacob and becomes his enemy from that point forward. When Isaac is old, blind, and near death, he delivers blessings upon his two adult sons. However, his wife Rebekah tricks him into pronouncing his irrefutable family blessings on the younger son Jacob instead of the older (Esau) as was customary. As part of his blessing to Jacob (whose name God later changed to *"Israel"*), he includes the promise, *"Cursed be everyone who curses you, and blessed be those who bless you!"* (Genesis 27:29b, ESV). The twelve tribes that eventually formed the nation of Israel came from Jacob—that is, from Israel, whose name they bear to this day.

WHO ARE THE JEWS? ARE THEY A RACE OR A RELIGION?

As we have seen, Jews are the physical descendants of Abraham, through Isaac, through Jacob. The twelve tribes formed from Jacob's twelve sons gave rise to all the Jews born into the world (although others have converted to Judaism over time). One of the challenges with discussing the Jews is they are defined both as a race and as followers of a religion. For our purposes, we will focus on the Jewish race and define it as those who are physical descendants of Jacob, and anyone who has a Jewish parent is considered Jewish by race.

For a people with thousands of years of history, there are relatively few Jews today. The Chinese and Indian civilizations are as ancient as that of Israel, and each has well over one billion members of its race, but there are only fourteen million Jews in the world—about 1 percent of the population of China or India. Six million of those fourteen million Jews live in Israel. (Israel is the land-size of New Jersey, and its population is about equal to Maryland. If you take the population of Maryland and scatter it across New Jersey, you have a good picture of the size of Israel today and the number of Jews who live there.) Why are there so few Jews in the world? Because they are the single most abused people group in the history of the world—like no other, they have been tortured, persecuted, and killed in enormous numbers throughout their history.

It is critically important to understand that God <u>Himself</u> says the covenant (both its blessings and curses) comes only through Abraham, Isaac, and Jacob, through whom the Jewish people and the Jewish nation sprang. There is a calling and a blessing upon Ishmael's descendants (the Arabs), but the promises of God are accorded to how we act toward the Jews and their nation Israel. According to the Bible, if we bless them, we will be blessed; and if we curse them, we will be cursed.

CURSE? WHAT IS THAT?

What does it mean in Genesis 12:3 when God says to Abraham, *"I will curse him who curses you"* (NKJV)? What does it mean to curse someone? (We are not talking about using a curse word or some type of profanity.)

Two different Hebrew words are used for the single English word "curse," which is used twice in this verse. The first word "curse" comes from the Hebrew word root לָלַק which means "to make light of," or "to despise." This can mean something as simple as taking something lightly, dismissing it as unimportant, or verbally scoffing at it. The second word comes from ארר and means "a bitter curse"—"speaking forth a sentence of Divine vengeance upon someone." God is stating that those who curse Israel (that is, those who dismiss Israel or the Jews as unimportant, take them lightly, or scoff at them) will be cursed by Him (that is, they will receive a bitter denunciation from Him and an assignment of His ju̇ment). On the other hand, those who bless Israel and the Jews blessed by God. So, if we are indifferent to Israel or are m̓ portive of her and of God's plans for her, we may be ̇ curse. This applies to us individually and to the na⁺

TO WHAT LAND WAS GOD REFERRING?

As we examine God's promises to Abraham, we see they identify a very specific piece of land: *"Then the Lord appeared to Abram and said, 'To your descendants I will give this land.' And there he built an altar to the Lord, Who had appeared to him."* (Genesis 12:7, NKJV)

God is very definite about the specific geography He promised to Abraham and his descendants. *"On the same day the Lord made a covenant with Abram, saying: 'To your descendants I have given this land, from the river of Egypt to the great river—the River Euphrates"* (Genesis 15:18, NKJV). God keeps repeating the promise for this *same* land: He reaffirms it to Abraham in Genesis 17:8, then to Isaac in Genesis 26:3–4, then to Jacob in Genesis 28:13, and then to Jacob's descendants in Genesis 35:12.

The land promised is from the Nile River to the Euphrates River. This parcel includes parts of modern day Egypt, Lebanon, Syria, Jordan, Iraq, Saudi Arabia, and all of Israel, including the Israeli lands of Gaza as well as what is now called the West Bank.

Interestingly, the specific place where God originally made and confirmed His land covenant, saying *"this land,"* was in an area north of Jerusalem between the towns of Bethel and Ai, which is the heart of the so-called West Bank (which the Palestinians want as their land). Ironically, the "West Bank" (a term never used in the Scriptures) is the region referred to in the Bible as Judea and Samaria—two areas demonstrably in historic Israel and still part of Israel today. Modern critics claim Israel is illegally "occupying" this land (because the Palestinians want it) and must give it up for the hope of an elusive peace.

Obviously, at the current time, Israel is nowhere near experiencing the fullness of the land promise God repeatedly gave and they once enjoyed. Israel did have this land—for millennia, but it has steadily been taken away from them. (For instance, the nation of Saudi Arabia was formed in 1926 from land designated as Israeli land.) So the claim that Israel is an occupier is ridiculous. God gave that land to the Jews; they possessed it for thousands of years but are struggling to retain even a small portion of it today.

SUMMARY

In the book of Genesis, God chooses a *specific* people, the Jews, to live in a *specific* land, Israel, and to serve as a blessing to all the nations and families of the earth. And here is the key point: God offers encouragement to those who align with this plan and pointedly warns those who stand against it.

CHAPTER 28

ISRAEL: FROM JESUS TO
THE TWENTIETH CENTURY

As noted earlier, the Jews have been pursued, shoved around, relocated, discriminated against, persecuted, and slaughtered more than any other people group on the earth. The Nazi holocaust of World War II was only a recent example of what has been occurring to Jews for millennia. Some may not care for history, but you need to know at least a little about this part of the story.

Let's quickly survey just the past 2,000 years of the more than 4,000-year-old story of the nation of Israel. This means we'll pick up with New Testament times.

ISRAEL UNDER SIEGE IN ANCIENT DAYS

At the time of the crucifixion of Christ in 33 AD, Rome controlled Israel. In 70 AD, the Romans destroyed the Jewish temple. When Emperor Hadrian later banned Jewish freedom and religious practices, the Jews revolted, but Hadrian crushed the revolt and killed the Jewish leaders in 136 AD. He also destroyed and plowed under the Temple Mount (the traditional center of Jewish life), and Jews were banished from Jerusalem. Hadrian then drew up a plan to build a new city on the ruins of Jerusalem, making it a center of pagan worship.

THE BIG NAME CHANGE THAT EXPLAINS IT ALL

To further humiliate the Jews, he sought to rename their nation. After learning that the Philistines were the oldest and fiercest enemy of the Jews, he renamed the country Palestina. It is critical you know this fact: the name Palestine was to honor the Philistines, the most-hated enemy of the Jews. For the next 500 years, Jews were allowed in Jerusalem only one day each year: the anniversary of the burning of the temple.

Let's be clear that Palestine has *no* relation to the current Palestinians; the Palestinians are *not* the descendants of the ancient Philistine inhabitants of the land of Judea. The Philistines of the Bible, who arrived in the land about the same time as the Israelites, were from Greece and *were not* Arabic, and they were gone from the Holy Land over a millennium ago. The current Arabic Palestinians have <u>no</u> relation to the Philistines and *no* ancient claim to the land.

CONSTANTINE AND AFTER

Early in the fourth century, Emperor Constantine claimed conversion to Christianity (although his subsequent practices made any such conversion seem unlikely—it seemed to be a "conversion" in name only). Under Constantine, Jerusalem began to regain lost prestige. The Church of the Holy Sepulcher (where Roman Catholics believe Jesus was buried) was consecrated in 335 AD. In 380 AD, by decree of Emperor Theodosius, Christianity became the official state-established religion of the Roman Empire.[204]

In the fifth and sixth centuries, the Roman Empire began to weaken. In 614 AD, the Persians took control of Jerusalem and destroyed many of its churches, but in 628 AD, the Romans (at that time calling themselves Christians) recaptured the city. And from then until the 1900s was a flurry of one conquering army after another.

Jews controlled Jerusalem for about 1,500 years until about 70 AD; then Rome controlled it until 600 AD; then Muslims took control, holding it until 1100 AD; from 1100 to 1250, the Crusades occurred with Christians attempting to regain control from the Muslims and power shifting back and forth; in 1250, Muslim Turks gained control until 1917, when the British gained control. This is where the story of Israel's rebirth begins.

By the way, claims that Jerusalem belongs to the Muslims are bogus, considering not only that Mohammed never visited Jerusalem but neither did Islam arrive there until:

- 2,600 years after the Jews were founded through Abraham
- 2,000 years after Joshua established the nation of Israel
- 1,600 years after David made Jerusalem the capital of Israel
- 600 years after Christianity was founded there
- And the Islamic Dome of the Rock was not built on the Temple Mount until 687 AD.

These are important dates to remember when Muslims lay claim to the land and city.

By the 1800s (the latter part of Turkish Muslim rule), Western interest and involvement in Palestine was growing. In the 1840s, an American naval expedition explored the Jordan River from the Sea of Galilee to the Dead Sea. Americans such as Mark Twain traveled the region, and President Abraham Lincoln expressed his desire to visit Palestine. Consular offices were established in Jerusalem, and visits occurred from celebrated American officials such as diplomat Lew Wallace (the author of *Ben Hur*).

British, French, and Germans became more plentiful in the region, and among several European nations, the maneuvering for position in Palestine grew more intense. In fact, in England, the Palestine Exploration Fund was established, which sponsored several surveys of Palestine in attempts to lay British claim to as much of the Middle East as possible and to counteract the efforts of the French to do the same.

CHAPTER 29

THE TWENTIETH CENTURY: THE ADVENT OF ZIONISM

By the middle of the nineteenth century, Jews comprised half the population of Jerusalem, and there was open support growing for the restoration of Palestine to the Jews. (In America, Founding Fathers such as John Adams and John Quincy Adams long before expressed their support for the reestablishment of Palestine as an independent Jewish nation[205] as had early American Jewish leader Mordecai Noah.[206]) From 1860 to 1870, the concept of Zionism began to take shape.

Recall that Zionism simply means the right of the Jews to return to their ancient Biblical homeland and reestablish Israel as an independent self-governing nation, with the right to defend itself. A Christian Zionist is a Christian who believes Jews have this right.

THEODORE HERZL

In 1894, an event occurred in France that would forever change the shape of the Middle East. A Jewish officer in the French military, Lt. Col. Alfred Dreyfus, was accused and convicted of treason. The trial was covered by a Jewish journalist from Vienna named Theodore Herzl, who was shocked by the magnitude and fervor of the anti-Semitism he observed against Dreyfus during those proceedings. Dreyfus was later exonerated, but Herzl became convinced that with the open anti-Semitism in Europe, trouble lay ahead for the Jews, and they would be extinguished unless they had their own country.

In 1896, he published his classic work *The Jewish State*, considered the testament of modern Zionism. In 1897, the first Congress of the World Zionist Organization was held, with a goal to gain the sponsorship and support of the European powers for an independent Jewish state. In 1903, the British obliged by offering Uganda as a state for the Jews, but the Zionist Congress refused the generous offer, instead resolving that the Jewish national home should be the Holy Land, where it had already been for so many centuries.

THE BRITISH TAKE PALESTINE

In 1917, during World War I, British General George Allenby entered Jerusalem and reclaimed it from Muslim control, 400 years after the Turks invaded it. England, holding possessions all over the world, including Egypt, controlled Egypt's strategic Suez Canal, which connected the Indian Ocean with the Mediterranean Sea, allowing rapid travel between two regions otherwise difficult to connect. England believed a British-controlled state in Palestine would help keep the canal secure, so an Anglo-Zionist alliance was forged, and a Jewish chemist named Chaim Weitzmann became instrumental in the process. (Weitzmann eventually became the first president of Israel.)

Despite Britain's win over the Turks and Germans in Palestine in World War I, the War in Europe was not going well for them. English Prime Minister Lloyd George felt that, to win the war, he needed to (1) get the Americans fully involved and (2) keep Russia from withdrawing altogether. Lloyd felt that securing Jewish influence in both these countries could make a considerable difference, so he sought Jewish help.

Meanwhile, Weitzmann kept up the pressure in England for what he called a *"British protectorate over a Jewish homeland."*[207] Lloyd saw this as helpful to his larger objective, so British Foreign Secretary Lord Balfour asked the Zionist organizations to draft a declaration for a Jewish homeland. This statement became known as the Balfour Declaration—a British promise for the creation of a Jewish state from British-held land in Palestine.

LEAGUE OF NATIONS CREATES NEW NATIONS

After the end of World War I, the League of Nations (which was formed in 1919 to help create greater international cooperation) approved the creation of several brand-new nations in the Middle East. For the Arabs, there would be the new countries of Syria, Lebanon, Iran, and Iraq. For the Jews, Israel (Palestine) would be set aside. The League of Nations gave England the authority, or the "Mandate," to govern Palestine.

ARABS RIOT, BRITISH BACKTRACK

The League of Nations (the precursor to the United Nations) endorsed both the Balfour Declaration and the Jewish homeland. The first high commissioner sent by England to govern Jerusalem was Sir Herbert Samuel. He subsequently appointed Haj Amin al-Husseini as the Grand Mufti of Jerusalem, the highest Muslim office in Palestine.

But the Muslim Husseini clan opposed British rule altogether and adamantly opposed sharing the land with the Jews. Arab nationalists, enraged by the Balfour Declaration and its call for a home for the Jewish people, set themselves to run both the Jews and the British out of the region and set up an Arab state encompassing all of Palestine.

In 1919, Haj Amin al-Husseini formed the "Palestinian Society" with a military arm to carry out actions against both the British and the Jews. He immediately began leading demonstrations and protests, demanding an end to the British Mandate and a repudiation of the Balfour Declaration.

In April 1920, when the religious holidays of Easter (Christian), Passover (Jewish), and Nabi Musa (Islamic) all fell in the same week, thousands of Muslims convened at the Al-Aksa Mosque as Jews were simultaneously worshiping at the Western Wall. The Muslims attacked the Jews in three hours of bloody rioting. When British troops finally arrived, they jailed the instigators, but upon their release the next morning, the rioting resumed and lasted for three more days, resulting in a number of deaths, with hundreds more injured.

During the ensuing investigations, the Jews proved the British military government was clearly favoring the Arabs to the detriment of the

Jews and in violation of the Balfour Declaration. Haj Amin al-Husseini, who instigated the violence, fled to Transjordan (the region that was soon to become the country of Jordan). He was sentenced in absentia by the British military court to ten years imprisonment, but in an attempt to calm the Arabs, Sir Herbert Samuel pardoned him.

THE MUSLIM STRATEGY

This incident began a new and successful strategy for the Arabs: riot and kill, blame it on the presence of Jews, and wait for the governing author- ity to agree to Arab demands to quell the violence. It worked time and again. In fact, after the violence, in order not to offend the aggressor Arabs, Samuel put restrictions on Jewish immigration and imposed other measures to impede Zionist progress. Muslims initiated the violence, but the Jews were punished.

ANNULLING A MANDATE: CREATING JORDAN OUT OF JEWISH TERRITORY

Still seeking to achieve peace among the Arabs, England created yet another new country for the Arabs out of land the League of Nations set aside for the Jewish homeland. With the stroke of Winston Churchill's pen (colonial secretary at the time), 78 percent of the territory under the British Mandate was taken away from its Jewish designates in Palestine to create the Muslim Kingdom of Transjordan (now simply Jordan)—an exclusively Arab area.

The new document changing the rules was known as the Churchill White Paper (1922). It said the Jewish national home was now to be restricted to the area west of the Jordan River (the Balfour Declaration had included land east of the Jordan River). Imagine: after World War I, *six nations were created for Arabs out of the Holy Land, but still none for Jews.* And the document further stated Jewish immigration should be limited to the economic capacity of the new smaller country (now less than one-fourth the size it was under the Balfour Declaration).

The Zionist Organization signed this new agreement with great reluctance, primarily doing so to avoid losing all British support because

Britain still ruled the region. The Arabs flatly rejected the paper, establishing another pattern to be repeated time and again: they wanted control of all of the Jewish land, not just part. In the meantime, they were glad to accept all new territory (such as the Transjordan)—as long as it came from land held by the Jews.

CHAPTER 30

FINALLY, A LAND FOR THE JEWS

On paper, Jews had a land officially designated for them, so from 1918 to 1924, the Jewish population of Palestine grew from 55,000 to 103,000 as Jewish people began returning to their ancestral homeland. And over the next four years, it doubled again.

As can be imagined, this growth was unacceptable to the Arabs. They believed something more severe needed to be done, so Husseini began consolidating his power base in Palestine. He removed all moderates from places of authority and eliminated every Arab opponent until he held unfettered control over the entire Muslim population of Palestine.

BAD NEWS NO. 1: MASSACRING THE JEWS

In 1929 on Yom Kippur (the holiest day of the year for Jews) as they were peacefully praying at the Western Wall, Husseini sent his hordes against the defenseless Jewish worshippers. When it was over, 133 Jews were dead and 399 injured. When Husseini was brought to account, he claimed Jews moving back into their designated homeland "provoked" the anti-Jewish massacre. So Britain issued a new white paper even more severely restricting Jewish immigration and purchase of land by Jews. Once again, Arabs attacked, and Jews were punished.

BAD NEWS NO. 2: FURTHER CARVING UP THE HOLY LAND

Despite Churchill's creation of Transjordan that dramatically shrank the land designated for the Jews, he was still very much pro-Zionist—he wanted to see an independent nation for the Jews. But during the last half of the 1930s, a labor government in England came to power, so Churchill retired from office, remaining out of the public eye for the next decade. The new labor government was much less sympathetic to Zionists and effectively negated the Balfour Declaration and its provisions.

Simultaneously, Hitler was on the rise in Europe, requiring more of England's time and attention. England hoped to enlist the help of Arabs, and one of the chief ways England could do so was by further restricting Jewish immigration into Palestine. But once again reaffirming the historic pattern, this appeasement only spurred the Arabs to yet more aggression.

BAD NEWS NO. 3: BRITAIN CHOOSES ARAB OIL; JEWS SLAUGHTERED

Finally recognizing the difficult situation it created in Palestine, in July 1937, Lord Peel's Commission in England issued a report acknowledging the commitments it made to both the Jews and Arabs were irreconcilable. Because England was not willing either to turn the Jews over to Arab domination or to put the Arabs under Jewish rule, they proposed further dividing the remaining land set aside for Israel into two separate portions: one Arab state (which would be joined to Transjordan) and one Jewish state. The historic cities of Jerusalem and Bethlehem would belong to neither but would be set aside as British enclaves (that is, as British holdings). The League of Nations and the Arabs rejected the idea, so the violence in Palestine continued.

On the one side, the Jewish community was trying to persuade the British to allow increased Jewish immigration; on the other, the Arabs were threatening to cut off access to Middle Eastern oil if Jewish immigration increased. The British chose oil and in 1939, released another white paper stating (1) Jewish immigration would be slowed and then halted, (2) Jews would only be allowed to buy land in areas where they were already the majority population, and (3) after the war, Britain would support an independent Palestinian state controlled by the Arabs to be made from designated Jewish holdings.

BAD NEWS NO. 4: HITLER AND WORLD WAR II

The new policy halting Jewish immigration to Israel, issued in the shadow of Hitler's vow to annihilate the Jews of Europe, effectively condemned millions of European Jews to death because they were no longer able to leave Europe. In fact, of Europe's eight million Jews, only 1.5 million survived the war.

During the War, Arabs took an active part: some fought with the Allies, but many fought with Hitler. In fact, a sign commonly displayed in the shops of Syria declared *"In heaven; God is your ruler; on earth, Hitler."*[208] Strikingly, *Mein Kampf* is still a best-selling book in parts of the Islamic world.[209]

In the wake of continuing Arab violence in Palestine in the early part of World War II, the British deposed the Mufti and abolished the Supreme Muslim Council. Husseini escaped Palestine before he could be arrested. He spent World War II as the guest of Hitler in Germany and Mussolini in Italy. In 1942, he succeeded in getting both to agree to the abolition of the Jewish homeland in Palestine, pointing out that Jews were their common enemies.[210]

BAD NEWS NO. 5: CHURCHILL OUT OF OFFICE

In October 1943, Churchill, having come out of retirement to serve as British Prime Minister, revisited a partition plan that would set aside area for the Jews, acknowledging, however, it could not be implemented until after the war. But after the war, Churchill was forced from office before the plan could be implemented. The new labor government was not sympathetic to the plight of the Jews in Europe, so immigration remained suppressed. Lord Bevin, the new British foreign minister, declared, *"The Jews have waited two thousand years; they can wait a little while longer."*[211]

THE REMARKABLE JEWISH RESILIENCY

But many Jews who survived the genocide efforts in Europe did not wait, attempting to sneak into the country on boats and by foot. But they were sent back to Europe, sometimes to the same concentration camps in which they had been tortured during the war. (Those camps were then being used as displaced persons camps.)

CHAPTER 31

THE MODERN REBIRTH OF ISRAEL

The words "miracle" and "miraculous" are often overused and much of what are called "miracles" are not. But the rebirth of Israel is a genuine miracle.

CHAOS IN THE HOLY LAND

As a result of so many bad decisions by the British, Jews and Arabs in Palestine began to fight them. In 1946, when the Irgun, a radical Jewish resistance group (denounced by leading Jewish authorities), bombed the King David hotel (which housed the central office of the British authority in Palestine), the British made possessing a weapon by any Jew a capital offense. Obviously, this made it extremely difficult for the rest of the Jews to defend themselves against the well-armed Arabs, who were readily supplied by their neighboring Arab cousins.

By early 1947, the British wanted nothing more to do with Palestine, so they informed the United Nations they would be leaving the region. The Soviets called for revisiting the partition plan that set aside a region for Jews and another for Arabs, and the United Nations created a committee to study the question. (As usual, the Arabs refused to participate.) The committee ruled in favor of partition, but Jerusalem was to be withheld from both Jews and Arabs and would become an international zone administered by the United Nations.

NOVEMBER 29, 1947: THE UN VOTE

When the plan came to a vote before the full United Nations, for all practical purposes, the Jews were blackmailed by the Vatican into giving up Jerusalem and handing it over to the United Nations. (The Catholic nations of Latin America made plain they would cast their votes in favor of partition *only* if the Jews let the city go.) On November 29, 1947, the United Nations voted (by a two-thirds majority) to approve the partition of Palestine, creating two states: one Jewish and one Arab. The plan was scheduled to go into effect in May 1948, but the Arabs continued to adamantly oppose it because it acknowledged the right of the Jews to exist as a nation in the Middle East.

THE BEGINNINGS OF WAR

Even though the UN approved the internationalization of Jerusalem, Jerusalem's citizens were well aware no nation would be willing to back the UN policy with military force—and military force would definitely be required if peace were to be maintained and Muslim attacks prevented. In this, the Arabs saw their greatest opportunity for victory: because only Jews and Arabs were willing to spill their own blood for Jerusalem, the rest of the world would stand by and watch, leaving Arabs free to take whatever steps they wished.

As May 1948 approached, the Jews were woefully unprepared for war. They still were not allowed to possess weapons and were unable even to defend their own humanitarian convoys attempting to restock food in Jerusalem. (Jews in Jerusalem were being starved; Arabs guarded the road to Jerusalem and attacked every Jewish truck en route.)

MAY 14, 1948, MIDNIGHT JERUSALEM TIME, 6:00 PM US EASTERN TIME ZONE

The British Mandate (that is, British control over the region) was set to end. By midday, Arab nations were mobilizing to pounce on the new Jewish state and eradicate it before it could begin. Egyptian forces were massed in the Negev (the southern region of Israel), Jordanian and Iraqi troops were positioned all along the Jordan River, and Syrian forces were marching from the north toward Palestine. In Tel Aviv, the founding fathers of the nation of Israel, led by David Ben-Gurion, voted six to four in favor of independence. At the United Nations, the Arab states were still trying to force a vote on a last-minute resolution to prevent the creation of a Jewish state.

MAY 14, 1948, 6:11 PM

Israel's only hope for legitimacy was if the United States recognized the new nation. America did so, but the circumstances surrounding that declaration were remarkable.

President Franklin Roosevelt, despite the UN vote, was firmly anti-Zionist, repeatedly declaring that he would not support Israeli statehood. He died in office only a week after he once again reaffirmed his opposition to a Jewish nation in Israel and only four weeks before Israel's declaration of statehood.[212]

On Roosevelt's death, Vice President Harry Truman became president. His view toward Israel was very different, and at 6:11 PM (only eleven minutes after Israel's announcement of its independence, and over the strong objections of those in his own cabinet, including his Secretary of State, General of the Army George C. Marshall), Truman boldly declared official support for the new nation.[213] Truman and the United States became the first in the world to officially recognize and express support for reborn Israel.

ISRAEL'S FIRST DAY: ATTACKED BY SIX NATIONS

When the UN also recognized Israel's independence, the Grand Mufti of Jerusalem (its Muslim leader) declared:

> The entire Jewish population in Palestine must be destroyed or driven into the sea. Allah has bestowed upon us the rare privilege of finishing what Hitler only began. Let the jihad begin! Murder the Jews. Murder them all![214]

The Arab countries launched an all-out effort to do exactly that. At midnight, Jordanian troops (trained and led by British General John Glubb) crossed the Allenby Bridge and headed for Jerusalem. The next morning, Egypt bombed Tel-Aviv. The war of independence was on.

Within hours of Israel's declaration of statehood, tens of thousands of soldiers from six Arab nations, armed with state-of-the-art British and French weapons, were arrayed against the men, women, and high-school students who made up the Israeli Army. The majority of those Israelis had never seen a day of real training, much less genuine battle. Forty-five million Arabs were intent on pushing 400,000 Jews—bunkered on a tiny strip of land comprising only one-eighth of 1 percent of the 6.1 million square miles of the Arab lands—into the sea. Few gave the fledgling nation of Israel much hope for survival.

JERUSALEM DIVIDED

After ten days, the Israelis still had not buckled. In fact, they held part of Jerusalem and a secure corridor leading west to the coast, as well as the northern, southern, and western areas of the small land mass of their partition within Palestine. Egypt held a small strip of land called Gaza (the southern part of Israel adjoining the Egyptian border). The Jordanians held Judea and Samaria (Israel's "West Bank") as well as the eastern half of Jerusalem, which included the old city, the holy sites, the Western Wall, and the abandoned Jewish Quarter. Jerusalem, for the first time in its long history, was now a divided city.

The war continued sporadically for the remainder of 1948, but Jerusalem ceased to be a focus of any serious fighting. Early in 1949, Israel and Jordan negotiated an armistice, agreeing to divide Jerusalem. The United Nations voted the city to be placed under control of a UN mediator, but he was promptly assassinated. The Jews moved their parliament from Tel Aviv to Jerusalem, announcing Jerusalem as the eternal capital of Israel.

Recognizing Jerusalem could be kept under UN control only by armed force, the United Nations set aside its resolution. By 1950, a new arrangement was reached: the city of Jerusalem would remain divided—one side belonging to Jordan, the other to Israel, just as Israel and Jordan agreed.

BOUNDARIES AND BORDERS

Outside Jerusalem, there were no internationally recognized borders, so the 1949 armistice lines became the *de facto* borders of Israel. By the way, when politicians refer to "the '67 borders" as the basis for a peace negotiation (as President Obama did in May 2011), they are referring to the original armistice lines—the places where the armies were when the bullets stopped flying in 1948 and that remained in place until 1967. But these lines reduce the nation of Israel to being only nine miles wide at its most strategic point—an untenable scenario for any nation to survive when surrounded by hostile enemies on every side, as Israel is.

After the armistice of 1949, King Abdullah of Transjordan annexed the Jordanian half of Jerusalem and the West Bank to his kingdom. It is significant that he (or Egypt or Syria) could easily have given some of their newly acquired land to the Palestinian Arabs among them, but they did not. The Palestinian Arabs did not want land from other Arabs; they wanted whatever land Israel was still holding.

It is important to note the West Bank and the other areas acquired by Jordan suffered greatly throughout the tenure of Jordanian occupation, for they were little more than a trophy for Abdullah. The Jewish quarter of East Jerusalem, which was in his control, lay in ruins. Nearly all its synagogues, schools, and buildings were destroyed in 1948, and they remained that way. But Jewish West Jerusalem (unlike the Arab-controlled areas of Jerusalem) as well as the remainder of Israel flourished.

Furthermore, Arab and Jewish refugees were offered citizenship by Israel. And Jewish refugees from across the world, having a relatively safe destination, streamed into Israel in such numbers its population doubled within three years.

AFTER THE WAR OF INDEPENDENCE

The Soviets were initially supporters of Israel's statehood, but when they began courting Arab interests in the Middle East, they withdrew their support. In 1955, they signed an arms deal with the Egyptians, and Egyptian President Nassar, emboldened by Soviet assistance, insisted that many of the British troops guarding the Suez Canal be pulled out. In 1956, he seized control of the under-protected canal, closed it to all international shipping to or from Israel, and blockaded the Straits of Tiran, effectively cutting off Israel from most of the world. He openly called for the destruction of Israel.

Britain and France mobilized against Egypt in a brief Sinai campaign, reopening the canal. The United Nations guaranteed it would keep the canal open, and for the next ten years, there was an absence of war in Israel.

GAZA

This did not mean, however, all was quiet and safe inside Israel. Far from it, for there were frequent terrorist incursions into Israel by the newly created Palestinian Liberation Organization (PLO), led by Yasser Arafat. (Significantly, the 1964 charter document of the PLO openly calls for the destruction of Israel.[215]) These terrorist attacks, coming from Egyptian-held Gaza (the southern part of Israel bordering Egypt) and the Jordanian-held West Bank (Judea and Samaria), were calculated to provoke Israeli retaliation. If Israel responded, it would serve as justification for Arab powers to launch an all-out war with Israel.

CHAPTER 32

THE MIRACULOUS SIX-DAY WAR

The birth of Israel in 1948 was miraculous: it was a nation coming back to life after being absent from the world scene for 2,000 years. The Six-Day War of 1967 was equally miraculous.

ON THE NORTHEAST

By the spring of 1967, the situation had markedly deteriorated. There was significant Syrian military buildup occurring in the Golan Heights (the Israeli-controlled region along the border with Syria).

FROM THE SOUTH

On May 22, Nasser of Egypt once again blockaded the Straits of Tiran, closing off the Israeli port of Eilat, shutting down Israel's supply of oil from the Persian Gulf. Israel considered this an act of war and notified the United Nations that, if it was not prepared to uphold the peace treaty negotiated in 1956, Israel would take matters into its own hands.

FROM THE EAST

A week later, on May 30, Jordan's King Hussein signed a mutual defense pact with Egypt. Arab inflammatory rhetoric was increasing, including radio broadcasts calling for an all-out jihad to avenge 1948. Nasser of Egypt vowed to destroy the nation of Israel and push the Jews into the sea once and for all. War was inevitable.

THE UNEXPLAINABLE WAR

On June 5, the Six-Day War began, with Israel launching a preemptive strike on Egypt's air force, effectively wiping it out. Simultaneously, Israeli ground forces attacked the Egyptian army amassed in the Sinai, virtually eliminating Egypt's capacity to fight. By the end of the second day of battle, Israel was in command of Gaza as well as the Sinai region of Egypt.

Jordan attacked Jerusalem, thereby opening the door not only for Israel to reclaim the other part of Jerusalem but also Judea and Samaria (the "West Bank"). After destroying the Jordanian air force, Israel pressed its ground attack, and by sundown on June 7, Judea, Samaria, and the Old City of Jerusalem were back in Israeli hands. Jews could once again pray at the Western Wall.

By June 8, Israel had captured the Suez Canal, thus ending Egypt's blockade against them. After another day, the Israelis controlled the entire Golan Heights in the north (the part of Israel from which Syria launched its attacks). On June 10, after only six days of fighting, the Arabs called for a cease fire and the war was over.

For Israel, she increased her land size four-fold (but she was still only a small part of what was set aside for her in the Balfour Declaration and of what she historically was). For the Arabs, it was a crushing and humiliating defeat. In a gesture of good will, Israel generously handed the sacred Muslim Temple Mount in the unified Jerusalem back over to Arab supervision in hopes it would engender peace. It did not.

AFTER THE 1967 WAR

In the aftermath of the Six-Day War, the Arab countries, still stinging from their defeat at the hands of a much smaller enemy, held a summit in Khartoum, Sudan. They signed a declaration specifying *"the main principles by which the Arab states abide"*[216]: (1) *no* peace with Israel, (2) *no* recognition of Israel, (3) *no* negotiation with Israel, and (4) the Palestinian people must have their "own" country, but it must be made from land belonging to Israel.[217]

In November 1967, the UN Security council adopted a resolution (written by the British and American delegates) calling for Israeli withdrawal *"from the territories occupied in the recent conflict."* Because the wording was somewhat ambiguous concerning withdrawal and because it called for *"acknowledgment of the sovereignty . . . of every state in the area"*[218] (which would include Israel), the Israelis viewed it favorably. But predictably, because it acknowledged Israel's right to exist, none of the Arab nations would approve it. They remained technically at war with Israel.

It would be another ten years and would take another war before just one Arab leader—Anwar Sadat of Egypt—finally made peace with Israel.

CHAPTER 33

THE RISE OF ANTI-SEMITISM AMONG CHRISTIANS

Having looked at the political and Biblical history associated with Israel, now we'll look at the history of the relations between Christians and Jews. Be forewarned: much of it is ugly. For centuries, unabashed anti-Semitism characterized the Christian church, and the centuries-long Christian hatred of Jews is well-documented.

REPUDIATING OUR JEWISH ROOTS

In the first century, the Jerusalem church was looked upon as the Mother Church of Christianity. There was no question the Church was Jewish. The Apostles, who were all Jews, continued in the style of worship of Jesus (also a Jew) based on the Hebrew Scriptures and practiced by Jews for centuries (including Jesus). Early Christians gathered to celebrate the Sabbath and the Biblical feasts. The Hebrew Scriptures—the totality of inspired Scripture at the time—were all affirmed by the Christian church.

CHRISTIAN REDUCTION OF JEWISH CIVIL RIGHTS

After the destruction of Jerusalem by the Romans in 70 AD and the scattering of the Jewish people, the Gentile side of the Church took a decidedly more negative stand against the Jewish side. They began to reject the Jewishness of the New Testament and even of Jesus. And in the century after the death of the Apostles, the attitudes of Church leaders against Jews began to visibly harden. Even though the Scripture specifically commanded to *"give none offence, neither to the Jews nor to the Gentiles"* (1 Corinthians 10:32, KJV), this command gradually fell by the way.

For example, around 150 AD, early Church father Justin Martyr noted the Jews' hands were *"high to do evil, because though ye have slain Christ, even so ye do not repent."*[219] This is an early precursor to the errant belief that took root and grew over succeeding centuries that Jews were Christ-killers.

(Just to be clear, the Jews were *not* the killers of Jesus, *our* sins were. We are responsible for His death, which He voluntarily chose to allow so we could be redeemed and reconnected to God the Father through His death. Jesus's death was part of *God's* plan for us; it was not some human-originated diabolical plan of the Jews.)

Holding wrong beliefs about the Jews, other early church leaders gradually became more vile in their rhetoric. For example, in 386–387 AD, Chrysostom, an early Church Father in the Greek church, apparently forgetting Jesus was Jewish, wrote his infamous eight hateful sermons against the *"pitiful and miserable Jews."*[220] He left no margin for misinterpretation: *"I hate the synagogue"*[221] and *"I hate the Jews."*[222] And the great Council of Nicea I (325 AD), from which arises the Nicean Creed (a statement of faith of core Christian beliefs), similarly avowed:

> We ought not, therefore, to have anything in common with the Jews. . . . we desire, dearest brethren, to separate ourselves from the detestable company of the Jews.[223]

With church leaders holding such anti-Semitic beliefs, it is not surprising Christian civil rulers followed their lead.

For example, Emperor Constantine (who professed himself a Christian) was anti-Semitic, and his policies were reflective of that belief. Not only did he make it illegal to become a Jew,[224] but he also began a systematic rejection of Biblical feasts, wrongly believing, for example, the Feast of the Passover came from the Jews. The Feast of the Passover was commanded by God (Exodus 12:12–16). Nevertheless, Constantine rejected the Biblical feast solely because the Jews kept it, explaining, "*Let us then have nothing in common with the detestable Jewish crowd.*"[225]

Subsequent "Christian" Roman Emperors followed suit, persecuting Jews and eliminating their civil rights:

- Emperor Constantius II made Christian–Jewish intermarriage a capital offense[226]
- Emperor Theodosius II prohibited Jews from serving in civil positions and made the construction of synagogues, as well as Jewish proselytization, a capital offense[227]
- Emperor Justinian banned Jews from testifying in judicial proceedings.[228]

Other Christian realms continued this abominable trend. For example, in Spain:

- The laws required that Jews "*observe no Jewish customs or rites,*" and if they disobeyed any Catholic tenet, they would be killed or enslaved[229]
- King Erwig commanded that any Jew who refused forced baptism into Christianity "*receive a hundred lashes*" and be exiled.[230] (On countless occasions across the centuries were numerous instances of Christians forcibly baptizing Jews.[231])
- The Spanish Seven-Part Code forced Jews to "*bear some distinguishing mark upon their heads.*"[232]

The reason for this requirement was this

Jews were formerly highly honored, and enjoyed privileges above all other races, for they alone were called the People of God. But for the reason that they disowned Him Who had honored them and given them privileges; and instead of showing Him reverence, humiliated Him by shamefully putting Him to death on the cross, it was proper and just that on account of the great crime and wickedness which they committed, they should forfeit the honors and privileges which they enjoyed.[233]

(Once again, Jews did *not* kill Jesus; the sins of humanity did.)

On the basis of these wrong beliefs, in 1099 AD, Christians forced Jews in Jerusalem into a synagogue and set it on fire, burning all alive;[234] in 1182, Philip Augustus of France banished all Jews and confiscated their property;[235] in 1492, Ferdinand and Isabella expelled all Jews from Spain;[236] and there are countless similar events of which most Christians are unaware but of which many Jews are fully aware.

CHAPTER 34

HERETICAL REPLACEMENT THEOLOGY

B y rejecting the Jewishness of Jesus and the lifestyle He led, these later Church fathers instituted the heretical belief system that Christianity no longer needed either Judaism or the Jews. It is not a stretch to go from that belief to thinking the Church has replaced both Israel and the Jewish people in the heart and plan of God.

THE ARROGANT HERESY

This Christian replacement of Israel (now known as "Replacement Theology") rested on the doctrinal error that God was finished with the Jews. This was not merely un-Biblical, it was unspeakably arrogant. The Jewish faith *can* exist without Christianity, but the New Testament makes explicitly clear Christianity will _not_ make sense without its Jewish foundation (see Romans 11:11–21).

The Church wrongly divested itself of its Jewish roots and heritage. And when one group of people no longer sees value in another, it does not take much to begin to look at them as outsiders, treat them differently, and eventually refuse to let them live among you. Significantly, Replacement Theology has laid the groundwork for multiple of the demonically devised genocidal campaigns against the Jews, often carried out under the claimed authenticity of "Christian" teachings.

If you study Church history, it is evident this tendency was gaining strength between the fourth and seventh centuries—the same period in which much of the power and effectiveness that characterized the New Testament and early Church was being lost. Significantly, this period of repudiating Jews and Judaism heralds the beginning of the Dark Ages— a centuries-long period of barbarism and cultural stagnation. In the Dark Ages, was the Church reaping what it sowed by its cursing of the Jews in the centuries before?

THE WORLD WAR II GENOCIDE OF THE JEWS

In the twentieth century, Hitler (like many before him) attempted to annihilate the Jewish people. One third of the world's Jews—and almost the entire population of Jews in Europe—were killed during the Holo- caust. Sadly, it is historical fact Hitler used Church reformer Martin Luther's writings to justify to the church of Germany his attempted annihilation of the Jews. [237]

For example, here is a quote Luther penned late in his life in 1543:

> What shall we Christians do with this damned, rejected race of Jews? . . . We cannot tolerate them. . . . Their synagogues or churches should be set on fire. . . . This ought to be done for the honor of God and of Christianity. . . . Their homes should likewise be broken down and destroyed . . . Passport and trav- eling privileges should be absolutely forbidden to the Jews. . . . All their cash and valuables of silver and gold ought to be taken from them.[238]

"YOU MAY NOT LIVE"

Every atrocity committed against Jews in the name of Christ made the name of Christ a name of hatred to the Jews. There is a saying attributed to Raul Hilberg, a preeminent Jewish scholar of the Holocaust, that says: *"The missionaries of Christianity had said in effect to the Jews: 'You may not live among us as Jews.' The secular rulers who followed them from the late Middle Ages then decided: 'You may not live among us;'*

and the Nazis finally decreed: 'You may not live.'"[239] This captures well
the history of Christian anti-Semitism.

Significantly, Hitler invoked the anti-Semitic writings of Christian
Church fathers to justify to the church of Germany his attempted annihilation of the Jews.[240] But Germany was not alone in her culpability
regarding the fate of Jews during the Holocaust. As already noted, Great
Britain—the governing power in Palestine—refused to let Europe's Jews
enter, sending them back to the ovens of German-occupied Europe.[241]
Other nations did the same.

For example, in 1939, as Hitler was beginning his military move to
subjugate Europe, the captain of the *St. Louis*, a German ocean liner,
carried 900 Jewish refugees away from Germany, seeking to find them
a safe haven elsewhere. After being turned away by Cuba, the United
States, and Canada, they finally returned to Europe, where up to one
third of them perished in the German extermination camps.[242] Jim's wife,
Rosemary Schindler Garlow, was involved with the US State Department
in 2009 on the seventieth anniversary of the ship, *St. Louis* when they
honored its few surviving Jews. At that gathering, the US acknowledged
this type of foreign policy should never again be allowed, but Rosemary
took the microphone and said what governmental officials either could
not or would not say: She asked for forgiveness for the sin committed
when the United States sent them back to Europe at gunpoint.

There is a connection between the Holocaust and the rise of anti-
Semitism in the ancient Christian Church. There is also a connection
between anti-Semitism and the birth of Islam, but time and space do not
allow us to elaborate here—or on the rebirth of "Replacement Theology"
among some evangelicals today. Nor can we take the time to trace the
treatment of Jews in Western Europe, Eastern Europe, and Russia with
the respective fall of those great states, but a careful review of history
will bear out that those nations that cursed the Jews or Israel did not fare
well, just as God had specifically forewarned in Genesis 12:3.

CHAPTER 35

FRIENDS OF ISRAEL

Even though anti-Semitism is growing in the Christian Church today (especially among what are considered mainstream Christian denominations and among some evangelical churches as well), the good news is simultaneously growing support for the Jewish people and the State of Israel.

CHRISTIAN ZIONISM

Recall Christian Zionism is the belief by Christians that Israel has the right to exist as an independent Jewish nation. As noted earlier, this belief predates the rebirth of modern Israel, and Christian Zionists included American Founding Fathers as well as early presidents and diplomats after them. Many Christian Zionists in the nineteenth century were enormously helpful in paving the way for the modern state of Israel.

William E. Blackstone (1841–1935) was one such leader. He was an American evangelist who, out of a pious wish to hasten the coming of the Messiah, initially focused on the restoration of the Jews to the Holy Land as a prelude to their conversion to Christianity. However, he became increasingly concerned with the Russian murders of Jews and believed neither Europe nor America would accept the large number of Jews who needed to flee Europe. He was convinced a return of the Jewish people to their ancient homeland was the only possible solution for the widespread global persecution of Jews.

In 1890, he organized the "Conference on the Past, Present, and Future of Israel," calling on the great world powers to return Israel to the Jews. Noteworthy resolutions of sympathy for the oppressed Jews living in Russia were passed with the support of prominent leaders, but Blackstone believed more needed to be done. He escalated his efforts, including a petition drive (later known as the Blackstone Memorial) that gathered the signatures of 413 prominent leaders in the United States, including John D. Rockefeller, J. P. Morgan, Cyrus McCormick, senators, congressmen, religious leaders of all denominations, newspaper editors, the Chief Justice of the US Supreme Court, and others. He presented the "Memorial" to President Benjamin Harrison in 1891, calling for American support of Jewish restoration to Israel.

Across the ocean, the list of prominent British Christians who supported the restoration of the Jewish homeland was long and impressive, including such famous names as Charles Spurgeon, Samuel Rutherford, and William Wilberforce. And the labors of evangelical Anglican Anthony Ashley Cooper, known as Lord Shaftsbury, helped pave the way for the Balfour Declaration.

There have been so many Christian Zionists over the last 200 years that Michael Evans, a modern American evangelical of Jewish descent, raised millions of dollars and in Jerusalem built the high-tech interactive Friends of Zion Heritage Center. It highlights many historic Christian Zionists and asks everyone who visits the Center and experiences its unique program to leave as a Christian Zionist. (This request has an excellent response from the multitudes of visitors.)

MODERN-DAY CHRISTIAN ZIONISTS

Israel today recognizes its best friends are Bible-believing Christians and Evangelicals. In 2017, Prime Minister Netanyahu told one such group, "*When I say we have no greater friends than the many, many millions of Christian supporters of Israel in the United States and also in other parts of the world, I mean it. I know you've always stood with us.*"[243] So many Biblically minded Christian groups have now come alongside Israel it has ushered in a new day in Jewish–Christian relations. Several excellent Christian groups are now doing admirable work in Israel. Here are some of the many.

CUFI

Christians United for Israel is the largest and fastest growing pro-Israel organization in the United States. It strives to act as a defensive shield against the lies, boycotts, bad theology, and political threats seeking to delegitimize Israel's existence and weaken the close relationship between Israel and the United States. With membership moving toward four million, it has frequent pro-Israel events and nights organized in cities across the nation to honor and pray for Israel. It also has over 100 campus chapters and holds campus events to counteract anti-Israel campus groups.

ICEJ

The International Christian Embassy in Jerusalem was established in 1980. It recognizes the Biblical significance of Jerusalem and its unique connection with the Jewish people, and although many international embassies have stayed in Tel Aviv, the ICEJ from the beginning has made its home in Jerusalem in recognition of the fact the city is the eternal capital of Israel.

Many additional excellent groups also operate within Israel, including *Bridges for Peace, Eagle's Wings Ministries, Christian Friends of Israel, the Ebenezer Fund*, and others. And one of the more amazing movements in burgeoning Jewish-Christian relations is the Israeli government-sponsored Christian event called *The Jerusalem Prayer Breakfast*.

A PENDING PROBLEM: THE AGING OF CHRISTIAN ZIONISTS

The organizations above (and many other excellent ones) represent millions of Christians around the world who have supported and continue to support Israel politically, economically, and spiritually. But as the membership rolls of these organizations attest, they are heavily populated by older folks.

So far, strong support for Israel is not the same in the upcoming generation of Christians, a larger percentage of whom, like their less religious peers, have often bought into the modern misuse of "social justice." To be clear, true justice is of God, it is important, and it is demanded by the Lord. But today's so-called "social justice" is rarely rooted in objective truth and therefore is often ill-informed, ahistorical, and often anti-Scriptural, having led many in the next generation of Christians to embrace falsehoods about Israel.

If the current trajectory continues, Christian Zionism and support of Israel will surely fade, but there are many reasons for optimism that this trajectory will turn in a more favorable direction. *CUFI On Campus, Covenant Journey*, and the *Philos Project* are only a few of the youth and young-adult–centered movements raising a new generation of Christian Zionists.

CHAPTER 36

THE ELEPHANT IN THE ROOM

All the organizations mentioned before have not only improved Christian–Jewish relations but have helped many Jewish people move to or live in Israel, thereby changing their lives forever. Despite this, there remain questions that trouble many Jews as they ponder such assistance. They wonder, *"What is the ultimate goal of these groups? Are they simply loving Israel and Jews, or is there a different endgame?"*

TO HASTEN THE COMING OF THE MESSIAH, EVANGELIZE?

After all, it is well-known many Evangelical groups see the reestablishment of Israel as a Biblical prerequisite for the coming of the Messiah. Are these groups only helping the Jewish people to hasten what they believe will be fulfillment of Biblical prophecy? Is their assistance just a camouflaged way to introduce Christian evangelism to Jews? Is Christian interest in Jews simply to trick them into believing in Jesus?

Apparently, the government of Israel (very conscious of these concerns) does not believe so. These groups have official approval to operate within Israel (but they are not allowed to proselytize Jews or partner with Messianic Jews in Israel). In fact, most, if not all the services provided through these groups go to Israelis who have not embraced Jesus as Messiah; and if evangelism were to become part of their ministry, official permission for them to operate in Israel might be withheld.

WHY SUPPORT ISRAEL?

Such restrictions create a paradox for some Christians in that they seem to violate the Great Commission of Jesus to go into the world and make disciples of all nations, beginning first in Jerusalem, and Israel, and then the rest of the world (cf. Matthew 28:18–20).

The obvious question for Christ-followers is: If there are official limitations placed on sharing Jesus, then why are Christians active in supporting Israel? Very simply, because *the Bible commands us to love and bless Israel.* God does *not* place conditions on that command; this is what He wants and what Christians must do. This needs to be repeated for emphasis: *The Bible commands us to love and bless Israel.* Period. End of story.

HISTORY OF CHRISTIAN PERSECUTION OF JEWS

There is also the sad reality that Christians have lost the credibility to do a lot of talking. For centuries, the last words Jews heard from Christians was *"Convert, or die!"* Most Christians are not taught this, but most Jews are. It was a very real and very significant part of their history, and unlike much of America today, Jews still know and study their history (but few Christians know the horrific and excruciating torture done by Christians to Jews).

For Christians, this is a season of proving ourselves to Jews by our actions. A wise person once said, *"Preach the Gospel; and if necessary, use words."*[244] This is similar to the adage *"actions speak louder than words."* This is a season when Bible-minded Christians ought to make sure actions displaying their love and commitment to Israel and the Jewish people are clearly evident.

They have few friends on this planet. It's basically God and Bible-believing Christians. God *will* come through for them, but will we? Frankly, they deserve our support with no strings attached. Love the Jews, including those who might be suspicious of you or your motives. Love them. Stand with the State of Israel. God expects it.

Prayer: Lord, no people group has experienced as much pain and suffering as the Jewish people. We pray the world will repent of its anti-Semitism. Show us—Christians and Jews—how to enjoy the relationship You long for us to have. And Lord, we lift the State of Israel. Protect her. Guide her leaders in Your ways. Bring back the Jews from all over the world to enjoy their prophesied homeland. May those who are part of the Church repent of any attempt to replace Israel's unique role. We pray for the peace of Jerusalem as it remains the eternal and indivisible capital of Israel. Amen

MILLENNIALS

Don't let anyone look down on you because you are young, but set an example for the believers in speech, in conduct, in love, in faith, and in purity.

1 TIMOTHY 4:12, NIV

The goal of this section is to understand the values and attitudes of this unique age group and explore ways to empower them for maximum Christian impact in the future.

CHAPTER 37

WHO ARE THESE OFT-MALIGNED INDIVIDUALS?

A subject much discussed today is Millennials. ("Millennial" describes the category of individuals generally born between 1981 and 1996, although some measurements include a birth year as late as 2000.[245] Generally, they are the grandchildren of the Baby Boomer generation and were born in the years approaching the new millennium that began in 2000—thus, "Millennials." Gen Z-ers are those following Millennials, and some date them as those born after 1995.)

So why all the attention on Millennials (and sometimes even on Gen Z-ers)? Because surveys show their attitudes and behaviors are dramatically different from those of any previous generation. In fact, they are so different (and sometimes so perplexing) Millennials are often the subject of jokes by comics. What makes this generation so unlike previous ones?

Several things. Wikipedia (one of the more unreliable sources on historical truth, but frequently a good reflection of modern beliefs) points out the Millennial Generation is distinguished by (1) *"an increased use and familiarity with communications, media, and digital technologies,"* and (2) *"an increase in a liberal approach to politics and economics."*[246] Consider these two characteristics.

First, Millennials were the first generation born into hand-held technology and smart devices. Previous generations saw incredible advances during their lifetime but can also remember when it was otherwise. Not so for Millennials. They have *always* known laptops, cell phones, gaming systems, and reality TV—they are complete digital natives.

Second, they have been educated in an increasingly left-leaning and secular progressive education system. Previous generations remember starting each school day with the Pledge of Allegiance and a prayer while receiving an education that actively encouraged or reinforced traditional values and Biblical morality. Again, not so for Millennials. Words such as "absolutes" and "moral values" were absent, being replaced with "choice" and "preferences."

The strong leftward tilt of Millennials was very evident in the 2016 presidential primaries. Young voters, by a margin of 75 to 17 percent, supported Bernie Sanders over Hillary Clinton.[247] They thus preferred full-fledged socialism (the position of Bernie Sanders) to progressive liberalism (the position of Hillary Clinton), even though they were unable to define socialism[248] or point to any socialistic nation in history characterized by prosperity, opportunity, or upward mobility for those in lower classes.[249] They were taught socialism was the best and most fair system, so they wanted it in America.[250] In fact, the majority of Millennials currently prefer Socialism, Communism, and Fascism to free-market capitalism.[251]

Although Millennials have some common characteristics, ideas, and desires, not all Millennials fit into the same box. Generally, there are four primary categories in which most Millennials claim residence.

THE FOUR CATEGORIES

1. *Socialists.* Millennials in this camp are looking for the government to offer services and products for free, make their life better, and keep the wealthy from "oppressing the poor" (which they believe is what the free-market system does in America). They feel entitled to what they don't currently have and are convinced socialism will create an "even playing field," also taking care of "poor people" and "immigrants."

2. *Social Justice Warriors.* This group is moved by social issues in which they perceive there has been an injustice. They are against what

they consider to be bigotry and intolerance of any kind. Although nearly every American would openly acknowledge they don't support injustice, intolerance, or bigotry, this newer generation has redefined these words and to whom they apply. Under their definitions, what they see as "injustice" is primarily committed by police officers, Christians, conservatives, pro-lifers, or National Rifle Association members.

For example, SJWs (Social Justice Warriors) view "intolerance" as being practiced by people who want to "narrow" the definition of marriage to one man and one woman, who believe the only genders are male and female, who think men should only use the men's restroom, or who believe an unborn child is a living human and should not be murdered. And "bigotry" is primarily committed by Christians, conservatives, and the nation of Israel.

Millennials in the Social Justice Warrior camp can be seen supporting movements such as Colin Kaepernick's National Anthem protest, Black Lives Matters marches, and anti-Israel movements on college campuses.[252] Although Millennials in this camp also may oppose human trafficking and partial-birth abortion, these are dwarfed by their support for other issues.[253]

3. *Libertarians.* Although most young people don't like boundaries in their lives (especially when imposed by authority figures), for generations, civil authority has been accepted as appropriate and necessary. But this is now questioned and largely rejected by this group.[254]

Almost without exception, Libertarian Millennials argue we should have a more limited government and greater freedom, but they desire their freedom to be without boundaries. They don't want any authority—whether parents, teachers, coaches, bosses, or government officials—telling them how they should behave or live their lives.[255]

This segment frequently pushes to legalize drugs, prostitution, and most forms of sexuality and sexual expression.[256] Although many in this camp say they are "personally against" much of this behavior, they are much more against any kind of government restrictions on behavior.

4. *Faith-driven Millennials.* This is the smallest of the four groups. Although "faith" is a motivating factor for this segment, and most in this group identify as Christian,[257] there is not a consistent pattern of belief or behavior characterizing them. Many believe faith and/or Jesus is to be "experienced" and that their personal spiritual experiences are to guide their lives, often without direct reference to or application of Scripture. Consequently, the clear majority of Millennials who identify as

Christians have never read the Bible[258] and do not know what it says on most issues. In fact, only 4 percent of Millennials have a Biblical worldview[259]—the lowest percentage of any generation.[260] But inside this group are many Christian Millennials fully committed to a genuine Biblical worldview and strongly motivated to see Biblical truth and morality upheld in the daily lives of Americans.

Although these four groups represent most Millennials, these are still general categories, so not every Millennial will fit neatly in one or the other of them. (And Gen Z-ers have many unique features that differentiate them from Millennials, but they are similar in many areas.[261] The solutions discussed later are appropriate for both groups.)

CHAPTER 38

SEXUALITY

There is a substantial gap between the values of Millennials and the understood societal mores (even if not followed) of their parents. With the Millennial culture's general rejection of traditional values, sexuality is seen as being without any boundaries:

- Sex is a normal part of dating in Millennial relationships,[262] and 58 percent believe casual sex is *"morally acceptable."*[263]
- 72 percent believe in cohabitation,[264] and as NPR noted, *"Cohabitation before marriage . . . is now almost a rite of passage . . . for the millennial generation."*[265] (Only 25 percent believe it is morally wrong for a couple to live together with no intention of getting married.[266])
- The rate of sexually transmitted diseases (STDs) among Millennials is soaring[267]
- Young Millennials have an extremely high rate of newly diagnosed HIV infections.[268] They also have the highest rate of undiagnosed HIV of any age group[269]
- 74 percent view homosexuality as *"morally acceptable."*[270]
- 81 percent support legal recognition of homosexual marriage,[271] and a sizeable percentage of Millennials say the statement *"that sex should only be within a marriage*

between a man and a woman" is an anti-gay sentiment.[272] Traditional male–female marriage is not highly esteemed

- 68 percent say having children outside marriage is morally acceptable[273]
- 57 percent of children born to Millennials are born outside marriage—the highest percentage of any generation on record.[274] This dramatically increases poverty among Millennials: 34 percent of *unmarried* Millennials with children live in poverty, compared with only 8 percent of *married* Millennials with children who live in poverty[275]
- Two-thirds see gender as fluid rather than fixed,[276] and half see gender as a spectrum of various identities.[277] For example, even Facebook now recognizes seventy-one different genders (although that number is changing constantly)[278]
- 57 percent of Millennials seek out pornography,[279] and 45 percent see it as *"morally acceptable."*[280]
- Millennials have created new standards of sexual norms known as "friends with benefits" (friends with whom they have casual sex) and "sexting" (sending sexually explicit pictures of their own bodies to potentially interested sexual partners). They even venture into sexual exploitations of classmates and peers, seemingly without the slightest regard for the impact their actions might have on their targeted victims[281]
- 59 percent of Millennials have never married—a percentage much higher than any previous generation.[282]

Concerning this last point, in 1960, 65 percent of those aged eighteen to thirty-two were married; today that number has plummeted to 26 percent.[283] The onset of both marriage[284] and adulthood[285] are being dramatically delayed, if not discarded.

Concerning sexual behavior, Millennials largely hold, *"If it makes someone happy and doesn't hurt me, it's okay. Who are we to judge what makes someone else happy?"* Individual preferences and personal pleasure are the measuring stick for right and wrong rather than truth, results, traditional values, or Biblical morality.

WHERE DID MILLENNIALS GET THIS?

None of this should be surprising, however, for these beliefs generally reflect those of the educational system in which Millennials have been raised—they have been taught they are free to choose whatever makes them happy. For example, on the issue of gender, from kindergarten all the way through the postsecondary level, students are encouraged to make their own choices, regardless of their biological sex. It is all about being "free" to choose whatever they think makes them "happy."

NOT JUST SEX, BUT DRUGS TOO

So, too, with drugs such as marijuana. It is touted as enjoyable and fun; it shouldn't be banned. *"After all,"* Millennials argue, *"beer and cigarettes are legal; why shouldn't we legalize marijuana?"* Ironically, this argument could be restated as: *"Since we have legalized other things proven to be addictive and to produce harmful health effects (i.e., liquor and cigarettes), both to the primary user and to those around him or her, we should also legalize marijuana!"* But instead of logic or consequences, personal desire has become the highest standard of measurement.

In short, Millennials want to touch it, taste it, and feel it without anyone else telling them what is right or wrong or what does or doesn't work. With the focus being almost solely on "me," the concept of entitlement has largely replaced responsibility. Personal feelings and beliefs take ascendency over everything else.

CHAPTER 39

PRESUPPOSITIONS AND VALUES

We have lost count of the number of parents who have come to us totally baffled at their Millennial. They unsuspectingly sent their children off to college (sometimes even to a so-called "Christian" college) only to have that child come home for Thanksgiving break speaking a different language and with totally different values. What happened?

NATIONAL BRANDING

For Millennials, things such as Biblical truth, moral absolutes, traditional values, or other seemingly common sense and reality-based positions are demonized. Why do they believe these things to be "hateful," "bigoted," "intolerant," and "unloving?" Very simply: national branding. Among Millennials, branding and labels currently carries more weight than fact or reality.

Let's revisit the 2016 Republican presidential primary. Of the seventeen original Republican candidates, most embraced the same core issues. For example, all of them ran as pro-life or held pro-life positions,[286] and each proclaimed government spending needed to be reined in.[287] So given the commonality between them, how does any one candidate stand out from the rest? Donald Trump ingenuously distanced himself from the others using branding.

For example, he branded Jeb Bush as "boring"[288]; it stuck. John Kasich became "1 for 41 John,"[289] referring to the fact he won only one state in the primaries, thus branding him as a loser. Senator Marco Rubio was branded "Little Marco"[290]; his support fell. And most notably, Trump branded Senator Ted Cruz as "Lyin' Ted"[291]—a label he could not escape during the rest of the campaign and that contributed greatly to his fall in the polls. Then, when Trump won the GOP primary and moved into the general election against Hillary Clinton, he dubbed her "Crooked Hillary,"[292] and the moniker stuck.

Branding is also apparent in the protests against conservative speakers on various college campuses.[293] Students have been told "conservatives" and "Christians" are "racist oppressors" who are "hateful," "intolerant," and "bigoted," so they react accordingly. It is irrelevant whether these conservative or Christian speakers are really what they are labeled. Their professors and social media branded the speakers and for Millennials; that branding sticks.

Secular Progressives (who dominate the arenas of academia and media) have repeatedly utilized this strategy with great success. Stick a negative label on your opponent or on their positions that disagree with yours, then repeat the label time and again until it is believed to be reality.

To see how well this has worked with Millennials, ask them to list key words they associate with topics such as Islam/Muslims, LGBTQ, socialism and communism, marijuana and drug use, and physician-assisted suicide; nearly all the words will be positive. Then ask them which words they associate with Christianity, America, the Constitution, the Founding Fathers, free-market economics, absolute truth, free speech, national borders, and traditional marriage; the words will nearly all be negative. With branding, you don't need reasons, sound logic, proof, or results; all you need are plenty of adjectives you can repeat until they stick.

Interestingly, the items in the latter grouping were not viewed as "hateful" or "discriminatory" by previous generations—and for good reason. The reality is the US Constitution explicitly guarantees equal civil rights to all races, but today Millennials believe the document is "racist" and discriminatory.[294] Christianity has provided more global benevolence and benevolent institutions than any other religion in the history of the world,[295] but Millennials view Christianity's adherents as "hateful" and "bigoted."

Millennials have also "learned" the Founding Fathers were terrible men who were "racist" and believed in white privilege.[296] It is true most of the Founding Fathers were white, and a majority did own slaves, but as previously noted in the section on racism, many of them freed their slaves after America separated from Great Britain, and the overwhelming majority of the Founders started and participated in antislavery societies or stood against slavery. But this doesn't matter. To Millennials, the Founders have been branded.

And even though churches are the most charitable organizations in America[297] and do more than any other to help the poor and those in need (including disaster relief, halfway houses, job training for released prisoners, food pantries for the hungry, shelters for the homeless, foster homes, hospitals and health care, addiction dependency support, and much else), Millennials largely believe churches are houses of "religious bigotry" and "intolerance." It is not surprising Millennials' attendance at religious services has plummeted.[298]

NO ABSOLUTES

We are now living in what is considered a postmodern culture. Postmodern means "*a radical reappraisal of modern assumptions about culture, identity, history, or language*"[299] resulting in a blanket rejection of all that went before. Truth and morality have become purely subjective, being individually determined. In fact, 74 percent of Millennials believe there is no absolute truth or moral absolutes.[300]

But if truth is individually determined, can something like crime actually exist? After all, the criminal did what he thought was right for him and what made him happy. And if truth is subjective, how can you tell anyone his or her behavior is wrong? Can stealing really be wrong if the person who stole believes it to be acceptable—if it makes him or her happy? So the actual issue is,who decides truth, or right or wrong? Who makes the standards for a society, and what are they?

A prevalent standard among Millennials is this As long you don't do harm to others, you can do what you want. But we have the same core problem: How do you define "*doing harm to others*," and who gets to establish the definition?

For example, if I see a rich man drop his wallet, do I need to return it? If he is rich and has lots of money, it's likely he didn't even know how much money was in his wallet, and for me to keep that money certainly does him no real harm. Or if I see something at Walmart (or Target or Lowes) I want but don't have the money to purchase, it does the store no real harm for me to take it. The big chain stores would not know something was missing, and the items on the shelves in the store are already marked up to compensate for such store losses.

Many Millennials would argue the actions described above are morally acceptable for they do no real harm. The reason for this twisted logic is that is what Millennials have been taught. For example, consider the Houston school district—the seventh largest school district in America, with 287 schools and nearly 12,000 teachers.[301] (By the way, the population of the city of Houston is greater than the population of twenty-six states in the United States.) One of our friends was a high school teacher in Houston. He is great with kids in the classroom and was nominated for teacher of the year.

During the in-service teacher training launching the school year, teachers were instructed that if a student asks a moral question, teachers were to respond, "Do whatever you think is right." Our friend asked, *"So you're telling me that if a student decides to rob a convenience store and they come to me and ask me what I think, I can't tell them stealing and robbing is wrong?"* The answer? *"Correct. You need to tell the student they need to do whatever they think is right."*

CHAPTER 40

HOPE ON THE HORIZON

Although Millennials hold many poor, impractical, and uninformed positions, there are some favorable positions they hold.

ANTI-ABORTION

One area where the majority of Millennials embrace a positive position is concerning abortion and the value of life. They are the most pro-life generation since the US Supreme Court delivered their abortion-is-okay-under-any-circumstance *Roe. v. Wade* decision in 1973.[302]

Some argue Millennials are more pro-life because today's science and technology allow us to know things about the unborn child (as well as abortion's harm on the health of the mother) we didn't know in previous generations. There is no doubt access to images of unborn children (including a mother's ability to take home images from a sonogram to stick on her refrigerator or post on social media) certainly humanizes the unborn child in the minds of most.

But the "advanced science and technology" argument is not persuasive. After all, if it were, there would be no more abortion supporters in America, for the science is clear the abortion is being performed on an unborn human child. In fact, as far back as April 30, 1965, *LIFE* magazine published amazing photographs taken inside the womb showing the humanity of the unborn child as it was developing across the weeks and months.[303] There was no question in 1965 it was an unborn human life, but the court still decided otherwise, and many abortion supporters also hold that view, notwithstanding all the scientific evidence to the contrary.

So the high opposition of Millennials to abortion is almost inexplicable, especially considering their education systems were so pro-abortion. Perhaps the real reason there is such high support for protecting unborn life among Millennials is because God has birthed in them His supernatural purpose to end the genocide of abortion in America. We'll see.

ANTI-HUMAN TRAFFICKING

Millennials should also be praised for their moral clarity on the issue of human trafficking. (Ironically, for a generation that largely believes there are no absolute rights or wrongs, they are almost unanimous in their affirmation that human trafficking is absolutely wrong—and in this they are absolutely right.) Many have found their voice in strong and open opposition to this modern form of slavery. On both these important issues, Millennials' hearts have motivated them to a position of certainty as well as of positive action.

THERE IS HOPE

Although much of the country ridicules the beliefs and actions of Millennials (and sometimes for good reason), Millennials have many redeeming features that should not be overlooked. On the whole, they care very deeply for and about people and are motivated to be a part of something significant (which is why they so quickly join causes and movements). They also dislike injustice and have great compassion.

But many Millennials simply haven't had the life experience or training to know they shouldn't believe everything their professors or the media or Wikipedia tells them. As a result, they are often misled, misguided, and even taken advantage of by interest groups and political parties that exploit them for political or socioeconomic purposes. But as a general rule, Millennials are incredibly big-hearted and motivated to be part of something bigger than themselves; these characteristics simply need to be informed and pointed in productive directions.

Before Millennials can be reached, they must be understood by those who have a heart for them. To use a military comparison, before engag-

ing in any battle (such as this one for the hearts and minds of Millennials), an accurate survey of the battlefield must be made. Without that,
we might attempt ineffectual solutions—like sending tanks into a swamp
or dropping paratroopers into dense jungles. Solutions must be crafted
that comport with the specific needs of the battle.

Here are seven key realities of this allegorical battlefield for the next
generation.

CHAPTER 41

REALITY NO. 1: MILLENNIALS BREATHE A DIFFERENT ATMOSPHERE

As a collective body, Millennials have grown up in an educational atmosphere particularly unfriendly to Christianity, Biblical truth, traditional values, and constitutionally limited government. In fact, most colleges and universities—even some so-called "Christian" colleges—are overtly hostile to these beliefs.

Millennials have also grown up in an entertainment atmosphere where:

- They thought reality television was genuine reality
- The music they listened to largely encouraged moral values that contradicted what most parents endorsed
- Every TV show from their childhood either had a positive, apparently happy and fulfilled homosexual character on the show or else promoted or normalized cohabitation and premarital sex in relationships
- The parents in the shows weren't smart, and the kids routinely displayed open disrespect for authorities
- The lead characters were guided by subjective morality.

Polling shows "peer pressure" has been a significant influence on youth, and for Millennials, it is no different,[304] except that a primary source of their peer pressure is social media—it is where their friends gather and share their unfiltered opinions. And sadly, several of the social media platforms have readily available and popular cesspools of twisted ideas.

In general, Millennials have been raised in an atmosphere devoid of absolute truth, not knowing *all* ideas have consequences that can and should be measured. They have been told certain things are good, but they have never been shown empirical data documenting whether that claim is true or not.

SOLUTION NO. 1: *INTRODUCE THEM TO NEW ATMOSPHERES*

Because our educational system no longer teaches students to engage in independent thinking, we should encourage Millennials to pursue and discover truth and reality rather than simply believe whatever they are told. Unless we encourage them to love truth, they will not develop the habit of seeking truth and may therefore stop short and accept the first thing they read on the internet.

One of the best ways of introducing Millennials to what they don't know is by asking questions that make them think—questions that will lead them to truth, such as *"How do you know?" "What is your source—where did you get your information?" "Is that all that is said about the issue, or is there another side to the story?"* and so forth. Such questions can challenge their positions and help them reach very different conclusions from what they might already hold by helping them discover what they were never told or by finding out many things they previously believed weren't entirely true or were even false.

The asking and answering of questions was central to American education for more than three centuries before Progressive educators changed that practice in the twentieth century. Before that, Jesus relied heavily on the use of questions, asking more than 300 questions in the Gospels.[305] (By the way, notice Jesus did not answer most of the questions He asked. Simply asking the question can often turn the thinking process in a different direction.) Young people often believe they know much more about a subject than they actually do, and by utilizing questions in conversations with them, we may help them quickly realize they don't know as much as they thought.

There are many specific areas where Millennials need to be exposed to truth and have their suppositions challenged. Among the things most have been taught (and most now believe) are the following:

- The minimum wage should be raised to unsustainable amounts (regardless of the skill and productivity, or lack thereof, of the worker)
- Socialism provides a superior economic system and provides high freedom and high equality whereas free-market economic principles provide low equality (although there are no examples to which they can point to support that premise)
- The United States should have open borders and allow legal status to all illegal immigrants (regardless of any crimes they may have committed or dangers posed)
- Authority figures, including police officers, are oppressive and abusive (although some examples of this do exist, they tend to be the exception rather than the norm—a point lost on, or unrealized by, many Millennials)
- All college should be free (they have no idea what the axiom, *"There is no such thing as a free lunch"*)
- The government should take care of the poor (even though seventy cents of every dollar the government collects for the poor funds the bureaucracy and never reaches the poor,[306] and the family, church, and individual are the most effective means of helping the poor)
- Islam is a religion of peace, and all religions are equal and equally valid (except, of course, Christianity—even though history and experience show otherwise).

None of the positions generally held by Millennials on these issues is sustainable in real life, but they need someone who will relationally engage them and respectfully ask them questions. Asking open-ended questions to which there are answers and then helping them find those answers is a major step toward slowly breaking down the indoctrination they have received.

If they are younger Millennials or Gen Z-ers, encourage them, if they are planning to attend institutions of higher learning (whether secular or religious), to look for a place where the pursuit of truth is encouraged—places that not only do not attack traditional values, Christianity, or America but also teach thinking. And when looking for a good college, an important question should be asked of the college president and professors: *"How do you determine truth?"* If their answer is to reference something subjective or if they respond that truth is determined by societal laws and customs, then you can know they will not promote objective truth, and this is a place you should avoid.

CHAPTER 42

REALITY NO. 2: MILLENNIALS ARE NOT TRADITIONAL

Most Millennials have been taught America's traditions and core values are racist, bigoted, and harmful to the world. And they simply don't study enough world or American history or traditions to know otherwise.

In fact, of the elite seventy-six universities in America (as listed in *US News & World Report*), fifty-three require no course at all in American history for *history majors*! Of the twenty-three that do require an American history course, eleven allow classes such as "Hip-Hop, Politics, and Youth Culture in America" or "Mad Men and Mad Women" to fulfill the American "history" requirement.[307] So only twelve of the seventy-six actually require a genuine American history course. (And if history majors are not required to study any American history, you can imagine how much less non–history majors get.) Further, only 3 percent of America's colleges and universities require students to take any course in economics,[308] so they know nothing about our free-market system or that socialism doesn't work. The Constitution is almost completely unknown, with only one of 1,000 being able to name the rights in the First Amendment.[309] In fact, because of what they have been taught, 53 percent actually oppose free-speech protected by the Constitution.[310]

What little Millennials do learn about American history, government, and economics comes largely from academia and the media, both of which hold a decidedly negative view on America's history and traditions. Millennials also receive the same type of skewed indoctrination against marriage, sexuality, family, Christianity, and traditional values.

Because what Millennials do know about America is generally bad and because they have limited life experience, there is very little appeal to them when someone talks about "restoring" or "returning" to "traditional values." In fact, that rhetoric turns most Millennials off because it sounds to them like they are going backward.

SOLUTION NO. 2: *OFFER A NEW VISION, BUT ONE BASED ON HISTORIC AND TRADITIONAL VALUES*

Understand that Millennials know nearly nothing about many of the cultural basics previous generations took for granted. If we know many positions the rest of the nation holds dear are viewed negatively by Millennials, it should change the way we approach talking with them.

Recall that much of what Millennials believe is based on how they "feel" on a specific issue. Facts or tradition is not where they will start, for they have been encouraged from kindergarten onward to "feel" and "decide for yourself." If we want to see Millennials embrace "traditional" positions (beyond their aforementioned laudable opposition to abortion and human trafficking), we need to know how to help them "feel" about other issues so they will decide for themselves to embrace traditional positions and Biblical truth.

For example, it would not be strategic to tell most Millennials we need to restore what the Founding Fathers established in America and get back to the Constitution. They have been taught these things are bad. However, if we were to suggest that in America we should promote equality—in fact, we should promote "*all people are created equal*" (the Declaration of Independence), people shouldn't be penalized for having an opinion and expressing it (the First Amendment Freedom of Speech), and an individual shouldn't be forced to do something he or she personally views as morally wrong (the First Amendment Free Exercise of

Religious and Rights of Religious Conscience)—most Millennials would quickly agree and be open to accepting and promoting them.

This doesn't mean you abandon traditional values, the Founding Fathers, the Constitution, the Bible, Christianity, or the many other things they have been taught are bad. Rather it means you simply take the old principles and put them in a new package.

CHAPTER 43

REALITY NO. 3: A NEW TYPE OF EDUCATION

Growing up, Millennials were repeatedly told the importance of getting a college degree. Many did, and parents are now finding more were indoctrinated than educated. This is because the purpose of education has dramatically changed for recent generations.

Formerly, education was to provide the skills necessary for work and citizenship. It trained students to engage in analytical thinking and showed them how to learn on their own. But today, education is no longer about job preparedness and analytical thinking—it teaches *what* to think rather than *how* to think.

This is called indoctrination, which is *"the process of teaching a person or group to accept a set of beliefs uncritically."*[311] It is the effort to make the professor's personal beliefs become the student's beliefs. Pursuit of truth is not the objective; for those who indoctrinate, they usually (1) don't like what the truth is and/or (2) don't care what truth is.

Dr. Martin Luther King Jr. saw early indications of this change and openly warned against it:

[I] often wonder whether or not education is fulfilling its purpose. A great majority of the so-called educated people do not think logically and scientifically. . . . To save man from the morass of propaganda, in my opinion, is one of the chief aims of education. Education must enable one to sift and weigh evidence, to discern the true from the false, the real from the unreal, and the facts from the fiction. The function of education, therefore, is to teach one to think intensively and to think critically. . . . If we are not careful, our colleges will produce a group of close-minded, unscientific, illogical propagandists, consumed with immoral acts. Be careful, brethren! Be careful, teachers![312]

Students now graduate with very clear and strong opinions on many subjects, but those opinions often routinely contradict empirical evidence to the contrary. For example, Millennials are very concerned about the environment and global warming[313]—but there has been no increase in the earth's temperature (thus, no global warming) since 1996.[314] Even though a broad spectrum of scientists now warn about the approach of a mini ice age,[315] most Millennials never heard this in college. So, too, with Socialism: They strongly support it despite all the evidence to the contrary—evidence they've never heard. The same with gender identity: They've been taught personal preferences trump biological truth, science, and reality.

Students have likewise been given only one side of many other issues—they've been taught the nirvana of universal single-payer health care, the evils of guns and the National Rifle Association, the admirable work done by Planned Parenthood, the racism of Israel and victimhood of Palestinians, and many other easily disprovable positions.

The Bible wisely notes *"The first to put forth his case seems right, until someone else steps forward and cross-examines him"* (Proverbs 18:17, ISV), but Millennials rarely get the other side of anything in their education. In fact, to help ensure they don't, many professors teach students that anyone holding an opinion different from what they've heard is bigoted and intolerant and should be rejected out of hand—that is, don't even listen to anyone who says anything different; immediately disregard or oppose them.

Not only does present-day education emphasize indoctrination over analytical thinking, it has also proven to be of little use in helping Millennials enter a productive career field. Currently, only 27 percent of graduates are able to get a job in their field of study[316]—three fourths can't get a job within their college degree. Part of the problem is colleges offer "career field" courses such as queer musicology, surfing, nannying, medieval sexuality, auctioneering, bagpiping, bowling technology, cannabis cultivation, Star Trek, sexy vampires, sexual hooking up, and many other majors and courses largely unusable in the real world.

College degrees fail three fourths of graduates, and adding insult to injury, it also gives them massive debt. Currently, 66 percent of college students graduate with an average debt of $37,172, leaving them with a monthly payment of $382.[317] That debt has a direct adverse impact in at least three areas: they put off home ownership (they can't afford a mortgage on top of their existing debt), they delay marriage (few want to undertake the added financial obligations of marriage and family), and although the majority of them would like to be an entrepreneur and have their own business,[318] their education debt stands in the way.

They were told to get into higher education; they did, and now they can't get a job, but they do get debt—along with views hostile to traditional American institutions, history, economics, and government. This often useless and substandard education (substandard when compared with the academic knowledge typical in previous generations) has caused professionals to add new words and meanings to "adolescence."

EXTENDED ADOLESCENCE

Traditionally, by definition, "adolescence" was the time before you became a legal adult at the age of eighteen[319]—the age at which you traditionally took on the responsibilities of life. But with Millennials, experts have had to create new terminology, which they now call "Prolonged" or "Extended Adolescence," recognizing the current reality it is somewhere between the ages of thirty and forty before the group known as Millennials begins to take on the responsibilities long associated with adulthood.[320]

As commentators on this new national phenomenon note:

It isn't until the age of thirty-five many of them will start to become responsible for themselves, financially productive, and consider having children of their own. In the meantime, they are happy to live with their parents, chop and change jobs, and indulge their tastes for nightlife and the latest consumer goods.[321]

Writing in *The Chronicle of Higher Education*, [Penn State historian Gary] Cross says "delayed social adulthood" means "in 2011, almost a fifth of men between twenty-five and thirty-four still lived with their parents," where many play video games: "The average player is thirty years old." The percentage of men in their early forties who have never married "has risen fourfold to 20 percent."[322]

It appears what Dr. King warned has now become reality:

> If we are not careful, our colleges will produce a group of close-minded, unscientific, illogical propagandists, consumed with immoral acts.[323]

SOLUTION NO. 3: *GET THE REST OF THE STORY*

Millennials must be told the rest of the story—the side they haven't heard. You can help them know that other side so they can make an informed decision. But don't try to beat them down with facts, studies, or statistics. Remember: Millennials are highly relational and are motivated by general relationships. Furthermore, they only know what they know, and if you aggressively attack that, they will believe you are attacking them personally. You need to approach them with the characteristics associated with God's wisdom:

> But the wisdom from above is first of all pure. It is also *peace loving, gentle* at all times, and *willing to yield to others.* (James 3:17a, NLT)
> But the wisdom from above is first pure, then *peaceable, gentle, open to reason* . . . (James 3:17a, NEV)

Don't be the proverbial "bull in the china shop." As the Bible reminds us, "*A gentle answer deflects anger, but harsh words make tempers flare*" (Proverbs 15:1, NLT).

This is the attitude you should have in approaching the individual Millennial (or any other person, for that matter). But the systemic source causing this problem must also be addressed: The cesspool that has become housed within education has to be cleaned out. How can we change the education system and institutions? We have to get our local legislators focused on this—we need free-market ideas at work in education, including competition between schools through parental empower-ment (also known as educational choice)—through defunding courses and degrees clearly designed for indoctrination or largely unworkable in the real world—through enacting educational standards focused on thinking and truth, and so forth.

We have to put our foot down on all the education money we spend to destroy the next generation and commit national suicide. Call your state legislator and tell him or her to withhold funding for schools and universities until there are systemic changes. Taxpayers should be fund-ing academic education, not philosophical indoctrination.

CHAPTER 44

REALITY NO. 4: NO BOUNDARIES AND FEW FACTS

As already noted, sexual boundaries are largely nonexistent with Millennials. There are several possible explanations for this:

- First, education has taught them their feelings are their only boundaries
- Second, there is nearly no knowledge either of the Bible or the nation's traditional Judeo-Christian sexual values, and when presented, both are portrayed as repressive and backward
- Third, with few exceptions, their entertainment programming presents nearly no sexual boundaries
- And fourth, many Millennials have come from dysfunctional or broken families where sexual boundaries were rare and there were few positive influences in their lives.

Whether it is one of these reasons, some, all, or other reasons, the reality is Millennials generally lack appreciation for traditional marriage or sexual boundaries and have been told by their professors, "health professionals," and social media that removing boundaries will make things better.

SOLUTION NO. 4: *SCIENCE AND FACTS SHOW THE BENEFIT OF BOUNDARIES*

Have discussions with Millennials about the negative consequences of sexuality without boundaries. Most Christian parents and grandparents aren't comfortable having these conversations with their kids or grand-kids, but do you know who is comfortable telling young people what sex should look like? Culture. Social Media. Hollywood. We must not let the other side have an uncontested free ride on sexuality. We must engage.

Millennials need to know God created sex, and He put helpful and beneficial boundaries on how and when it should take place. Countless areas demonstrate whenever something is used outside how it was designed, there will be problems—so, too, with sex. The Bible teaches God made sexual union *only* for the context of a sacred lifelong union (marriage) between one man and one woman.

One of the great advantages we have (and must utilize) is to contrast the results of the world's way of approaching sexuality with God's. Jesus told us to judge a tree by the fruit (that is, the results) it produces. He explained a good tree would produce good fruit and a bad tree bad fruit (Matthew 7:15–20). So just look at the results of each approach.

As an example, a high percentage of Millennials practice cohabita-tion, explaining they want to make sure any potential spouse "is compat-ible" before they get married,[324] kind of like test-driving a new vehicle before buying it. Despite the apparent logic of this approach, statistics show just the opposite: Those who cohabit before marriage are more likely to have a divorce later.[325] So cohabitation may hinder the long-term personal happiness they want.

Likewise, modern culture tells them they should practice "safe sex" and thus fully enjoy the pleasure of sex. However, science affirms the only truly "safe sex" is not having sex until you're married, and then having sex only with your spouse. But a high percentage of Millennials are sexually active, and as a consequence, large numbers of them have STDs.[326] Significantly, however, up until the 1960s when sexuality was generally within the boundaries God established, there were only two known sexually transmitted diseases;[327] today there are some twenty-seven,[328] and several are permanent and incurable.[329]

Interestingly, an article titled "Revenge of The Church Ladies" acknowledged:

> One of the nation's most liberal sexual studies ever conducted, and summarized in a book called *Sex in America*, revealed that religiously active middle-aged women who were in mutually monogamous life-time partnerships (I call that marriage) were more sexually satisfied than those with little or no faith present in their lives. And I like to call *that* the "revenge of the church ladies!"[330]

This study would wreck most Millennials' thoughts about sexuality and sexual satisfaction. But as it turns out, science repeatedly shows that observing the boundaries God put on human sexuality is what makes us happiest and brings the most sexual satisfaction.

We need to begin teaching Millennials how to *"judge a tree by its fruit"* and to engage in behavior with positive and proven outcomes, not ones satisfying for a brief moment but often bringing many negative consequences in the future. We need to promote how easy it is to do the "right thing" (i.e., following the boundaries of sex inside marriage between one man and one woman) and how many problems it solves.

CHAPTER 45

REALITY NO. 5: THEIR WORLD IS FILLED WITH WEAK EXAMPLES

Many Millennials are convinced marriage is unnecessary today, having been taught society has evolved past the need for the institution of marriage—that marriage worked for people in early times when they needed help to survive, but we are no longer at that point. This is certainly a massive understatement as well as a faulty view of God's design for marriage, but in defense of Millennials, many marriages they see don't contribute much to society in general or to individual happiness in particular. Certainly, we can tell them there are wonderful benefits to marriage—for example, married couples are the most financially stable of all demographic segments today.[331] But financial stability doesn't matter to Millennials if it also means being in an unhappy marriage, which is what most Millennials see around them.

Also, Millennials are, by far, the most Biblically illiterate generation in American history—they don't know even the minimal cultural and historical aspects of the Bible every previous generation knew. Numerous studies confirm this Biblical illiteracy,[332] and we see almost daily examples of it:

- A friend who is the president of a Christian university recently confided to us Christian students who attend the school—students raised in church and in church youth groups—no longer know the difference between Moses (who received the Ten Commandments) and Jonah (who was swallowed by a big fish)
- A friend who runs a large national conglomerate has begun to mentor a church-going Millennial who never before heard the names Adam and Eve—nor had he heard of other legendary Bible figures who for centuries were known by all, including both religious and secular citizens
- A student in a college Biblical studies course related that when a classmate heard "Sodom and Gomorrah," she assumed they were a married couple from the Bible rather than the two infamous cities God destroyed for their homosexuality.

It is a problem Millennials know so little of the greatest literary, historical, and theological book ever written. It is also a problem only 4 percent of them have a Biblical worldview[333]— only 16 percent of the Boomer and Builder generations do[334]—and only 10 percent of Christians overall.[335] Furthermore, 90 percent of Christians who say they have a Biblical worldview actually don't.[336] Millennials don't see folks around them who know and live by the Bible and its teachings—their world is largely devoid of such positive examples.

Millennials have significant problems that must be addressed with their views on both marriage and the Bible.

SOLUTION NO. 5: *MODEL THE RIGHT EXAMPLE*

It is silly to expect the next generation, or our kids and grandkids, to do and be something we did not first model for them. The best thing to help change a Millennial's perspective on marriage is not just telling them what the Bible says about marriage but rather showing them what a Biblical marriage looks like—what it looks like to faithfully love and support someone, cheering for their success and serving them to help them accomplish what God has called and gifted them to do and be.

And even for those who really do have a sound and healthy marriage, the next generation needs to see you keeping your marriage as a primary focus in your life. By attending marriage seminars and marriage conferences (no matter your age or the number of years you've been married), you will be communicating that your marriage relationship is something so important to you, you *always* want to make it better than it already is.

Model to Millennials what a healthy marriage looks like, and show what it means to read the Bible, study the Bible, live by the Bible, and apply the Bible—model for them what Biblical literacy and a Biblical worldview actually look like. And once you are living it, you can help explain it to them. Actions do speak louder than words, and you should use both (as long as your actions don't contradict your words).

CHAPTER 46

REALITY NO. 6: NO CONCRETE REALITY

Millennials live in a constantly changing culture, including with language, inventing new words (micro-aggressions, snowflakes, trigger warning, safe spaces) and redefining old ones. For example, the Bible and history teach us the word *love* represents something sacrificial and unselfish—it places the interests of others ahead of our own—it causes us to think about how we want to be treated and then treat others the same way (i.e., to live by Jesus's "Golden Rule" of Matthew 7:12). But the modern definition of *love* is no longer about self-sacrifice but rather about sex. Thus, we hear, "*If two people love each other, who are we to tell them who or how they can love?*" This is not talking about serving others but rather about who should have a sexual relationship with whom.

Similarly, the traditional definition of tolerance was being able to endure and put up with someone or something you disagreed with. But the new definition requires those around you to affirmatively praise you for what you do or believe, and if they don't offer you positive approval for whatever you do or say, they are "intolerant." (There are thousands of examples where people are now labeled "intolerant" simply for disagreeing with someone else.)

And one of the few religious things Millennials are told is *"The Bible says not to judge,"* and *"judging"* other people is one of the greatest of human evils. Of course, if you simply think about that argument, it is not even logical. Should we not judge a mass-murderer? Or a mother who murders her toddler? Or a pedophile or child rapist? Of course we should—and Millennials would agree, if the question was posed to them. But they hear that phrase in the context of total acceptance of all beliefs, behaviors, and lifestyles, and anyone who disagrees is "judging."

Significantly, this modern meaning of *"Don't judge"* is the *opposite* of what Jesus taught in Matthew 7:1–2, NASB when He used that phrase. He said: "Do not judge so that you will not be judged. For in the way you judge, you will be judged; and by your standard of measure, it will be measured to you." Jesus was setting forth a standard of measurement: He was telling them not to be hypocritical—they should live up to the same standard by which they measure others. And significantly, only a few verses later (Matthew 7:15–20), Jesus specifically *commanded* His disciples to judge—to judge a tree by its fruit—that is, to examine people's lives and ideas and see what results they produce.

So the redefining of traditional words is a common feature in the Millennial culture. And if you don't understand this, it will be like you speaking to them in French but them hearing you in Russian; they will completely miss what you are trying to communicate. It will be as if you said "red" but they heard "green" because of the redefinition of words.

SOLUTION NO. 6: *JUDGE THE RESULTS*

What overcomes words is demonstration of facts, so show Millennials how to do exactly what Jesus said: judge a tree by its fruits. Show them how to find and evaluate statistics, studies, and evidence as to whether an idea, practice, policy, lifestyle, or behavior works as advertised, regardless of how it is defined or what they have been told it means. Significantly, polling shows a source of major frustration for Millennials once they get into the workplace is so many things didn't work out the way they were taught they would.[337]

Through the use of historical polls and studies, as well as logic and experience, help Millennials learn to distinguish what works and what doesn't before they have to slam into a wall. Of course, remember to do this in conjunction with other solutions already mentioned, including building genuine and honest relationships (this is key), asking questions that guide them to the truth, and so forth. But the bottom line is helping them learn to judge a tree by its fruit will help establish a measuring system beyond their feelings and perhaps will develop in them a lifelong love for objective truth.

CHAPTER 47

REALITY NO. 7: MILLENNIALS ARE HIGHLY RELATIONAL

Although Millennials are part of a group, and although that group has very distinguishable characteristics, they are nevertheless very individualized in how they view themselves and interact with others. Because of this, they must be individually reached. Reflective of this, more than any previous generation, Millennials want direct personal contact with their boss[338]—they like and desire to be in mentoring relationships.[339] They also don't read books or watch traditional television.[340] Everything is on-demand, which tailors not only to their individual preferences but also their personal timetables. With other generations, a wide-reaching appeal to the group can be effective, but not so with Millennials. If you don't grasp the relational nature of Millennials, then crafting any solution will likely miss the mark and be ineffective.

SOLUTION NO. 7: *DEVELOP INDIVIDUAL FRIENDSHIPS AND MENTORING RELATIONSHIPS*

Understand that it has taken decades of indoctrination to lead Millennials in the wrong direction, and we shouldn't imagine that with one conversation the problem can be resolved. It will require us being intentional, going out of our way, and spending time to share our life experiences and our insight. Reaching Millennials will be a long and engaging task, and in a culture accustomed to things happening very quickly, slow processes can be frustrating. But as Paul exhorts us, *"Let us not become weary in doing good, for at the proper time we will reap a harvest if we do not give up"* (Galatians 6:9, NIV).

Changing Millennials will require us to do what Jesus did to change the world: He spent one-on-one time with those he was mentoring. Over recent generations, we have turned to mass evangelism and mass discipleship, trying to reach groups instead of discipling individuals; and interestingly, the church is weaker today than at any point in our history. Significantly, Jesus spent more time with His handful of disciples than He did with the masses who followed Him, and ultimately it was that smaller group He personally discipled who changed the known world. The Bible specifically instructs us to handpick some others and teach them what we know so they in turn can do the same for others (2 Timothy 2:2). What God has for us is to be passed down from individual to individual, not from group to group.

Millennials desire personal and genuine relationships with people, and they aren't looking for people who have their lives together or have all the answers. They enjoy getting to know people who aren't perfect but who are genuine. Let's repeat that: They enjoy getting to know people who aren't perfect but who are genuine. By spending time with an individual who is open and real, even if it is someone with whom they disagree, they can quickly soften their opinions. So intentionally pursue time engaging Millennials, getting to know them through relationships. Once there is a level of trust, Millennials are very open to know what you believe and why you believe it. The bottom line is that Millennials are a very reachable generation—one by one, over time.

CHAPTER 48

ADVICE TO MILLENNIALS AND OLDER GENERATIONS

M ay we offer some advice to both Millennials and to older adults?

TO MILLENNIALS AND GEN Z-ERS

To all Millennials or Generation Z-ers who might be reading this: Don't lose heart at what you are seeing around you. God has called and created you with a great destiny! In fact, you can be part of the solution to the problems around you. And just like the older generation, you, too, must do your part. God has given you a voice and influence; use it with those around you. Learn to ask questions so you can discover truth and use questions to challenge your friends' positions and help them discover truth.

When you challenge an idea that seems wrong, don't be contentious, but instead remain calm and genuine in your pursuit of answers. Nobody likes to have his or her position challenged; but if you do it in a nonaggressive and nonconfrontational way, you might make your friends think about why they believe what they believe, and they may even question whether what they believe is right.

Also, spend more time reading God's Word. It was written to help us know how God has called us to live. If you've never read your Bible before, start with the Gospel of John; from there, read James. Those are two of the best places to help you learn about your faith. After you've read those books, read them again; then begin reading other books in the Bible, such as Acts and Luke. As you read them, look specifically for things you can apply to your life—for ways for you to live life differently based on what you are reading. Then share with your friends what you are learning. Don't think you don't have the voice or influence to make a difference. You do. And *"Who knows but that you were brought to the kingdom for such a time as this?"* (Esther 4:14, ISV)—you were born for this time in our history. Make the most of it!

TO OLDER GENERATIONS

Millennials have become the target of many frustrated adults and, at times, rightfully so. But where did Millennials learn and adopt so many bad habits? Frank Martin is an NCAA Division 1 basketball coach. While coaching at South Carolina, he was asked if it was hard to coach student athletes in this current generation. His answer caught the attention of many Americans and quickly went viral. Here's what he said:

> You know what makes me sick to my stomach? When I hear grown people say that kids have changed. Kids haven't changed. Kids don't know anything about anything. *We've* changed as adults. *We* demand less of kids. *We* expect less of kids. *We* make their lives easier instead of preparing them for what life is truly about. *We're* the ones that have changed.[341] (emphasis added)

We could argue about elements of his statement, but he certainly makes a valid point. He later tweeted:

> In today's society we demand less from children, expect less from them, and then we blame them when they make mistakes as adults.[342]

The truth of what he expresses in these statements should motivate us to change what we do as adults. Frankly, we have created a system that has miserably failed them, and we allow that system to continue to fail them (and now Gen Z-ers) at a high cost to them and to ourselves.

Although there is blame to be placed both on previous generations as well as the current ones, passing blame doesn't bring any solutions or resolution. Now is the time to roll up our sleeves and reach out to Millennials—let's repair much of what we've let the culture do to them.

Recognize Millennials were raised in a world that gave them trophies just for showing up. Hence, they are used to being rewarded and praised, regardless of their behavior and performance. This is readily seen in their attention to social media. They will post a picture and continually check throughout the day to see how many of their friends "liked" the image. If they don't get enough "likes" (i.e., praise) they feel they are failing. The lesson we need to learn from this is if we are going to reach and connect with Millennials, we need to learn to encourage them, regardless of whether they have gone above or beyond what is required.

Successful leaders and bosses have learned to motivate their young employees not through criticism but rather through praise and positive feedback. Right now, Millennials are generally moved by their emotions and heart rather than static or cerebral information (numbers, facts, or truth). As we learn to become better encouragers and to connect with Millennials on a personal level, we will discover they are motivated and open to change through relationships. So don't complain about Millennials (or any of the younger generations); instead, become friends with them and invest in their lives, and let's also get serious about changing the current so-called "education" system and culture that has so dismally failed them and the nation.

Prayer: Lord, you created all persons, including young adults. You see the full potential of this age group, so help us each to see as you see and to interact with each other in intergenerational ways that cause truth to be handed down from one generation to the next, like successfully handing off and receiving a baton in a relay race. May those of us who are handing off the baton do so gracefully, and those of us receiving the baton do so willingly and graciously. Amen.

A BIBLICALLY FOUNDED NATION

Blessed is the nation whose God is the Lord.

PSALM 33:12, NIV

The goal of this section is to understand with historical accuracy the distinct Judeo-Christian foundation of America and discover ways to return to our Biblical underpinnings.

CHAPTER 49

A NATION FOUNDED ON JUDEO-CHRISTIAN VALUES

The title of this section will certainly raise eyebrows for many. What it suggests certainly runs afoul of the modern mantra that America was founded as a secular nation. It also comes dangerously close to suggesting America was founded as a Christian nation. Those today who commit the cultural sin of suggesting America has a strong Biblical and Christian founding usually will be immediately hit with stiff opposition and demeaning name-calling.

In fact, one of the few things on which strident atheists (such as Sam Harris) and modern Christian theologians (such as Mark Noll, Nathan Hatch, and George Marsden) can agree is that America did *not* have a Christian founding.[343] Perhaps the title of the book by Cornell University professors Isaac Kramnick and Lawrence Moore best sums up the modern belief about the American Founding: *The Godless Constitution.*

But just because the modern culture has reached agreement on this doesn't mean it is so. As John Adams observed, *"Facts are stubborn things."*[344] Much of today's belief about religion in the Founding Era is based on modern opinion rather than actual historical fact.

FACTS

This chapter will give you some of the "stubborn" and irrefutable historical facts, even providing footnotes to original and primary sources so you can check them for yourself. If you do, you will discover the truth about the religious nature of our American Founding—and that it is definitely not secular or Godless.

Founding Father John Adams (a principal leader in the birth and establishment of America as an independent nation) summarized what previous generations of Americans knew and believed when he declared:

> The general principles on which the fathers achieved independence were. . . . the general principles of Christianity. . . . Now I will avow that I then believed (and now believe) that those general principles of Christianity are as eternal and immutable as the existence and attributes of God.[345]

EVEN THE IRRELIGIOUS GET IT

A generation later, South Carolina governor James Hammond described America as a Christian nation.[346] Upon hearing that, a small group openly attacked him and demanded a retraction and apology. Hammond was shocked by their reaction, telling them:

> Unhappily for myself, I am *not* a professor of religion—nor am I attached by education or habit to any particular denomination—nor do I feel myself to be a fit and proper defender of the Christian faith. But I must say that up to this time, I have always thought it a settled matter that I lived in a Christian land and that I was the temporary chief magistrate of a Christian people! That in such a country and among such a people I should be publicly called to an account, reprimanded, and required to make amends for acknowledging Jesus Christ as the Redeemer of the world, I would not have believed possible if it had not come to pass.[347]

The historical evidence was so clear that both religious and nonreligious leaders in early America agreed America was founded on Biblical and Christian (that is, Judeo-Christian) principles.

CHAPTER 50

WHAT THE EXPERTS BELIEVE

THE BIBLE: OUR FOUNDING DOCUMENT—ACCORDING TO PRESIDENTS

Only a generation ago, even *Newsweek* concluded *"historians are discovering that the Bible, perhaps even more than the Constitution, is our Founding document."*[348] Although such a pronouncement has become heretical today, for the previous two centuries, it was merely stating the obvious—a fact openly acknowledged by our national leaders:

In the formative days of the Republic, the directing influence the Bible exercised upon the fathers of the Nation is conspicuously evident. . . . We cannot read the history of our rise and development as a Nation without reckoning with the place the Bible has occupied in shaping the advances of the Republic.[349] PRESIDENT FRANKLIN ROOSEVELT

For we can truly be said to have founded our country on the principles of this Book. The Holy Bible was the most important possession that our forebears placed aboard their ships as they embarked for the New World.[350] PRESIDENT LYNDON B. JOHNSON

[T]he teachings of the Bible are so interwoven and entwined with our whole civic and social life that it would be literally— I do not mean figuratively, I mean literally—impossible for us to figure to ourselves what that life would be if these teachings were removed.[351] PRESIDENT TEDDY ROOSEVELT

It [the Bible] is the rock on which our Republic rests.[352] PRESIDENT ANDREW JACKSON

Across the centuries, these and many other pre ʻdents—whether liberal or conservative, Republican or Democrat—agreed that the teachings of the Bible were America's foundation.

THE FOUNDERS SPEAK ABOUT THE BIBLE

That the Bible was so influential in the American Founding was not surprising given the Founders' respect for that book:

[The Bible] is a book worth more than all the other books that were ever printed.[353] PATRICK HENRY

[T]he Bible contains more knowledge necessary to man in his present state than any other book in the world.[354] The great enemy of the salvation of man, in my opinion, never invented a more effective means of extirpating [eliminating] Christianity from the world than by persuading mankind that it was improper to read the Bible at schools.[355] BENJAMIN RUSH, SIGNER OF THE DECLARATION

[N]o book in the world deserves to be so unceasingly studied and so profoundly meditated upon as the Bible.[356] The first and almost the only book deserving such universal recommendation is the Bible.[357] JOHN QUINCY ADAMS, PRESIDENT

The Bible is the best of all books, for it is the Word of God and teaches us the way to be happy in this world and in the next. Continue therefore to read it and to regulate your life by its precepts.[358] JOHN JAY, ORIGINAL CHIEF JUSTICE OF THE US SUPREME COURT, AN AUTHOR OF THE FEDERALIST PAPERS

Suppose a nation in some distant region should take the Bible for their only law book and every member should regulate his

conduct by the precepts there exhibited. . . . What a Utopia—
what a Paradise would this region be![359] PRESIDENT JOHN
ADAMS, SIGNER OF THE DECLARATION, PRESIDENT

There are many additional declarations from other Founding Fathers.

TODAY'S ANTI-HISTORICAL SELF-APPOINTED "EXPERTS"

Most citizens today have been told the Founding Fathers were a collective
group of atheists, agnostics, and deists. Are these claims true?

Significantly, there are more than two hundred individuals who can
be considered Founding Fathers. (This would include the fifty-six signers
of the Declaration of Independence, the fifty-five who framed the Constitution, those in the first Congress who framed the Bill of Rights, and
so forth.) Yet ask someone today to name twenty, or even ten, of those
two hundred, and be prepared to wait perhaps years for an answer. For
example, from among the signers of the Declaration, most can go no
further than identifying Benjamin Franklin and Thomas Jefferson—
meaning they have been taught to recognize the least religious Founders
but not the others.

THE FOUNDERS SPEAK ABOUT THE CHRISTIAN FAITH

There are scores of quotes, unknown or ignored today, from other
Founding Fathers about Christianity, including these

> My only hope of salvation is in the infinite transcendent love
> of God manifested to the world by the death of His Son upon
> the Cross. Nothing but His blood will wash away my sins [Acts
> 22:16]. I rely exclusively upon it. Come, Lord Jesus! Come
> quickly [Revelation 22:20]![360] BENJAMIN RUSH, SIGNER OF THE
> DECLARATION

> I . . . [rely] on the merits of Jesus Christ for a pardon of all my
> sins.[361] SAMUEL ADAMS, SIGNER OF THE DECLARATION

> Christ Jesus . . . is the only Savior of sinners . . . . as He Himself
> says (John 14:6): "I am the way, and the truth, and the life: no
> man cometh unto the Father but by Me." . . . If you are not

reconciled to God through Jesus Christ—if you are not clothed with the spotless robe of His righteousness—you must forever perish.[362] JOHN WITHERSPOON, SIGNER OF THE DECLARATION

I have a tender reliance on the mercy of the Almighty, through the merits of the Lord Jesus Christ.[363] ALEXANDER HAMILTON, SIGNER OF THE CONSTITUTION

God commands all men everywhere to repent [Matthew 3:2; Mark 1:15]. He also commands them to believe on the Lord Jesus Christ, and has assured us that all who do repent and believe shall be saved [Acts 3:19].[364] ROGER SHERMAN, SIGNER OF THE DECLARATION AND CONSTITUTION

There are many more examples like these, which clearly are not consistent with so-called atheist, agnostic, and deist Founders. The overwhelming majority of Founders were strongly Christian, but today's tendency in education and academia is to make the exception into the rule—that is, to take Benjamin Franklin and Thomas Jefferson (who expressed beliefs in conflict with basic Christian doctrines) and tell the nation all the other Founders believed like they did. But if historical truth were accurately taught, we would show how strongly Christian most Founders were and then point to Jefferson and Franklin as exceptions rather than vice versa.

CHAPTER 51

EVIDENCE OF AMERICA'S CHRISTIAN FOUNDATION

STATE CONSTITUTIONS

Just as the statements of individual Founders affirm their Christian beliefs, so, too, does their collective voice. One evidence of this is seen in the language they placed into the original state constitutions they penned. For example, Delaware's 1776 constitution (whose authors included Declaration signers George Read and Thomas McKean and Constitution signer John Dickinson) stipulated:

> Every person who shall be chosen a member of either house, or appointed to any office or place of trust . . . shall . . . make and subscribe the following declaration, to wit: "I, _____, do profess faith in God the Father, and in Jesus Christ His only Son, and the Holy Ghost, one God—blessed forevermore; and I do acknowledge the Holy Scriptures of the Old and New Testament to be given by Divine inspiration."[365]

Massachusetts' 1780 constitution (written with the help of Declaration signers Samuel Adams, John Hancock, Robert Treat Paine, and John Adams, as well as Constitution signer Nathaniel Gorham) similarly required:

> Any person chosen governor, lieutenant-governor, counselor, senator, or representative, and accepting the trust, shall—

before he proceed to execute the duties of his place or office—make and subscribe the following declaration, viz. "I, _____, do declare, that I believe the Christian religion and have a firm persuasion of its truth."[366]

And other constitutions penned by the Founders contained similar clauses.[367]

BIBLES PROVIDED

The Bible was important to the Founders, and they believed it important to the country. In fact, in 1781, Robert Aitken, the official printer of the Continental Congress, asked Congress for permission to print Bibles on his presses in Philadelphia.[368] Pointing out the proposed Bible would be *"a neat edition of the Holy Scriptures for the use of schools,"*[369] Congress approved his request and appointed a congressional committee to oversee the project.[370] On September 12, 1782, that Bible received the approval of the full Congress[371] and soon began rolling off the presses. Printed in the front of the Bible was a congressional endorsement declaring, in part:

> Resolved, that the United States in Congress assembled . . . recommend this edition of the Bible to the inhabitants of the United States.[372]

Of the events surrounding the printing of that Bible, one early historian observed:

> Who . . . will call in question the assertion that this is a Bible nation? Who will charge the government with indifference to religion when the first Congress of the States assumed all the rights and performed all the duties of a Bible Society long before such an institution had an existence in the world![373]

AN OFFICIAL ANNOUNCEMENT

In 1783, when England officially declared an end to the hostilities against Americans, the peace treaty between the two nations was signed by Americans John Adams, John Jay, and Benjamin Franklin and then approved by the full Congress. That final document, like so many others of the American War for Independence, was explicitly Christian, with its opening line declaring:

> In the name of the most holy and undivided Trinity.[374]

This is an undeniably and explicitly Christian declaration—and it is the title our Founding Fathers placed on the document establishing America as an independent self-governing nation.

DEFINITION OF A "CHRISTIAN NATION"

The evidence presented thus far makes clear (and much more similarly affirms) America was indeed a Biblical, or Judeo-Christian, nation. But although critics vociferously assert otherwise, they avoid giving any historic definition of what a Christian nation is. They generally offer ludicrous standards that have never been a part of the American experience (such as a nation in which all citizens are Christians, or in which the laws require everyone to believe Christian theology, and so forth). Fortunately, however, there is an historic definition of what a Christian nation actually is, delivered long ago by US Supreme Court Justice David Brewer (1837–1910).

Significantly, he began the definition by first stating what a Christian nation is *not* (which is exactly what critics today wrongly say it is):

> [I]n what sense can it [America] be called a Christian nation? Not in the sense that Christianity is the established religion, or that the people are in any manner compelled to support it. On the contrary, the Constitution specifically provides that "Congress shall make no law respecting an establishment of religion, or prohibiting the free exercise thereof." Neither is it Christian in the sense that all its citizens are either in fact or name Christians. On the contrary, all religions have free scope within our borders. Numbers of our people profess other religions, and many reject all. Nor is it Christian in the sense that a profession of Christianity is a condition of holding [federal] office or otherwise engaging in public service, or essential to recognition either politically or socially. In fact, the government as a legal organization is independent of all religions. Nevertheless, we

constantly speak of this republic as a Christian nation—in fact, as the leading Christian nation of the world.[375]

So, if being a Christian nation is not based on any of the above criterion, what makes America a Christian nation? According to Justice Brewer, America is *"of all the nations in the world . . . most justly called a Christian nation"* because Christianity *"has so largely shaped and molded it."*[376] So America is a Christian nation because its values, society, and institutions have been shaped by Christian principles. This definition was reaffirmed by American legal scholars and historians for generations,[377] but is widely ignored by today's revisionists, who try to define a Christian nation by every superficial and false measurement Justice Brewer identified and discarded. But Brewer clearly identified the evidence he used to reach his conclusion:

> [T]he calling of this republic a Christian nation is not a mere pretense, but a recognition of an historical, legal, and social truth.[378]

"Historical, legal, and social truth." Already, much of this evidence has been presented, but it centered primarily on the American Founders. Consider additional evidence from the judicial, legislative, and executive branches of our federal government.

EVIDENCE FROM THE JUDICIAL BRANCH

Let's begin with what courts have said.

In a unanimous decision in 1844, the US Supreme Court held:

> [C]hristianity . . . is not to be maliciously and openly reviled and blasphemed against to the annoyance of believers or the injury of the public. . . . Such a case is not to be presumed to exist in a *Christian country.*[379]

In 1892, the Court, after reviewing scores of historical documents and precedents, delivered a unanimous ruling declaring:

> [N]o purpose of action against religion can be imputed to any legislation, state or national because this is a religious people. . . . [T]his is a *Christian nation.*[380]

In 1931, the Court rearticulated the same message as its previous decisions:

> We are a *Christian people* . . . according to one another the equal right of religious freedom and acknowledging with reverence the duty of obedience to the will of God.[381]

These *"Christian country," "Christian nation,"* and *"Christian people"* declarations were subsequently cited by countless lower federal courts for decades, including well into the modern era.[382] Additionally, federal courts regularly invoked Christian principles as the basis of their rulings on foreign affairs,[383] domestic treaties,[384] marriage,[385] citizenship,[386] and other areas.

State courts were just as forthright. For example:

> [O]ur laws and institutions must necessarily be based upon and embody the teachings of the Redeemer of mankind. It is impossible that it should be otherwise. And in this sense, and to this extent, our civilization and institutions are emphatically Christian.[387] ILLINOIS SUPREME COURT, 1883

> Our great country is denominated a Christian nation. . . . Our state has even sometimes been referred to by cynics as being in the "Bible Belt." It cannot be denied that much of the legislative philosophy of this state and nation has been inspired by the Golden Rule and the Sermon on the Mount and other portions of the Holy Scriptures.[388] MISSISSIPPI SUPREME COURT, 1950

> [I]t is well settled and understood that ours is a Christian Nation, holding the Almighty God in dutiful reverence. It is so noted in our Declaration of Independence and in the constitution of every state of the Union. Since George Washington's first presidential proclamation of Thanksgiving Day, each such annual proclamation reiterates the principles that we are such a Christian Nation. . . . [W]e consider the language used in our Declaration of Independence, and in our national Constitution, and in our Constitution of Oklahoma, wherein those documents recognize the existence of God, and that we are a Christian Nation and a Christian State.[389] OKLAHOMA SUPREME COURT, 1959

There are scores more similar declarations.

JUDGES' COUNSEL TO THOSE SENTENCED TO DEATH

Furthermore, a longstanding practice of federal and state courts (a practice unknown today) was if a defendant at trial was convicted and sentenced to death, the judge would often deliver a Gospel message as part of the official proceedings. For example, in 1778, after Founding Father and signer of the Declaration Thomas McKean (a judge) sentenced John Roberts to death for treason, he told him:

Before you launch into eternity, it behooves you to improve the time that may be allowed you in this world: it behooves you most seriously to reflect upon your past conduct; to repent of your evil deeds; to be incessant in prayers to the great and merciful God to forgive your manifold transgressions and sins; to teach you to rely upon the merit and passion of a dear Redeemer, and thereby to avoid those regions of sorrow—those doleful shades where peace and rest can never dwell, where even hope cannot enter . . . . May you, reflecting upon these things and pursuing the will of the great Father of Light and Life, be received into [the] company and society of angels and archangels and the spirits of just men made perfect [Hebrews 12:23]; and may you be qualified to enter into the joys of Heaven—joys unspeakable and full of glory [1 Peter 1:8]![390]

In 1812, Joseph Story (one of America's most famous US Supreme Court Justices) delivered a Gospel message to two defendants convicted of murder and piracy, telling them:

[A]fter what has happened, how you can appear before that dread tribunal and that Omnipotent Judge Who searcheth the hearts and trieth the reins of all men [Psalms 7:9]. From His sentence there is no appeal, and before Him you must soon appear to render an account of all the deeds done in the body [2 Corinthians 5:10; Romans 2:3-8]. . . . Let me entreat you— tenderly and earnestly entreat you, as dying sinners—to turn from your wicked thoughts, to ponder on the errors of your ways, and with penitence and humiliation to seek the altars of our holy religion. Let me entreat you to pray for mercy and forgiveness from that righteous God, Whom you have so justly offended.[391]

In 1861, a ship captain was sentenced to death for his participation in the slave trade. After delivering the sentence, federal judge William Davis Shipman told him:

Remember that you showed mercy to none, carrying off as you did not only those of your own sex but women and helpless children. Do not flatter yourself that because they belonged to a different race from yourself your guilt is therefore lessened. . . . As you are soon to pass into the presence of that God of the black man as well as the white man, Who is no respecter of persons [1 Peter 1:17], do not indulge for a moment the thought that He hears with indifference the cry of the humblest of His children. . . . Turn your thoughts toward Him Who alone can pardon and Who is not deaf to the supplications of those who seek His mercy.[392]

EVIDENCE FROM THE LEGISLATIVE BRANCH

Just as the judiciary openly invoked Biblical and Christian principles, so, too, did Congress. For example, from the time of the Continental Congress until the twentieth century, Congress regularly approved federal funds for Christian missionary work among Indian tribes.[393] And in 1853–1854, Congress delivered unambiguous declarations about America as a Christian nation:

HOUSE JUDICIARY COMMITTEE: Had the people, during the Revolution, had a suspicion of any attempt to war against Christianity, that Revolution would have been strangled in its cradle. . . . In this age there can be no substitute for Christianity; that, in its general principles, is the great conservative element on which we must rely for the purity and permanence of free institutions. That was the religion of the Founders of the republic and they expected it to remain the religion of their descendants.[394]

SENATE JUDICIARY COMMITTEE: We are Christians, not because the law demands it, not to gain exclusive benefits or to avoid legal disabilities, but from choice and education; and in a land thus universally Christian, what is to be expected, what desired, but that we shall pay a due regard to Christianity?[395]

Two years later, in 1856, the House of Representatives declared:

> [T]he great vital and conservative element in our system is the belief of our people in the pure doctrines and divine truths of the Gospel of Jesus Christ.[396]

FINE ART IN THE LEGISLATIVE BRANCH

Scores more acts of the federal legislature can be cited. In fact, between 1840 and 1855, Congress commissioned and placed four massive paintings in the Rotunda of the US Capitol[397] to reflect the Christian heritage of the nation:[398]

- The baptism of the Indian princess Pocahontas, the first convert to Christianity in Virginia
- The embarkation of the Pilgrims leaving Holland headed toward America, gathered in prayer around an open Geneva Bible
- DeSoto at the Mississippi River, planting a cross and dedicating the land to God
- Columbus off the coast of Florida, praying and dedicating the land to God.

Furthermore, each state is allowed to place two statues of their greatest heroes inside the US Capitol. So prominently displayed within the Capitol are dozens of ministers and Christian leaders, ranging from Father Damien of Hawaii to Roger Sherman of Connecticut and from Rev. Jason Lee of Oregon to James Garfield of Ohio.[399]

EVIDENCE FROM THE EXECUTIVE BRANCH

The executive branch, like the judicial and legislative branches, was equally forthright with similar declarations. For example:

> America was born a Christian nation—America was born to exemplify that devotion to the elements of righteousness which are derived from the revelations of Holy Scripture.[400] PRESIDENT WOODROW WILSON

In these last 200 years, we have guided the building of our Nation and our society by those principles and precepts brought to earth nearly 2,000 years ago on that first Christmas.[401] PRESIDENT LYNDON BAINES JOHNSON

Let us remember that as a Christian nation . . . we have a charge and a destiny.[402] PRESIDENT RICHARD NIXON

[T]his is a Christian Nation. More than a half century ago that declaration was written into the decrees of the highest court in this land.[403] In this great country of ours has been demonstrated the fundamental unity of Christianity and democracy.[404] PRESIDENT HARRY TRUMAN

Numerous other presidents likewise affirmed America as a Christian nation.[405]

The evidence not only from the American Founding but subsequently from all three branches is unequivocal in its affirmation America was founded (and long operated) on Judeo-Christian Biblical principles.

CHAPTER 52

SO-CALLED "EVIDENCE" AMERICA WAS NOT FOUNDED ON CHRISTIAN PRINCIPLES

If you ask a critic to provide their proof America was not founded on Christian principles, they frequently point to Article XI of the 1797 treaty between the United States and the early Muslim nation of Tripoli, which states:

> The government of the United States is in no sense founded on the Christian religion . . .

On its face, this clause appears to be nondebatable and final: America was not founded on Christian principles. But what the critics fail to mention is that, to make Article XI say what they want, they have to lift fifteen words out of an eighty-one-word sentence and then use those fifteen words completely out of context.

Here's the background they don't want you to know.

At the end of the American War for Independence when peace was achieved, Americans were still being attacked and killed by Muslim terrorists overseas. Five Muslim countries (Tunis, Morocco, Algiers, Tripoli, and Turkey) were making indiscriminate attacks against what they called the "Christian nations" (such as England, France, Spain, Denmark, and the United States). Muslim warships attacked American merchant ships wherever they found them, seizing the cargo as loot and killing or enslaving their Christian seamen.[406]

In 1784, Congress dispatched American diplomats John Adams, Benjamin Franklin, and Thomas Jefferson to negotiate with the Muslims,[407] and in 1786, when Adams and Jefferson candidly asked the Ambassador from Tripoli the motivation behind the unprovoked Muslim attacks against Americans, he responded:

that it was founded on the laws of their Prophet [Mohammed]—that it was written in their Koran that all nations who should not have acknowledged their authority were sinners; that it was their right and duty to make war upon them wherever they could be found and to make slaves of all they could take as prisoners; and that every Musselman [Muslim] who should be slain in battle was sure to go to Paradise. [408]

Given their "spiritual" incentive to enslave and make war, Muslim attacks against American ships and seamen were frequent.

When George Washington became president, he, too, dispatched diplomatic envoys to try to negotiate terms with the Muslim nations.[409] Several treaties of "Peace and Amity" were reached,[410] routinely acknowledging the conflict as being one between Muslim nations and a Christian one,[411] and America regularly attempted to assure the Muslims that as Christians, we had no religious hatred of them—that we were not like the European Christian nations that (1) had a state-established church and (2) attacked them simply because they were Muslims.

The 1797 treaty with Tripoli (Tripoli has generally become the nation of Libya today) was one of the many treaties in which each country recognized the religion of the other and in which America invoked rhetoric designed to prevent a "Holy War" between Christians and Muslims.[412] The full, unedited Article XI of the 1797 treaty states:

As the government of the United States of America is not in any sense founded on the Christian religion as it has in itself no character of enmity against the laws, religion or tranquility of Musselmen [Muslims] and as the said States [America] have never entered into any war or act of hostility against any Mahometan [Muslim] nation, it is declared by the parties that no pretext arising from religious opinions shall ever produce an interruption of the harmony existing between the two countries.[413]

As you can see, critics end the sentence after the words "Christian religion," thus stopping the sentence in mid-thought and placing a period in the middle of the sentence where no punctuation exists. But when Article XI is read in its entirety, the clause simply assures the nation of Tripoli that America was not one of the Christian nations with an inherent hostility against Muslims and that we would not allow the differences in our *"religious opinions"* to lead to hostility.

But if this is not clear enough, consider the language in other documents from that same conflict.

By the last year of George Washington's presidency, despite the treaties, there were still so many attacks from the Muslims he urged Congress to build a US Navy to defend American interests on the high seas.[414] When John Adams became President, he vigorously pursued those plans, earning the title "Father of the Navy,"[415] but he continued diplomatic efforts as well.

In 1799, he appointed General William Eaton as Consul to Tunis (one of the five attacking Muslim nations). After arriving there, Eaton reported to Secretary of State Timothy Pickering how pleased one of the Muslim rulers had been to receive the payments promised him by the *"Christian nation"* of America.[416] Eaton also explained why the Muslims were such dedicated foes:

Taught by revelation that war with the *Christians* will guarantee the salvation of their souls . . . their [the Muslims'] inducements to desperate fighting are very powerful.[417]

He further reported the Muslims found American targets inviting because they believed *"the Americans are a feeble sect of Christians."*[418] When John Marshall became the next Secretary of State in 1800, Eaton informed him:

It is a maxim of the Barbary [Muslim] States that "The *Christians* who would be on good terms with them must fight well or pay well."[419]

But when Thomas Jefferson became President in 1801, he decided he would no longer "pay well" to the Muslim nations, so he withheld further monetary payments. Tripoli therefore declared war against the United States (and Algiers threatened to do so),[420] thus constituting America's first official war as a new nation. Jefferson selected General Eaton and Commodore Edward Preble to lead the Navy and Marines against the terrorists.

Shortly before he did so, Jefferson told a US Senator, "*We are already about the 7th of the Christian nations in population, but holding a higher place in substantial abilities.*"[421] So even Jefferson called America a "Christian nation."

Eaton commenced his campaign against Tripoli, and entries in his own journal repeatedly affirm that it was a fight between a Christian nation and Muslim enemies.[422] He successfully crushed the Muslim forces in Tripoli and freed captured Christian seamen. An account of his military excursion was subsequently written and published as

The Life of the Late Gen. William Eaton . . . Commander of the *Christian* and Other Forces . . . which Led to the Treaty of Peace Between The United States and The Regency of Tripoli[423]

Significantly, the American leader of the American military expedition noted he was leading the *Christian* forces.

So the numerous treaties and the official correspondence from the Barbary Powers conflict (including Article XI from the 1797 Treaty of Tripoli) affirms it was *always* viewed by *both* sides as a conflict between Muslim nations and the Christian nation of America.

CHAPTER 53

AMERICA: EXCLUSIVELY CHRISTIAN OR PLURALISTIC?

Doesn't being a Christian nation smack of exclusivity? Aren't we plural-istic? and don't we want freedom of religion? Absolutely!—which is why being a Biblical Christian nation is so important, for it is the Bible that sets forth the principles of religious toleration, noncoercion, and the rights of religious conscience.

Consider, for example, Joshua's words to the children of Israel as they entered the Promised Land:

> And if it is evil in your eyes to serve the Lord, choose this day whom you will serve, whether the gods your fathers served in the region beyond the River, or the gods of the Amorites in whose land you dwell. But as for me and my house, we will serve the Lord. (Joshua 24:15, ESV)

Joshua offered the people a choice. He announced he and his family were going to serve God, but the people were free to choose differently. Each could decide whether to serve the god of the Egyptians, the god of the Amorites, or the God of Israel. The choice was theirs. Of course, each had to live with the consequences of their choices, for good or bad; each had a free choice.

NONCOERCION

God established this noncoercive approach as His *modus operandi* from the very beginning.

After creating Adam and Eve and placing them in the Garden of Eden, He allowed them a choice that meant the difference between continued fellowship with Him or separation from Him. There was neither force, pressure, nor coercion applied to their decision; it was completely their own voluntary choice. They chose poorly and then lived with the results. God could have prevented them from making the wrong choice, but instead, He allowed them to freely choose.

Consider, too, Elijah's contest against the prophets of Baal atop Mount Carmel (1 Kings 18). Not only did he offer the people their choice of which god to follow, he also permitted the followers of Baal to take additional time to express their faith (1 Kings 8:25–29). When they finished, Elijah presented his case for the God of Israel, and the people made their choice. Elijah, too, embraced religious choice and competition; and the New Testament is likewise filled with examples following the same pattern, demonstrated by Jesus, the Apostles Peter and Paul, ministers such as Philip and Timothy, and others.

THE FREE MARKET OF RELIGION

American Christian leaders, following these Biblical teachings, also embraced a free-market approach to religion (which was very different from the European model). They did not do this because they were indifferent to Christianity or because they believed all religions equal, for they held an opposite position on both points. They protected freedom of religion because of Biblical teachings, understanding individuals must make their own voluntary choice, even if it meant the difference between Heaven and Hell. American Christians thus welcomed numerous religions to America (including Jews, Muslims, Buddhists, and others), but they were also faithful to use their free speech to share the Gospel and offer each individual a choice of Heaven through Jesus Christ.

JEWS SPEAK

Even today, those from other religions openly applaud the religious liberty the Bible and Christianity provides. Notice some representative quotes from American *Jewish* leaders:

This is a Christian country—it was founded by Christians and built on broad Christian principles. Threatening? Far from it. It is in precisely this Christian country that Jews have known the most peaceful, prosperous, and successful existence in their long history.[424] JEFF JACOBY, COLUMNIST

[C]hristian America is the best home our people have found in 2,000 years. . . . [T]his remains the most tolerant, prosperous, and safest home we could be blessed with.[425] AARON ZELMAN, AUTHOR, HEAD OF CIVIL RIGHTS ORGANIZATION

[I] believe that it is good that America is a Christian nation. . . . Too many Americans do not appreciate the connection between American greatness and American Christianity.[426] DENNIS PRAGER, BEST-SELLING AUTHOR, NATIONAL COLUMNIST, TALK-SHOW HOST

Clearly this nation was established by Christians. . . . As a Jew, I'm entirely comfortable with the concept of the Christian America.[427] The choice isn't Christian America or nothing, but Christian America or a neo-pagan, hedonistic, rights-without-responsibilities, anti-family, culture-of-death America.[428] [J]ews—as Jews—must oppose revisionist efforts to deny our nation's Christian heritage.[429] DON FEDER, COLUMNIST

Without a vibrant and vital Christianity, America is doomed, and without America, the west is doomed. Which is why I, an Orthodox Jewish rabbi, devoted to Jewish survival, the Torah, and Israel am so terrified of American Christianity caving in.[430] God help Jews if America ever becomes a post-Christian society! Just think of Europe![431] RABBI DANIEL LAPIN, BEST-SELLING AUTHOR, TALKSHOW HOST

And there are many others.

TODAY: PROCLAIMING HISTORICAL ERROR

The evidence that America was founded, and for centuries operated as a Bible-based Christian nation, is clear and unequivocal. Although critics scream otherwise, former US Supreme Court Chief Justice William Rehnquist correctly observed, *"no amount of repetition of historical errors . . . can make the errors true."*[432]

CHAPTER 54

THE CONSTITUTION AND THE DECLARATION OF INDEPENDENCE

Even if the Founders relied on the Bible and Christianity, does that necessarily mean our founding documents and the Constitution were also influenced by the Bible? Many say not, including the two professors who penned the book *Godless Constitution*. They firmly assert the governing documents were not influenced by religious principles.

By the way, on what historical sources did those professors rely to prove their claim? Significantly, in their *"Note on Sources"* at the end of their book, these professors candidly admit: *"we have dispensed with the usual scholarly apparatus of footnotes."*[433] There are no footnotes—they use *no* historical documentation to prove their "historical" claims. What a startling admission, but this is reflective of what often occurs in far too much of academia and media today.

Is there any way to know for sure what specific ideas influenced and shaped the Framers' unique concepts in our Founding documents? —was there any reliance on religious sources? Political scientists embarked on an ambitious ten-year project to analyze writings from the Founding Era (1760–1805) with the goal of isolating and identifying the specific political authorities quoted during that time.[434] If the sources of the specific quotes could be identified, the origin of the Founders' political ideas could be documented.

Selecting some 15,000 representative writings, the researchers isolated 3,154 direct quotations and then documented the original sources of those quotations. The research revealed the single most cited authority in the writings of the Founding Era was the Bible: 34 percent of the documented quotes were taken from the Bible (a percentage almost four times higher than the second most quoted source).[435]

Additionally, the notion that the Constitution is secular (or as the professors claimed, "Godless") is easily disproved by specific clauses in the Constitution.

SUNDAYS EXCEPTED

For example, the Constitution stipulates that when Congress passes a bill, the president has ten days to sign the bill—not counting Sundays, or as the Constitution says, "*Sundays excepted.*"

Significantly, no other religion in the world observes a Sunday Sabbath except Christianity. As the Supreme Court of California noted (1858), the Sabbath observed by various religions included "*the Friday of the Mohammedan, the Saturday of the Israelite, or the Sunday of the Christian.*"[436] The South Carolina Supreme Court (1846) similarly noted:

> Christianity is a part of the common law of the land, with liberty of conscience to all. It has always been so recognized. . . . The U. S. Constitution allows it as a part of the common law. *The President is allowed ten days [to sign a bill], with the exception of Sunday.* The Legislature does not sit, public offices are closed, and the government recognizes the day in all things. . . . The observance of Sunday is one of the usages of the common law recognized by our U. S. and state governments. . . . Christianity is part and parcel of the common law.[437]

For decades, the specific recognition of the Christian Sabbath in the Constitution was cited by state and federal courts as proof of the Christian nature of our governing documents.[438]

OATH-TAKING

The five oath-taking clauses in the Constitution also show its religious nature, for the Founders repeatedly affirmed oath-taking as a solely religious activity. For example, James Madison called an oath *"the strongest of religious ties,"*[439] Constitution signer Rufus King explained oaths were a *"principle which is proclaimed in the Christian system,"*[440] John Adams said they were *"sacred obligations,"*[441] Declaration signer John Witherspoon said taking an oath *"indeed is an act of worship,"*[442] and George Washington warned to never let oath-taking become a secular activity.[443]

THE YEAR OF OUR LORD

Furthermore, the Constitution declares in Article VII that it was written *"in the year of our Lord,"* 1787. Most legal documents of that day gave only the year; a few added *"in the year of the Lord,"* but the drafters of the Constitution personalized that phrase, making it *"in the year of our Lord."*

THE FEDERAL GOVERNMENT'S BIBLICAL FOUNDATIONS

Other clauses of the Constitution also demonstrate a reliance on Biblical principles:

- The natural-born citizen presidential requirement
    - The Bible's directive on who can be the national leader says: *"**One from among your brethren** you shall set as king over you; **you may not set a foreigner over you,** who is not your brother"* (Deuteronomy 17:15, ESV)
    - The Constitution says: *"**No person except a natural born citizen** . . . shall be eligible to the office of **President**"* (Article II, Section 1, Paragraph 5)
- Capital punishment
    - Concerning the death penalty, the Bible says: *"Whoever is deserving of death shall be put to death on **the testimony of two or three witnesses;** he shall not be put to death on the testimony of one witness."* (Deuteronomy 17:6, NKJV)

- Concerning treason (the capital punishment offense specifically named in the Constitution), the Constitution says: *"No person shall be convicted of treason, unless on **the testimony of two witnesses** to the same overt act"* (Article, Section 3, Paragraph 3)
- Attainder
  - The Bible says: *"The son shall not bear the guilt of the father, nor the father bear the guilt of the son. The righteousness of the righteous shall be upon himself, and the wickedness of the wicked shall be upon himself"* (Ezekiel 18:20, NKJV). The family is not to be punished for the wrongdoing of a single member of the family
  - Attainder (common in European governments at the time) punishes a *family line* for a crime—if one person in the family commits treason, then the bloodline of the entire family becomes "corrupt" and for generations thereafter no member of the family can own property or enjoy other rights. But the Constitution, echoing the Bible's teaching, says: *"No attainder of treason shall work corruption of blood or forfeiture, except during the life of the person attainted"* (Art. III, Sec. 3, Clause 2).

And notice also the three branches of government—judicial, legislative, and executive—is set forth in Isaiah 33:22, ESV (*"the Lord is our judge, the Lord is our lawgiver, the Lord is our king"*); and the type of tax exemptions the Founders gave to churches (tax exemptions that still exist today) is found in Ezra 7:24, NIV (*"You have no authority to impose taxes, tribute or duty on any of the priests, Levites, musicians, gatekeepers, temple servants or other workers at this house of God"*).

The concept of republicanism set forth in Art. IV, Sec. 4 (that is, of selecting our leaders at the local, county, state, and federal levels) has its origins in Exodus 18:21, NIV (*"select capable men from all the people . . . as officials over thousands, hundreds, fifties, and tens"*) and also Deuteronomy 1:13. In fact, Noah Webster (the Founder personally responsible for Art. I, Sec 8, ¶8 of the Constitution) specifically cites Exodus 18:21,[444] as do Declaration signers John Witherspoon[445] and Benjamin Rush.[446]

And on multiple occasions, John Adams directly affirmed the principle undergirding the constitutional separation of powers was found in Jeremiah 17:9, NKJV (*"the heart is deceitful above all things and desperately wicked; who can know it?"*)[447]—a point similarly made by signers of the Constitution George Washington and Alexander Hamilton.[448]

THE BILL OF RIGHTS

After the writing and ratification of the Constitution, the Founders penned the Bill of Rights, which became the capstone of their work on the Constitution. Of this, US Supreme Court Chief Justice Earl Warren (1953–1969) declared:

> I believe the entire Bill of Rights came into being because of the knowledge our forefathers had of the Bible and their belief in it: freedom of belief, of expression, of assembly, of petition, the dignity of the individual, the sanctity of the home, equal justice under law, and the reservation of powers to the people. . . . I like to believe we are living today in the spirit of the Christian religion. I like also to believe that as long as we do so, no great harm can come to our country.[449]

There is abundant documentary evidence to demonstrate what Chief Justice Warren avowed concerning the Bill of Rights.

For example, even Supreme Court Justice Stephen Breyer (one of the most secular-minded justices in Supreme Court history) openly acknowledges *"The right of an accused to meet his accusers face-to-face [in the Sixth Amendment] is mentioned in, among other things, the Bible."*[450] In proof of this, Breyer cites *Federal Practices & Procedure, Federal Rules of Evidence*, which devotes more than twenty pages to document the ways in which the Bible directly shaped numerous of the Due Process Clauses (the Fourth through the Eighth Amendments) of the Bill of Rights.[451] The Bible likewise influenced other Amendments in the Bill of Rights.

INFLUENCED BY GOD

Finally, numerous Founders directly involved with the Constitution's writing and ratification openly testified they believed the Constitution was directly influenced by God. For example, James Madison testified the Constitution was the result of *"a finger of that Almighty Hand"* which had so often been manifested to them throughout the Revolution.[452] (Significantly, several Founders invoke the unique Bible phrase *"finger of God,"* which is used in the Bible to represent miraculous manifestations of His authority and power, as in Luke 11:20, Exodus 8:19, Deuteronomy 9:10, Daniel 5:5, and Exodus 31:18.) Alexander Hamilton, also, declared the Constitution was *"a system which, without the finger of God, never could have been suggested and agreed upon."*[453] George Washington avowed the Constitution *"appears to me, then, little short of a miracle,"*[454] and *"it will demonstrate as visibly the finger of Providence as any possible event in the course of human affairs can ever designate it."*[455] Benjamin Franklin believed the writing of the Constitution had been *"influenced, guided, and governed by that omnipotent, omnipresent, and beneficent Ruler, in Whom all inferior spirits live, and move, and have their being"* [Acts 17:28].[456] And Founding Father Benjamin Rush avowed the Constitution *"in its form and adoption is as much the work of a Divine Providence as any of the miracles recorded in the Old and New Testament."*[457] So the Founders definitely did not see the Constitution as a secularly produced document.

The evidence is unequivocal America's government was intentionally and deliberately founded on, and for centuries operated by, general Biblical and Christian principles.

PRACTICAL IMPLICATIONS

The blessings Americans have experienced across our long history are unprecedented.

For example, the average life of a constitution in recent centuries is only seventeen years,[458] but Americans have been under our Constitution since 1789. (In that same period, France has had fifteen different constitutions; Haiti, twenty-three; Venezuela, twenty-five; Ecuador, twenty; Thailand, seventeen; and so forth.[459]) Political instability generally characterizes the rest of the world—except America.

And our creativity is unsurpassed. America has only 4 percent of the world's population, but every year we produce more patents (a measurement of inventions and discoveries) than the other 96 percent of the world.[460] And our 4 percent produces an amazing 25 percent of the world's gross domestic product (GDP).[461] We are more creative, stable, and prosperous and enjoy more personal and political freedom than any other nation in the world.

As poet Katherine Lee Bates rightly acknowledged in her landmark 1895 song, *"America! God shed His grace on thee!"* We truly have been blessed by God—so much so even the loudest critics in America don't relocate to other countries; they prefer to stay here and complain rather than live anywhere else. Sure, America's not perfect—we've had warts on our nose throughout our history, but fewer than any other nation, and we've also done more good for the world than any other nation.

Our Judeo-Christian foundations, and the institutions and policies proceeding from them, are what made us so unique. Significantly, the foundation is the most important part of any structure: if the foundation is imperiled, the entire structure is jeopardized. America's blessings—if they continue—will be contingent on the extent to which Americans understand our Biblical heritage and the effort we are willing to put forth to preserve those principles in public life and policy today.

Prayer: Lord, our nation was founded upon your Word. But we have turned from Your ways in so much of our national life. We repent. We long for Your blessing—we need Your blessing. Show us how to return nationally to the acknowledgment that You are Lord of this land, and Your Word is the guiding force in public affairs. Amen.

LET THE CHURCH BE THE CHURCH

*For it is time for judgment to begin with
God's household . . . .*

1 PETER 4:7, NIV

The goal of this section is to show the areas in which the modern
Church has betrayed its Biblical calling and point out ways it can
return to its proper role and function.

CHAPTER 55

WHAT HAPPENED TO BIBLICAL CHRISTIANITY IN AMERICA?

UNDERSTANDING THE PROBLEM

America has had an explosion of megachurches in the past decade, many with attendance in the tens of thousands. We also have Christian colleges rapidly expanding in size, some with up to 100,000 students. Some Christian books sell in the millions, and there are Christian radio and television networks worth billions of dollars. We have never seen anything like this. Yet all these visible indicators are misleading; something else is also going on that tells a very different story.

For example, although the number of megachurches has increased at a brisk rate (from 600 in 2000 to 1,642 today[462]), at the same time, national church attendance is steadily falling (from 41 percent down to 36 percent[463]), and the median size of all churches is only seventy congregants.[464] So the impressive growth of megachurches is a false positive.

And although some Christian colleges are rapidly growing, many have become so secular it is not unusual for kids who attend them to abandon the faith. In fact, a coalition of approximately two-hundred Christian colleges and universities has experienced loss of its members because they can no longer agree on things as simple as the Biblical definition of marriage and acceptable sexual behavior.[465] It is our understanding that this organization offered associate membership status for those so-called "Christian" schools that, in direct opposition to plain Biblical teachings, affirmed homosexuality and homosexual "marriage." Several authentically Biblical colleges appropriately left the organization in protest. At that point, the two anti-Biblical colleges left the organization, but the once stellar reputation of the coalition was tarnished.[466]

The same is true for the other seemingly positive measurements. Many simply are not accurate portrayals of the actual Christian landscape.

We speak in many conferences, addressing numerous pastors each year. When we ask local pastors how many of them pastor in communities measurably more righteous today than a generation ago, no one has ever raised their hand. So, despite the billions of dollars spent and millions of hours expended in Christian ministry, the nation is less reflective of Christian values than ever before. To be blunt, the nation is going to hell.

America has shown great resiliency in the past, surviving other challenges, including numerous wars and even a bloody Civil War. Yet all great nations eventually came to an end, including the Assyrians, Aztec, Greeks, Romans, Persians, and many others. They came. They flourished. They rose to world status. They remained strong for generations. They assumed they would always be in power. They all fell.

THE DOWNWARD SPIRAL

The same fate may await the United States. America is in serious trouble today. Only the most naïve dare deny it. The same indicators that heralded the fall of other great nations are now present all around us. What are some of those indicators?

Moral Compass. Moral boundaries and sexual limits are rapidly disappearing. The sexual behaviors widely accepted and practiced in America today range from group sex to homosexuality, bestiality to sex with siblings, public sex to polygamy, nymphet sex to voyeurism, polyamory to incest, and much more.[467] We are now in the condition the Bible describes as *"In those days . . . everyone did what was right in his own eyes"* (Judges 17:6, 21:25, ESV).

A landmark study published by Dr. J. D. Unwin, a noted professor at both Oxford and Cambridge, investigated more than eighty different civilizations and cultures across 5,000 years of recorded history. He found the degree of stability and longevity each experienced was directly proportional to the rigor of sexual morality it practiced. Whenever marriage became disrespected, divorce easy, and sex outside of marriage widely accepted, for 100 percent of those civilizations there was no "*example of a group retaining its culture after it has adopted less rigorous [sexual] customs.*"[468] The Bible is clear that rejecting Biblical standards of sexual morality brings judgment on a nation (cf. Deuteronomy 27:20–23, Leviticus 18:22–25, Colossians 3:5–6, etc.). God's blessings will not reside on any nation that rejects His moral standards, as America now openly does.

Innocent Blood. Sadly, murder abounds in America today, whether it is taking babies' lives in the womb, young men in gangs killing each other (and innocent bystanders), or extinguishing the elderly and handicapped through euthanasia. However, in earlier America when Biblical values still influenced the culture, murder of any kind was extremely rare. In fact, the state of New York experienced only eight murders over the span of sixteen years[469]—a murder every two years. But today, New York has almost two murders a day[470]—and there are some forty-seven murders daily across the United States.[471] The Bible repeatedly condemns the shedding of innocent blood, and history demonstrates that God always removes His blessings from the land where it occurs. America is now such a land.

Education. America spends more on education than nearly any other nation in the world.[472] Yet today, 19 percent of high-school graduates are illiterate[473]—after twelve years of school, and an average approaching $140,000 spent per student,[474] one of five graduates can't read. And in international testing, American high school students regularly finish last, near the last, or in the bottom half of students in math and science testing. We are academically outperformed by what are considered third-world nations such as Vietnam, Slovenia, and Latvia.[475] American education is abysmal, but as Jeremiah 8:9, NIV reminds us, "*Since they have rejected the word of the Lord, what kind of wisdom do they have?*"

Debt. Each American pays an average of $15,202 per person in taxes each year.[476] But the current federal debt of $20 trillion dollars is so great that if it were to be equally divided among citizens, every American would have to come up with an additional $61,539 per person in taxes in order to retire the current debt.[477] But that does not include the additional financial obligations that federal law has made well into the future, which is called the debt liability. To retire this already committed debt, each person in America will have to pay an additional $260,300 beyond their annual taxes.[478] So if America is to survive, it will have to find a way to retire its debt; yet to do so may drive American families and businesses into widespread bankruptcy and poverty. Significantly, when God blesses a nation, it lends rather than borrows (see Deuteronomy 15:6), but America is now just the opposite: it is a borrowing nation—big time.

Proud Decadence. When a nation loses its conscience, its sensitivities become calloused and its threshold of embarrassment largely disappears. Today, what does it take—how far do you have to go, and what do you have to do—to cause society to become ashamed or mortified? A collective insensitivity permeates the culture. But as the Bible affirms, *"Since they have rejected the Word of the Lord . . . they have no shame at all; they do not even know how to blush"* (Jeremiah 8:9, 12, NIV). This certainly seems to accurately describe American culture today.

So, despite what we would like to believe, America is in trouble. She is not what she was even a generation ago. Selfishness has been substituted for service, arrogance for humility, entitlement for hard work, and personal pleasure for duty and responsibility. And even worse, many Americans are either oblivious or ambivalent to this precipitous slippage.

WHAT HAPPENED

The de-Christianizing of American public life and the open rejection of our historic Biblical foundations has resulted in a nation exploding in crime, sexual anarchy, wrecked homes and lives, now leaving massive human pain and carnage in its wake. Who is to blame for the dramatic downturn of American culture?

One could certainly blame the aggressive secularists who show up everywhere (even the smallest communities in America) demanding the removal of anything allegedly "offending" their lack of religious sensibilities. It matters not whether it might be a seemingly innocuous invocation before a meeting; a coach, player, or student offering a short prayer at an athletic event; or any image of Jesus being displayed on the day that, by federal law (Christmas Day),[479] officially celebrates His own birthday.

There are many other groups and movements where it is tempting to place the blame for the coarsening of American culture. But truth be told, the fault cannot be laid solely at the feet of the secularists—or the

Progressives, or liberal academia, activist judges, hostile media, tone-deaf politicians, or any of the other groups openly attacking our foundations. No doubt each of these has contributed much to the damage done to the nation, but America is in deep trouble primarily because the Church in America today has become largely impotent and irrelevant—it no longer functions collectively as salt and light and is neither a preservative in the culture nor a guiding beacon for the nation to follow.

CHAPTER 56

THE STATE OF THE
CHURCH

Be sure you know the condition of your flocks,
give careful attention to your herds.

PROVERBS 27:23, NIV

This chapter documents current tendencies in the Church, relying particularly on recent information from national pollster George Barna—one of the most cited pollsters in American history. (Both Jim and David serve on a board with George, and both consider him a close friend and associate.[480]) Barna is a devout Bible-believing, Bible-practicing Christian concerned about the condition of the Church.

When it comes to polling, most firms allow respondents to self-label their religious identities, such as Born-Again, Evangelical, and so forth. But not Barna. Instead, he asks enough questions to categorize each respondent on the basis of his or her religious beliefs and behaviors.

For example, if people say they are "Born Again"[481] but have never had a life-changing experience with Jesus Christ (a prerequisite for being Born Again), then Barna does not place them in the Born-Again category, regardless of what they call themselves or what other pollsters accept. Similarly, if people say they are "Evangelical" but don't believe the Scriptures are the Word of God, Barna will not categorize them as Evangelicals. Instead, Barna follows Jesus's command to identify people by the fruit they produce (Matthew 7:16), and he labels them according to their beliefs (although at the same time openly acknowledging that only God knows a person's heart and that labels are only estimates of where a person stands spiritually).

Specifically relevant to this chapter, Barna has spent the last several years polling within the Church, asking pastors and Christians questions about where they stand on quintessential Biblical teachings and Christian beliefs, such as these:

- Is the Bible accurate in all the principles it teaches?
- Does absolute moral truth exist?
- Did Jesus live a sinless life on earth?
- Can people earn their way into Heaven by doing good works?
- Is satan a real or imaginary being?
- Is God the all-knowing, all-powerful Creator of the world, Who still rules the universe today?[482]

These are some of the most basic teachings of the Bible, but Barna found more than 70 percent of the 384,000 churches in America today rejected such elemental Christian tenets.[483] He describes the 100,000 or so remaining churches that still embrace these Biblical teachings[484] as *"theologically conservative."*[485] He then spends extensive time polling within this group, and the results are very disturbing, to say the least.

90% OF PASTORS AGREE ... BUT 90% OF PASTORS WON'T!

ON THE GOOD SIDE, more than 90 percent of these theologically conservative pastors agree the Bible addresses specific issues facing Christians today (such as abortion, same-sex marriage, gambling, immigration, and so forth).[486] BUT ON THE BAD SIDE, only 10 percent of these pastors are willing to address these issues that they admit the Bible addresses. Why? Barna reports:

[T]hey are concerned about being seen as political, not wanting to risk the loss of numbers of people or donations, and concern about the status of the church's nonprofit designation. . . . Conservative churches have a Biblical mandate to teach these things but are choosing to ignore the opportunity in favor of remaining safe. . . . When Millennials and others describe Christian churches as *"irrelevant,"* they are not talking about styles of music and dress codes as much as they are attacking the focal point of church services: the teaching. These days, people value their time too highly to invest it in hearing lectures on topics that do not intersect with their life questions and daily struggles.[487]

WHAT CHRISTIANS NEED TO HEAR

ON THE GOOD SIDE, at least 70 percent of congregants in theologically conservative churches say there are fourteen different topics they want their pastors to address (the percentage of church-goers who want to hear these issues covered from the pulpit appears after the topic):

- Abortion (91 percent)
- Religious persecution/liberty (86 percent)
- Poverty—personal duty, church role, government role (85 percent)
- Cultural restoration (83 percent)
- Sexual identity and same-sex marriage (82 percent)
- Israel (80 percent)
- Christian heritage of America (79 percent)
- The proper role of government (76 percent)
- Bioethics (76 percent)
- Self-governance (76 percent)
- The church in politics (73 percent)
- Islam (72 percent)
- The media (70 percent)
- Senior citizens and end-of-life issues (70 percent).[488]

ON THE BAD SIDE, despite the extremely high desire of parishioners to hear about these issues from the pulpit, only 6 percent of pastors addressed as many as six of those topics, and only half even addressed the two easiest ones of abortion and same-sex marriage.[489] Furthermore, the number of pastors addressing these topics has fallen by half since 2014.[490] The Bible-believing church is rapidly growing silent about the culture and the relevancy of God's Word to it.

MEASURING SUCCESS

ON THE GOOD SIDE, pastors recognize the need to track results to see if what they are doing is working. But ON THE BAD SIDE, when theologically conservative pastors are asked about how they determined the success of their churches, their top-five measurements are (1) church attendance, (2) dollars donated, (3) number of programs offered, (4) number of staff people hired, and (5) square footage of facilities available for ministry use.[491]

According to Barna, these measurements are inadequate because:

> Jesus did not die to fill auditoriums, raise money, offer religious programs, hire employees, and build more extravagant campuses. If He had, these would be the perfect measures of the "success" of a church. Because that was not His mission, we need to evaluate other kinds of behaviors and beliefs.[492]

But you get what you measure. So today's emphasis on quantity rather than quality results in the current obsession with megachurches even though the overall Church in America is steadily deteriorating. There is nothing inherently wrong with a large, nice church building, but attendance and structure are not indicators of a truly Biblical and successful church.

ADDITIONAL MEASUREMENTS

There are other indicators of the sad condition of the Church today:

- When Americans are asked the *"most important things their local churches needed to do to make a positive contribution to people's lives and to the life of the community,"* the number one answer is, *"I don't know."*[493]

- Only 14 percent of professing Christians read the Bible on a daily basis[494]
- Of more than seventy moral behaviors studied, there are rarely substantial statistical differences in *moral* behavior between Christians and non-Christians[495]
- Only 6 percent of Americans have a major life goal of *"being a better Christian,"* only 2 percent *"having a better relationship with God,"* and only 2 percent *"going to Heaven."*[496]
- Personal evangelism is dying—few Christians, including only 39 percent of Born Again Christians, feel a responsibility to share Christ with others. In fact, more than half of Christians have never even heard of the Great Commission (Jesus's direct charge to His followers to share Biblical faith and teachings with others).[497] Consequently, whereas 45 percent of adults were Born Again in 2006,[498] today that number has plummeted to only 31 percent. And the younger the generation, the lower the percentage who have a personal relationship with Jesus Christ[499]
- The basic theological beliefs of America's Born-Again Christians are particularly troubling: Half believe Jesus sinned while on earth, more than half belief the Bible does not contain absolute moral truths, 60 percent believe someone can earn his way to Heaven by being good, 62 percent do not share their faith with others, and 67 percent believe people can get to Heaven without Jesus.[500] (Of course, the Bible teaches just the opposite on all of these.)

The above statistics indicate that American Christianity today is rapidly moving the wrong direction—a major reason the nation is also moving the wrong direction.

PREACH JESUS

The classic line used by many pastors for not addressing Biblical issues such as protecting unborn life and supporting man–woman marriage is *"I just preach Jesus!"* The implication is if you preach on Biblical truths that apply to daily personal and national life, you are not preaching Jesus.

It is certainly good to offer an invitation to receive Christ as Savior during church services, but pastors should also teach about the subject Jesus taught about the most: "the kingdom of God"—that is, they should teach about what happens when Jesus is truly Lord of *everything*.

"Preaching Jesus" is a good thing unless:

- It becomes an excuse for offering only the milk of the Word and never the meat
- It avoids the "so-called controversial" aspects of the Gospel, such as homosexuality, life in the womb, and marriage
- It prevents the pastor from mentioning "sin" or "sins"
- It causes people who have come to Christ to stay shallow and not conform their personal lifestyles to Biblical standards
- It hinders people from having a distinctly Biblical worldview and viewing the issues of our day through a Scriptural lens.

To preach Jesus is fine, but preachers must also preach what Jesus preached: the application of Biblical truth to every aspect of life, including to current issues in the life of our nation.

AN ISSUE OF EGO AND ECONOMICS

When pastors measure their own value to the church on the basis of church attendance or the financial giving that occurs under their leadership, then the possibility of offending people and causing members to leave the church (and take their tithe dollars with them) weighs heavily on them. In such cases, those who worship the idols of "nickels, noses, and numbers" will diligently avoid "unpopular" themes, even though Jesus and the Bible address them.

CHAPTER 57

THE CHURCH IN CULTURAL CHANGE, CHAOS, AND REALIGNMENT

The dramatic theological and political changes over recent decades have significantly altered long-standing alignments of the Church.

THE GRAND DIVIDE

For generations, there was an almost unbroachable fissure between Protestants and the Catholic Church—called the insurmountable "Grand Divide" (see illustration).

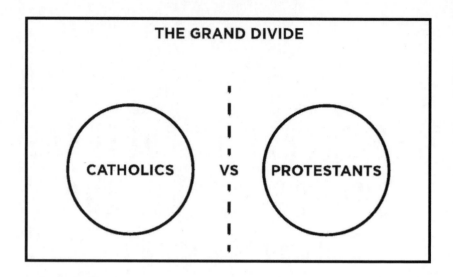

THE GREAT SPLIT

Another dramatic change occurred over the decades from the 1880s through the 1950s. Theological liberalism (the rejection of belief that the teachings of the Bible are God's inspired Word) began to divide Catholics among themselves as well as Protestants among themselves, thus causing each of the two major groups to subdivide—"The Great Split" (see below).

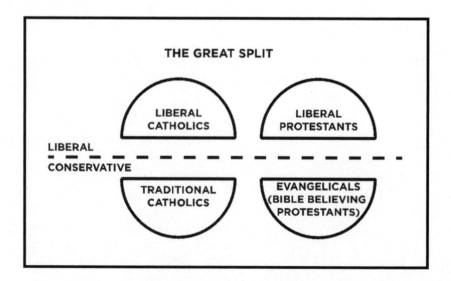

THE GRAND REALIGNMENT

But more change was on the way.

In the 1970s, the church in America (first the Catholic and later the Protestant) was shocked when the Supreme Court legalized the murder of preborn babies in its *Roe v. Wade* decision. Then four decades later, traditional Catholics and conservative Protestants (including most evangelicals) were stunned when the Supreme Court openly endorsed homosexuality, overturning hundreds of years of American law and directly repudiating clear Biblical standards of sexual morality.

When liberal Protestants voiced their open support of homosexuality, evangelicals found they had more in common with traditional Catholics who valued the sanctity of life and the sacredness of Biblical sexuality than with liberal Protestants who supported ripping babies to shreds in the womb and who also endorsed sodomy (which God openly calls *"an abomination"*—Leviticus 18:22, 20:13, ESV). Traditional Catholics and evangelicals who shared common Biblical values on life and traditional sexual morality thus began working together—"The Great Realignment" (see below).

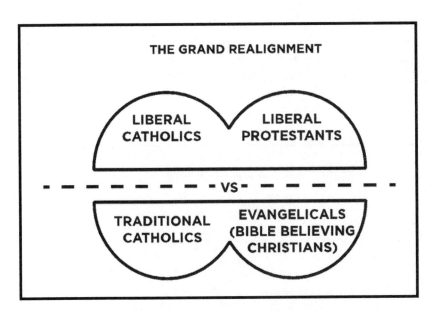

THE GRAND REALIGNMENT

LIBERAL CATHOLICS   LIBERAL PROTESTANTS

- - - - - - - - VS - - - - - - - -

TRADITIONAL CATHOLICS   EVANGELICALS (BIBLE BELIEVING CHRISTIANS)

THE FISSURE

Then came the Supreme Court's decision creating homosexual "marriage." It overturned the institution established by God in the Old Testament and reaffirmed by Jesus in the New. In the Court's view, God and Jesus were wrong on this issue. Interestingly, those today who continue to embrace the 5,000-year-old Biblical definition of marriage have repeatedly been told by the critics they *are on the wrong side of history."* Perhaps. But they are definitely on the right side of eternity.

Historically, the term "evangelical" had described conservative Protestants holding a solid belief in the preeminent authority of the Scriptures. But, after the Court's announcement of its new definition, many so-called "evangelicals" abandoned (or are in the process of abandoning) the Bible on this issue and have placed the Court's opinion above God's.

For example, the governing board of what is indisputably the most highly visible association that networks evangelicals nationally had difficulty passing a statement affirming marriage as being one man–one woman. And others who may not have openly abandoned marriage and Biblical sexuality have certainly grown strangely silent on the issue. Perhaps they are afraid of being labeled a "homophobe" or "intolerant," or maybe they don't want to face the ire that will undoubtedly come from supporters of the militant LGBTQ movement. Regardless, whether from abandonment or silence, the result is a distinct and very visible fissure among evangelicals over the formerly unquestioned authority of the Bible on this issue (see below).

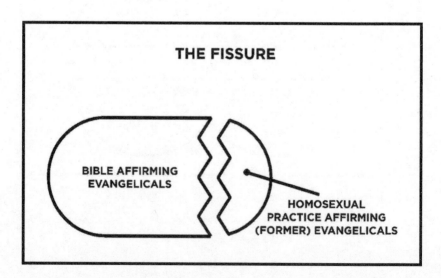

THE FISSURE

BIBLE AFFIRMING
EVANGELICALS

HOMOSEXUAL
PRACTICE AFFIRMING
(FORMER) EVANGELICALS

It is unlikely the term "evangelical" as it has been known will survive. In fact, many key evangelical voices are calling for the term to be dropped because it no longer describes a Bible-minded Christian and is thus largely meaningless. As a replacement, we suggest the use of the initials "ABC" Authentically Biblical Churches, Authentically Biblical Christians, and Authentically Biblical Colleges, for there is now a need to separate the ABCs from the CINOs (Christians in Name Only) and EINOs (Evangelicals in Name Only).

THE FORMING COALITION

Although traditional Catholics and ABCs have been working together for several years in a number of areas, their coalition is expanding (see below). Many Bible (Tanakh) believing orthodox Jews are joining arms with evangelicals, for they share common convictions on life, marriage, love for Israel, opposition to anti-Semitism, and other key Biblical teachings.

The once clear and easily identifiable labels have begun to lose their traditional meanings, and the jury is out on whether the American church as we have known it will survive. *This is a precarious moment*, but it could be the Church's greatest moment—if there is a return to the acceptance of the Scriptures and core Biblical truth.

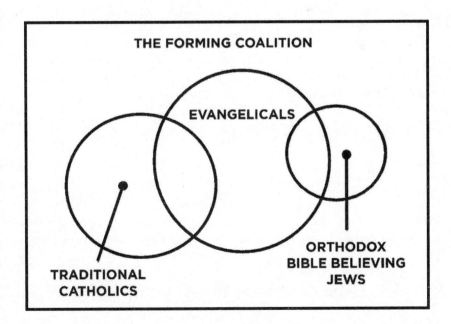

THE FORMING COALITION

EVANGELICALS

TRADITIONAL CATHOLICS

ORTHODOX BIBLE BELIEVING JEWS

CHAPTER 58

PAYING ATTENTION

Pay close attention to yourself and to your teaching.

1 Timothy 4:16, NASB

onsidering where we currently find ourselves, God's Word gives six specific solutions. Several will directly challenge prevailing Christian thinking today, but if we don't, then we will continue to have the same dismal results we currently get. Here are the six solutions.

1. KNOW WHY YOU WERE CREATED

And God created man . . . (Genesis 1:27, ASV)

Why are we here?—and what are we supposed to be doing while we are here? In recent centuries this question was answered in the famous *Westminster Shorter Catechism*, written in 1646 by Scottish theologians:

Q. What is the chief end of man?
A. Man's chief end is to glorify God, and to enjoy Him forever.

An intelligent answer, but is this what the Bible says? Not really. God has never had any shortage of beings to glorify Him—that's what angels did before man was created, and that's what they still do now. Man has a different purpose.

In Genesis 1–2, God made all of creation—the plants, fish, birds, and animals. The Bible then tells us when God finished, He looked at His creation and saw He had no one to "tend the garden," so He created man. Man was made to take care of God's stuff (Genesis 2:5, 15).

What is "God's stuff"? Everything. According to the Bible, "*The earth is the Lord's, and all its fullness, The world and those who dwell therein.*" (Psalm 24:1, NKJV). This "everything" includes business, government, media, arts and entertainment, education, the family, and religion. God put man here to "tend the garden"—that is, to take care of all these areas. (This is sometimes referred to as the "cultural mandate.") It is tragic when pastors and Christian leaders focus only on a narrow portion of the Gospel, ignoring this clear Biblical directive.

So, contrary to much current belief and teaching, God did not put us here to sit around, enjoy ourselves, bask in His love, and wait for His return so we can praise Him throughout eternity. It's time for Christians to get in the game and get busy in the various spheres of cultural influence so His will be done on earth as it is in Heaven (Matthew 6:10).

2. KNOW WHY THE CHURCH IS HERE

So Christ Himself gave the apostles, the prophets, the evangelists, the pastors, and teachers to equip His people for works of service . . . (Ephesians 4:11–12, NIV)

Having established the purpose of man (*"to tend the garden"*), what is the purpose of the Church? According to Ephesians 4, it is to *"equip His people for works of service"*—that is, to prepare His people to "tend the garden" in all spheres of influence. But this won't happen if the Church keeps sidestepping these areas and won't train God's people how His principles apply in each.[501]

3. FEED MY SHEEP

Jesus said, "Feed my sheep." (John 21:17)

One thing about sheep is they let you know when they are hungry. (David has been a rancher for years, and among other livestock, he has raised countless sheep.) Sheep often know what they need, whether a mineral block, salt block, sulfur block, or something else.

Currently, 65 percent, or two of three Christians (that is, two of three "sheep") say they are hungry for more information on what the Bible teaches in relation to current cultural and political issues.[502] The shepherds should listen—especially when what the sheep are hungry for is what God has already told shepherds they should be feeding them.

Multiple studies have shown *"one of the primary reasons that people are dropping out of churches in record numbers is because they believe it to be irrelevant to life these days."*[503] If the shepherds won't feed the sheep and give them fresh food that meets their needs, the sheep will abandon the flock, find a different flock, or leave the flock and be picked off by the wolves so plentiful throughout our culture—and the shepherds will be at fault.

4. A WATCHMAN, OR A SILENT WATCHDOG?

For the leaders of my people—the Lord's watchmen, His shepherds—are . . . like silent watchdogs that give no warning when danger comes. (Isaiah 56:10, NLT)

For years, Christians and Christian leaders have been aware of the general ways in which the enemy has moved the nation in the wrong direction: secularism, entertainment challenging traditional sexuality and families, an aggressive LGBTQ movement, moral relativism, open persecution of Christians, and countless other things.

Christians and Christian leaders have also seen the specific steps by which these general changes have advanced: Supreme Court decisions striking down traditional marriage and advancing homosexuality; government schools teaching sex education that contradicts what the Bible says, punishing students for living out their faith at schools, and pushing transgenderism; college professors and universities that make it their mission to secularize Christian students (some studies show that more than 70 percent of Christian students renounce their faith while at college[504]); entertainment that highlights dysfunctional families, attacks Christian values, and normalizes homosexuality, cohabitation, casual sex, and much more.

These are some of the easily identifiable dangers that have come at Christians in recent years. But how many Christian leaders have been the watchmen God told them to be? How many have taken a stand, loudly sounded the alarm, and boldly warned against these specific dangers?

It would be an interesting exercise for pastors to search their sermon archives and find the sermon they preached when the US Supreme Court declared it unconstitutional for students to see the Ten Commandments on school grounds. Or their sermon after President Obama turned on Israel and created the worst relations between the United States and Israel in modern history. Or the sermon warning the congregation about the normalization of homosexuality in the hit show *Will and Grace* (or about similar shows that openly attacked Biblical values such as *Modern Family, Big Bang Theory, Cheers, Family Guy, Two and a Half Men, South Park, Politically Incorrect,* and many more). Or the one telling congregants secular education for children directly violates every Biblical instruction for educating students. These are all dangers a Biblical watchman would have warned others about.

Of course, no one wants to be the first to blow the trumpet. It's not comfortable to be the watchman. Nevertheless, it is what God demands of us as Christians in general, and of pastors/shepherds in particular.

We each have a responsibility to warn those around us, and God specifically tells us if we don't, He will hold us *personally* accountable for whatever evil befalls those we did not warn (Ezekiel 3:17–21 and 33:1–9).

Become a good watchman, not a useless silent watchdog.

5. BE A SHEPHERD, NOT A HIRED HAND

I am the good shepherd. The good shepherd lays down his life for the sheep. He who is a hired hand and not a shepherd, who does not own the sheep, sees the wolf coming and leaves the sheep and flees (John 10:11–12, ESV)

This is a corollary to the point above, which contrasted a watchman with a silent watchdog. The comparison here is between a shepherd (who *"lays down his life for the sheep"*) and a hired hand (*"sees the wolf coming and leaves the sheep and flees"*). The question is the same as before. With all the dangers coming at Christians in recent years, did you throw yourself in front of the charging wolf and confront it, or did you turn away and ignore the approaching danger? Sadly, nine of ten pastors openly acknowledge they have retreated to the safety of their church grounds, refusing to engage the battle or to equip their congregants for it.[505] (David knows what it is to rush out to confront a predator such as a coyote seeking to destroy some of his vulnerable sheep. Oh, that today's pastors would have a similar commitment to protect their flocks from the "cultural coyotes" similarly seeking to inflict harm and damage.) Sadly, by their own admission (and based on Jesus's definition), nine of ten pastors are hired hands and not shepherds.

6. INDIVIDUALLY SHARE THE GOSPEL

He who wins souls is wise (Proverbs 11:30, NASB)

Hebrew scholars point out that the Scriptures talk very little about "rights" but much about "responsibilities."[506] Without a sense of responsibility or duty, the focus on our so-called "rights"—on what we believe is owed us (such as the "right" to healthcare, free education, a fair salary, and so forth)—leads to selfishness, which produces a sense of entitlement (the mentality that currently afflicts much of America).

Our early Founders were very cognizant of the Biblical teaching of responsibility and duty and therefore placed a strong emphasis on it. For example, James Wilson (a signer of both the Declaration of Independence and the Constitution) affirmed, *"To each class of rights, a class of duties is correspondent."*[507]

To illustrate this, Americans have a constitutional right to free speech, but they have a corresponding duty to be truthful with what they say, and although they have a constitutional right to keep and bear arms, they also have a duty not to shed innocent blood. There is also an equivalent duty associated with the other rights we possess and enjoy.

For many American Christians, the entitlement mentality of spiritual rights without duties has become part of our modern thinking. Too many are cognizant of, expect, and enjoy our spiritual blessings (that is, our rights), but not much time is spent emphasizing our duties.

One indispensable spiritual duty every Christian has is the duty to share with others the testimony or the good news of what Jesus Christ has personally done for them. Jesus once told a man, *"Return home and tell how much God has done for you."* That man then went *"and told all over town how much Jesus had done for him"* (Luke 8:39, NIV). This is what every Christian should also do.

It is vital that each of us talk to others about Jesus, for, as He pointed out, "Whoever acknowledges Me before others, I will also acknowledge before My Father in heaven" (Matthew 10:32–33, NIV). Jesus won't speak up for us if we won't speak up for Him. But only one third of Christians share their faith with others. This is one of the many things that has to change.

If Christians and the church don't start doing these six things, any hope for a reversal of the current trends is unlikely.

CHAPTER 59

LOOKING BACKWARD TO SEE THE WAY FORWARD

Remember the days of old; consider the
generations long past.

DEUTERONOMY 32:7, NIV

A quote attributed to President Woodrow Wilson says:

> A nation which does not remember what it was yesterday, does
> not know what it is today, nor what it is trying to do. We are
> trying to do a futile thing if we don't know where we have come
> from, or what we have been about.[508]

There are many things we can see in the past that still work today.
After all, the same general problems and issues are faced by each gen-

eration; only the technology changes from one to the next. Much can be learned today from the role of the Church in previous generations.

Significantly, America would never have become a great nation and a world leader for good in so many areas had it not been for the direct involvement of pastors and the Church in the affairs of the nation. Their influence was directly felt through the sermons they preached as well as the hands-on leadership they exercised in all areas of the culture, including in political and governmental areas.

By so doing, these earlier American pastors were merely following countless Biblical examples of God's ministers addressing the pressing issues of the day and openly calling out bad public policies and leaders:

- Elijah confronted King Ahab and Queen Jezebel over issues such as their unjust use of eminent domain and religious persecution (1 Kings 21:1–24, 1 Kings 18:18), and Micaiah regularly challenged Ahab over wicked public policies (1 Kings 22:7–18)
- Isaiah came against King Hezekiah over national security failures and issues related to the treasury (2 Chronicles 32:27–31, 2 Kings 20:12–19)
- Eliezer and Jehu confronted King Jehoshaphat over his blunders in foreign relations and ill-advised foreign alliances (2 Chronicles 19:1–2, 2 Chronicles 20:35–37)
- John the Baptist called out King Herod over his divorce and marriage practices (Mark 6:18–19) and condemned civil leaders for their hypocrisy (Matthew 3:7)
- Samuel confronted King Saul over not fulfilling his assigned responsibilities (1 Samuel 13:1–14, 1 Samuel 15)
- Daniel confronted Nebuchadnezzar over his pride and arrogance (Daniel 4:1–27) and Belshazzar over his moral debauchery (Daniel 5:17–28)
- Azariah (along with eighty other priests) opposed King Uzziah for usurping religious practices through an improper expansion of government powers (2 Chronicles 26:16–21).

There certainly is no Biblical model where God had His ministers remain silent with civil leaders or about civil issues. Furthermore, His

ministers frequently partnered with civil leaders in constructing good
public policies and providing sound guidance on many issues:

- Elisha gave the King of Israel counsel regarding military
  intelligence and military policy (2 Kings 6)
- Nathan provided guidance to David on architectural
  issues (2 Samuel 7:1–13)
- Ezra delivered strong counsel on marriage policy (Ezra
  9–10), and Governor Nehemiah implemented that counsel into public policy (Nehemiah 8:1–6, 13:23–27)
- King Joash pursued good policies as long as the priest
  Jehoiada provided him counsel, but when Joash lost godly
  input, his policies became wicked (2 Chronicles 24:1–2,
  15–19)
- Isaiah provided guidance on national security issues and
  foreign policy to King Hezekiah (Isaiah 37).

The Bible is loaded—and almost overflowing—with accounts of
God's ministers speaking into the civil arena and speaking directly to
(and about) civil leaders. (Significantly, US Senator James Lankford of
Oklahoma, a well-known former Southern Baptist leader, contends that
there is not a single book in the Bible that does not in some way speak
to or about governmental issues.) With such clear Biblical examples, for
generations American ministers did the same.

For example, in several New England colonies and states, it was
common practice to open annual state legislative sessions with a sermon,[509] and those sermons on legislative matters were often printed and
sent throughout the state at government expense.[510] Such sermons were
preached in front of numerous Founding Fathers.[511] Ministers had great
impact on the thinking and worldview of that day.

In fact, John Adams specifically identified the Rev. Dr. Jonathan
Mayhew as one of the individuals *"most conspicuous, the most ardent,
and influential"* in the *"awakening and revival of American principles
and feelings"* that led to American independence.[512] Mayhew preached
practical sermons, applying the Bible to issues in the news,[513] including
a famous sermon on the Biblically authorized use of civil disobedience[514]
that led to a motto of the American War for Independence: *"Rebellion
to Tyrants is Obedience to God."*[515]

Adams also identified the Rev. Samuel Cooper as another influential
leader in securing American independence.[516] Cooper's sermons

addressed, among other things, constitutional issues, military events, and current events in the news.[517] And the Rev. Charles Chauncy (another pastor whom John Adams specifically praised[518]) preached about the Stamp Act[519]—an unpopular 1765 tax imposed on the Americans by the British.

Additional subjects also addressed by early pastors included sermons on foreign affairs, science, the role of judges, economic policies, American history, military battles, education, sexual morality, principles of government, and other topics touching day-to-day life.[520] As John Adams affirmed:

It is the *duty* of the clergy to accommodate their discourses to the times—to preach against such sins as are most prevalent and recommend such virtues as are most wanted [lacking].[521]

After the American Founding, the same practices were still readily evident in the pulpit.

For example, in the 1800s, sermon topics included dueling, architecture, how to grow old, transportation, solar eclipses, alcoholism, the War of 1812, the duties of an American citizen, elections, marriage, medicine, slavery, immigration, the War with Mexico, the trans-Atlantic telegraph, and many other subjects.[522] (Hundreds of these original sermons can be viewed at www.wallbuilders.com under Library/Historical Sermons.) The impact of such sermons directly shaped American public policy, resulting in a massive expansion of personal liberties, including the end of child labor, the beginning of women's rights, and the abolition of slavery.

Perhaps the Rev. Charles Finney (one of the most noteworthy ministers in the mid-1800s) best summarized the influence of the pulpit on America when he reminded ministers of his day:

Brethren, our preaching will bear its legitimate fruits, [but] if immorality prevails in the land, the fault is ours in a large degree. If there is a decay of conscience, the pulpit is responsible for it. If the public press lacks moral discrimination, the pulpit is responsible for it. If the Church is degenerate and worldly, the pulpit is responsible for it. If the world loses its interest in religion, the pulpit is responsible for it. If Satan rules in our halls of legislation, the pulpit is responsible for it. If our politics become so corrupt that the very foundations of our government are ready to fall away, the pulpit is responsible for it. Let us not ignore this fact my dear brethren, but let us lay it to heart, be thoroughly awake to our responsibility in respect to the morals of this nation.[523]

The repeating cadence is obvious: whether for good or for bad, *"the pulpit is responsible for it."*

SALVATION

It goes without saying, all the aforementioned pastors also preached traditional sermons about spiritual life and growth, but unlike today's pastors, they did not avoid sermons on issues that arose in the news, state, or nation. "Salvation" applies to more than merely saving human hearts. It also pertains to the restoration of that which has been lost in all of culture. Through relevant preaching, congregants become Biblically informed and equipped on the issues.

CHAPTER 60

KEEPING FIRST THINGS FIRST

Jesus said . . . "Go and make disciples of all nations . . . teaching them to obey everything I have commanded you."

MATTHEW 28:18–20, NIV

The last mandate Jesus gave His followers while on earth is called the Great Commission (Matthew 28:18–20)—to go and make disciples of all people. To *"disciple"* is to engage in the process of teaching, training, preparing, and equipping. For centuries, this was the primary objective for Christians, whether individually or collectively.

THE COSTLY SHIFT: HOW MANY?

In the early twentieth-century, the Church's traditional understanding of this Great Commission shifted from discipleship to evangelism. Mass crusades therefore became common, such as those led by Billy Sunday, a professional baseball player who came to Christ and worked to evangelize others. In that period was introduced what became known as the Sinner's Prayer—a simple prayer to ask Jesus into a person's life. The prayer became an easy way to count converts and know who had been reached in the services. But becoming a convert is only a starting point, not an arrival destination; yet for many churches today, making converts has become almost the singular focus of their ministry. This is not the Great Commission as defined by Jesus.

The change from making disciples to making converts resulted in the Church shifting from qualitative measurements (that is, measuring how spiritually mature an individual became) to quantitative measurements (counting the quantity, or numbers, of those who said the prayer or did something else measurable). Because quantitative numbers now drive so many church operations, Sunday and Wednesday night services are largely a thing of the past because the number of those attending such services are so much lower. But if the objective were discipleship, we would take every opportunity to teach, train, and disciple individuals regardless of how small the crowd might be. (Some churches are proactive in discipleship, but most are not or are producing "Christians" whose core beliefs and thinking are hardly different from that in the culture at large.)

TRANSCENDENT TRUTH APPLIED TO ALL OF LIFE AND CULTURE

If the Church still followed the Great Commission (that is, if we taught others what Jesus specifically taught His disciples), it would be addressing what Jesus addressed, which definitely includes current issues. After all, Jesus taught against no-fault divorce and on God's definition of marriage (Matthew 19); the economic principles of profit, reward, and taxation (Matthew 25); employer/employee relationships and contracts (Matthew 20); and the right to face your accuser (John 8, which became a central feature of civil court procedures in the western hemisphere[524]). Pastors today certainly ought to be teaching what Jesus taught.

Jesus was focused on discipleship—on changing the thinking paradigm of His followers. Discipleship is usually a slow, difficult, laborious, and even uncomfortable process. Nevertheless, Jesus spent more time instructing His handful of close followers than He did the massive crowds, and it was the highly trained qualitative group that changed the world, not the larger quantitative group.

As the statistics have shown, very few Christians today are truly His disciples—few live by Jesus's teachings, and even fewer read or study His word. Converts may be getting their "fire insurance," so to speak (that is, getting their spiritual ticket punched for Heaven rather than Hell), but they are not transforming the world and its culture, which is the objective of true Christianity. What is needed today is more disciples.

THE RISK OF OFFENDING

In this new era where numbers supposedly indicate church success, anything that jeopardizes or reduces those numbers (such as offending hearers in the crowd) is largely avoided. But that is not a Biblical viewpoint. Notice that although Jesus drew large crowds, He was also regularly offending them and losing many. It is not that He was deliberately trying to offend people; rather, He spoke an uncompromising truth, in love (Ephesians 4:15), and for some people, the truth is difficult to handle.

Thus, on one occasion, the crowd complained, *"'This is a hard teaching. Who can accept it? . . . From this time many of His disciples turned back and no longer followed Him"* (John 6:60, 66, NIV). And another time, His disciples pointed out, *"Do you know that the Pharisees were offended when they heard this statement?"* (Matthew 15:12, NASB). But Jesus was unapologetic, pointing out He simply declared the truth to them (v. 13).

Speaking the unvarnished truth and showing how God thinks about certain issues—that is, teaching what God thinks is right and wrong—will routinely offend many, but that doesn't necessarily mean they will all leave. Recall how many times Jesus's own disciples were offended but kept coming back to Him to learn more and how frequently new crowds gathered around Jesus to hear His teachings after other crowds abandoned Him.

If the Church today is to succeed in making disciples and not just converts, we will have to change from the current quantitative measurements and re-embrace the qualitative ones Jesus used. It also means we will have to change the type of meals we offer on the church menu, moving away from offering so much milk to adding more solid food (see 1 Corinthians 3:1–3 and Hebrews 5:12).

As long as the church primarily feeds milk, it will continue to have baby Christians. Eating solid food is part of growing up, and as polling has confirmed, Christians want more solid food. Of course, this means pastors may have to do additional study and research on the Bible and current issues because pastors can't teach what they don't know.[525] But strengthening disciples has the effect of increasing converts, for in a healthy flock, it is the sheep and not the shepherd who produce other sheep—healthy disciples lead others to Christ, and strong and healthy sheep cause the flock to increase.

Churches should no longer be judged on how many attend but rather on how many move into truly Biblical thinking and how many become activated to "tend the garden" in all spheres of today's culture.

A REASON FOR HOPE: RELATIONAL ON PURPOSE

Significantly, Millennials and Gen Z-ers may end up being the catalyst for national revival. Even though they are the most secular and Biblically illiterate generation in our history, unlike recent generations, they are transformed and most successfully brought back to truth through one-on-one relationships—through discipling.

Although the church at large has moved away from this one-on-one approach (or the use of small accountability groups), studies continue to affirm that the most effective way for someone to grow spiritually is through individual coaching or discipling and that most preaching is far less productive in creating lasting spiritual fruit.[526] So God may have sent America a generation that will force the Church to fulfill the Great Commission's mandate of making disciples and not just converts, thus helping the Church (and thereby the nation) become spiritually strong and healthy again.

CHAPTER 61

SOLUTIONS

What can be done by the average Christian who attends a church where the leadership does not address or give distinctly Biblical positions on the key issues of the day? There are four things you can do.

1. BE INQUISITIVE

Begin asking questions of your church leaders. Lots of questions. Ask politely but firmly the church's and the pastor's stance on the issues of our day. See if they have any written policy statements on these issues. Perhaps they do, but maybe those statements have been buried and have never seen the light of day. Also, there is a difference between an official position voted on by a denomination or a local congregation decades ago and the current functioning policy of the church.

For example, a church can say it is pro-life based on some official statement made in 1973, after the *Roe v. Wade* court decision legalizing abortion on demand. But today, the authentically pro-life church will involve itself in things, such as volunteering in pregnancy centers, assisting young unwed mothers, helping adopt children from unwanted pregnancies, marching and praying in front of the killing centers of our nation, unabashedly affirming candidates (including from the pulpit) who are truly pro-life, and challenging and confronting those who support the ripping apart of babies in the womb.

And the difference between a church that says it is pro-marriage and one that truly is is whether the pastor will openly address the topic of homosexuality. If the church leadership is truly pro-marriage, they will unabashedly hold an open and uncompromising Biblical position against homosexuality while still reaching out in a loving manner to those who struggle with same-sex attraction. They will also unhesitatingly raise the issue of traditional marriage with government officials and will not be silent in identifying candidates who are truly pro–Biblical marriage and those who are not. (By the way, it is completely legal to do this from the pulpit.)

Be very cautious of going to a church where they "let you" put information on a table tucked away in some invisible corner of the church foyer so you can make people aware of the issues. They shouldn't just "let *you*"; *they should be addressing those issues up front, from the pulpit.*

2. PRAY

The Bible tells us to devote ourselves to prayer (Colossians 4:2), to pray continually (1 Thessalonians 5:17), and to pray on all occasions (Ephesians 6:18). Pray for your local church, for your pastor, for the Church in general, and for Christians to develop a backbone and step up and become leaders.

Additionally, Jesus clearly said that His followers would not just pray but would also fast (see, for example, Luke 5:35). A truly Biblical church will therefore call periodic fasts as well as times of prayer. (Jim openly attests that some of the richest times experienced by his congregation were when they chose to go on extended fasts, some lasting even forty days.) But don't stop with just praying, or even with fasting and praying. As Founding Father John Hancock urged Christians in his generation:

> I conjure [urge] you—by all that is dear, by all that is honorable, by all that is sacred—not only that ye pray but that ye act.[527]

3. ACT

As statistics have already shown, pastors today are often reluctant to address current issues that are also clearly addressed in the Bible (such as the sanctity of life, the sacredness of marriage, and the State of Israel) for fear of becoming too "political." We have even heard pastors openly explain that if they address such issues, they may be seen as over-identifying with the Republican Party because it openly holds the same positions. But the Bible took those positions millennia before there was a Republican Party (or any party), so they were Biblical issues long before they were political ones. An ABC pastor will hold all candidates of every party accountable to the standard of Biblical truth. Just because a party holds the position the Bible holds on a particular issue is no reason to go silent on what the Bible says. Biblically correct positions should be praised, and Biblically incorrect positions should be pointed out and denounced, regardless of the group with which they may be associated.

The best way to encourage your pastor to openly tackle such subjects is to let him or her know you are interested in how the Bible applies to current topics and in learning what the Bible teaches about them—that is, you want to be equipped so you can speak to your friends, coworkers, and others in the culture on what the Bible says about that issue.

And if you can identify other congregants who share your interest in experiencing such teaching (and the data certainly indicate it should not be difficult to find many such people around you if you are in a church led by a theologically conservative pastor), then develop a way for all of you to communicate your shared interest to the pastor.

You might also provide your pastor with publicly available information, such as published articles or links to television broadcasts or websites, conveying research showing the enormous numbers of committed churchgoers who want their church to be more active in receiving training in these areas. (Barna's full study on this is available at www.wallbuilders.com; search for "*What God's People Want to Know.*")

Understand that, if your pastor does address such topics, it is likely he will experience pushback from some congregants. But the data show it will probably come from people who are less likely to take the Scriptures at face value—those who are less likely to possess a Biblical worldview. Pastors need to recognize that criticism for addressing such topics may actually come from those who are theologically at odds with what the church may stand for (even if they have been attending for years), thus providing an entirely different interpretation of that criticism. Therefore, addressing these issues may serve as an impetus for many in the congregation to develop a more Biblically centered worldview.

If you become aware your pastor is being criticized for addressing a current issue, make a special effort to encourage him and thank him for helping equip Christians for *"works of service"* (Ephesians 4:12). Be sure to let him know (and let your friends in social media know) you appreciated the times he addressed a current issue from a Biblical perspective and you hope to continue experiencing more of that kind of teaching. Succinctly stated, publicly defend him or her.

4. LEAVE

Of all the paragraphs we are writing, this is by far the most painful. It took us many years to arrive at this conclusion.

If your church and pastor will not take a strong stand on what the Bible takes a strong stand on, then leave that church. Some always argue that by staying in such churches, they hope to impact them, but we have watched this process for decades and have never seen it work.

We cannot count the numbers of times people have come to us and asked us to *"Please talk to my pastor."* We won't. Not anymore. We tried many times before, but it never worked.

(By the way, it did not work 400 years ago when both the Pilgrims and the Puritans tried to stay in their churches and change them. They finally left and came to America, where they practiced Biblical teachings. Those teachings worked, thus helping shape the best features of young America.)

If your pastor is largely silent on the issues or perhaps is even on the wrong side of the issues and if he or she won't change when you ask, then he or she holds that position on purpose. They are not going to change, so leave. Staying only facilitates them in their wrongness.

Recall that church measurements today are built around numbers. So a drop in attendance (and consequently in offering amounts) is a message they may understand. Go to a church where the pastor is fully Biblical, and then support him or her.

Barna estimates that of the approximately 100,000 churches that can be described as theologically conservative, only half of the pastors have a verifiable, measurable Biblical worldview, and far fewer are willing to take a public stand if it might involve a perceived risk or open opposition. Sadly, millions of Americans are supporting pastors who will not stand, which only hastens the destruction of America. Bluntly stated, there are many local churches that should not receive your support; so if you are a serious follower of Christ, get linked with a pastor who demonstrates Biblical courage. Compromise is rampant, and it is also contagious, so run from it.

If the millions of Americans who claim to be evangelical were to shift their allegiance to ABC pastors and congregations, the result would be positive cultural shifts in many areas. The church must once again become the proactive change agent so desperately needed in America right now.

CHAPTER 62

GOOD NEWS

After all of this negative information, there are still many reasons to be encouraged, and we will get to those shortly. But seeing the precarious situation of the Church and nation today is likely to make the cry for a national revival increase among many, particularly in older generations.

Longing for a national revival is fine—just so long as you understand that from an historical standpoint, a revival is generally a very slow process that spans decades, requires lots of hard work from those involved, and occurs largely *outside* the church. Usually, it is not until late in the revival when the church at large (made up of countless local congregations) finally decides to get on board with what is going on.

OUTSIDE THE INSTITUTIONAL CHURCHES

Perhaps you have heard of national revivals such as the Evangelical Awakening in England and the First and Second Great Awakenings in America. The Rev. John Wesley was a leader in the English revival, and in America, the Rev. George Whitefield was a leading figure in the First Awakening, and the Rev. Charles Finney in the Second. Each of these men largely preached in outdoor meetings. Why? Certainly, they could accommodate larger crowds that way, but primarily they began doing so because churches would not allow them to preach in their facilities.

Significantly, the loudest critics in these national revivals were not the secularists but rather pastors. John Wesley and his lay preachers were pelted with stones thrown by professing Christians. And pastors encouraged their congregants to similarly pelt George Whitefield with rotten vegetables and stones and even get in the trees over him and pee down on him.[528] At times of revival, churches often begin as the biggest opponents to what God wants to do in the nation, for it is new and not part of their accepted traditions at the time.

Jesus talked about this in terms of old and new wineskins (Mark 2:21–22). Old wineskins become fixed and rigid in their ways and can't handle new things—they refuse to mold or conform themselves to what God is trying to tell them to do at the time, so they resist and try to keep doing what they've become accustomed to. This is where much of the church is today—and this is where the Church at large was every time the nation needed a revival, until late in the game when it finally began to spiritually embrace what it so long rejected and fought against.

EXCITING INDICATORS: GOOD THINGS COMING

Returning to the good things we are seeing today, there are many.

For example, there is an outpouring of prayer unlike anything in decades. We have never seen so many prayer groups—*serious* prayer groups—functioning in our nation. It is a genuine prayer movement. Although rarely covered by the media, tens of thousands of Christians regularly fill arenas and stadiums for times of prayer and fasting—no speakers; just prayer and fasting. It is a national phenomenon.

And there are more Biblical and evangelical Christians in Congress today than at any time in the modern era. Certainly, there is still much visible wickedness coming out of Congress, and this is what most people see and know about. But the number of truly righteous, Biblically committed members is larger than at any point in recent history.

Countless Bible studies and personal accountability groups flourish on Capitol Hill. In fact, there is an official Congressional Prayer Caucus with scores of Members of Congress gathering every week at first votes, getting on their knees and praying for the nation. They jointly stand together against attacks on religious expression anywhere across the nation, weighing in with state and federal courts and other governmental entities. They zealously fight for the right of Christians to express their faith publicly.

There is also an unprecedented spiritual movement among elected officials at the state and local levels. Dozens of state legislatures have formed their own official Prayer Caucuses, and they, too, are extremely active in defending public Christian expressions in state courts, at city councils, and local school boards. In fact, more than 700 counties and cities have now officially adopted "In God We Trust" as their local motto, with police and sheriffs cars now proudly displaying that acknowledgement of God. States such as Indiana have made the motto part of the state license plates, and states such as Arkansas, Mississippi, Tennessee, and Florida now post bold acknowledgments of God in tens of thousands of classrooms throughout the state. All of this is largely unpublicized, but it's like nothing we've seen in decades.

And skyrocketing every year is the number of families choosing to homeschool their children[529] so they can raise them with Christian and Biblical teachings and values, thus bringing up a new generation of committed Jesus followers.

And even the number of pastors who are now beginning to really get it is also increasing. Both of us are personally involved in national networks of spiritually active and civically involved pastors, and the numbers of these uncompromising, Biblically centered pastors who are stepping out as a community voice and moral leaders are steadily growing. In fact, large numbers of pastors are now even running for elected office.

LET'S GO FOR IT

There are other positive indicators, but right now many of them are largely outside the traditional church. Thus, pastors and Christians have many decisions to make. Will they remain in what they believe is a safe silence, or will they begin to dive into God's Word, conform their life to its teachings, take a bold public Biblical stand, and begin fulfilling God's purpose of "*tending the garden*" by getting involved in the culture? It's a choice each of us must make.

THIS PRECARIOUS
MOMENT

When Swiss-French architect Charles-Édouard Jeanneret visited New York City, he quipped, *"New York is a catastrophe, but a magnificent catastrophe!"*[530] These words may well describe America today.

We affirm America's magnificence, but this book addresses the catastrophe. America is worth saving, but what will *you* do?

The dilemma before us is similar to that faced by a group in the Bible who also were experiencing severe national problems affecting their personal lives. As they contemplated their course of action, they asked themselves:

Why do we sit here until we die? (2 KINGS 7:3, NASB)

They correctly concluded personal complacency wouldn't solve any problems. So, too, with each of us. We must become engaged. There were specific solutions presented in each section—something you individually can do to become part of the solution. It is our prayer you will be actively engaged, for you <u>can</u> make a difference! But there is more good news.

You might think the nation too far gone to be restored, especially if you read the Bible verse, *"When the foundations are being destroyed, what can the righteous do?"* (Psalm 11:3, NIV). This makes it sound as though the good people are powerless, wringing their hands and not knowing what to do, but that's not what this verse really says.

One rendering of this verse in Hebrew reads, "*When the foundations are being destroyed, what is the Righteous One doing?*" In other words, in this dark season. God is still up to something, and we need to join Him in this work. This is winnable. This is our moment—even in *This Precarious Moment.*

Prayer: Lord, you are the Head of the Church. We have too often reduced what was supposed to be Your Church to something much less. Many who call themselves Christian don't care for Your Word and make no pretense about violating Your ways. Others love Your Word, but are largely silent about its precepts, having capitulated to the culture. Give us the courage that Peter and John displayed before the Sanhedrin when they refused to be silent about Truth, thus causing their critics to correctly observe of their boldness that they had been with Jesus. May we love the wounded and broken of this world but not be silent regarding the sins for which forgiveness can be experienced. God, help the Church to once again act like the Church. Amen.

ENDNOTES

1. Karen DeYoung and Carol Morello, "U.S. Embassy in Israel will move to Jerusalem in mid-May, State Department says," *The Washington Post*, February 23, 2018 (at: https://www.washingtonpost.com/world/national-security/us-embassy-move-to-jerusalem-could-come-as-early-as-mid-may-official-says/2018/02/23/83c254c4-18b2-11e8-8b08-027a6ccb38eb_story.html?utm_term=.62516786581c).
2. "Trump becomes the first sitting US president to visit the Western Wall," *The Washington Examiner*, May 22, 2017 (at: http://www.washingtonexaminer.com/trump-becomes-the-first-sitting-us-president-to-visit-the-western-wall/article/2623785).
3. "Trump and Netanyahu ready united assault against Iran nuclear deal," *The Gaurdian*, September 18, 2017 (at: https://www.theguardian.com/us-news/2017/sep/18/trump-netan-yahu-iran-nuclear-deal-united-nations-general-assembly).
4. "Netanyahu to Obama: Iran deal threatens Israel's survival," *The Times of Israel*, April 3, 2017 (at: https://www.timesofisrael.com/netanyahu-to-obama-iran-deal-threatens-israels-existence/); "Iranian Army Chief: We Will Turn Tel Aviv and Haifa into Dust," *The Jerusalem Post*, September 18, 2017 (at: http://www.jpost.com/Israel-News/Iranian-General-We-will-turn-Tel-Aviv-and-Haifa-into-dust-505406).
5. "'The U.N. bullies Israel,' Haley tells Netanyahu in Jerusalem," *The Washington Post*, June 7, 2017 (at: https://www.washingtonpost.com/world/the-un-bullies-israel--haley-tells-netanyahu-in-jerusalem/2017/06/07/c4796a58-4b7a-11e7-b69d-c158df3149e9_story.html?utm_term=.bcea6723e5f5).
6. "U.S. vetoes U.N. call for withdrawal of Trump Jerusalem decision," *Reuters*, December 18, 2017 (at: https://www.reuters.com/article/us-usa-trump-israel-un/u-s-vetoes-u-n-call-for-withdrawal-of-trump-jerusalem-decision-idUSKBN1EC25N).
7. "U.S.-Israel Relations Have Never Been Better Than Under Trump, Ambassador Dermer Says," *Haaretz*, October 18, 2017 (at: https://www.haaretz.com/us-news/1.817986).
8. George Barna, "What God's People Want to Know," *WallBuilders*, March 21, 2017 (at: https://wallbuilders.com/gods-people-want-know/).
9. Kelly Shattuck, "7 Startling Facts: An Up Close Look at Church Attendance in America," *Church Leaders*, December 14, 2017 (at: https://churchleaders.com/pastors/pastor-articles/139575-7-startling-facts-an-up-close-look-at-church-attendance-in-america.html).
10. In English, the first attested usage is in 1902 by Richard Henry Pratt: "Segregating any class or race of people apart from the rest of the people kills the progress of the segregated people or makes their growth very slow. Association of races and classes is necessary to destroy racism and classism." ("The Ugly, Fascinating History Of The Word 'Racism,'" *National Public Radio*, January 6, 2014 (at: https://www.npr.org/sections/codeswitch/2014/01/05/260006815/the-ugly-fascinating-history-of-the-word-racism); Isabel C. Barrows, *Proceedings of the Twentieth Annual Meeting of the Lake Mohonk Conference of Friends of Indians 1902* (New York: The Lake Mohonk Conference, 1903), p. 134, Fourth Session, October 23, 1902.) For more information on the etymology

of racism, see: "Racist," *Douglas Harper Online Etymology Dictionary* (at: https://www .etymonline.com/word/racist); "Racism," *Merriam-Webster* (at: https://www.merriam-webster.com/dictionary/racism) (accessed on April 18, 2018).

11. *Random House Dictionary* (Random House, Inc. 2017), "racism" (at: http://www.dictionary .com/browse/racism).

12. *The American Heritage New Dictionary of Cultural Literacy, Third Edition* (Houghton Mifflin Company, 2005), "racism" (at: http://www.dictionary.com/browse/racism).

13. See, for example, Tyler Durden, "San Francisco State Builds Segregated Dorms Where African-Americans Can "'Safely Live And Talk,'" *Zero Hedge*, September 20, 2016 (at: http://www .zerohedge.com/news/2016-09-20/san-francisco-state-builds-segregated-dorms-where-african-americans-can-safely-live-); "Segregated 'blacks only' housing at California university reignites old debate," *RTQuestionMore*, September 8, 2016 (at: https://www.rt.com/ usa/358711-california-state-university-segregated-housing/); "University of San Francisco to host blacks-only student orientation," *The College Fix*, August 15, 2017 (at: https:// drudgenow.com/article/?hop=https://www.thecollegefix.com/post/35536/).

14. See *Random House Dictionary* (Random House Inc., 2017) definitions for "Caucasian" (at: http://www.dictionary.com/browse/caucasian?s=t), "Mongoloid" (at: http://www .dictionary.com/browse/mongoloid), "Negroid" (at: http://www.dictionary.com/browse/ negroid?s=t), "Australoid" (at: http://www.dictionary.com/browse/australoid?s=t).

15. "ethnicity," *thesaurus.com* (at: http://www.thesaurus.com/browse/ethnicity?s=t).

16. "How Many People Groups Are There?" *Joshua Project* (at: https://joshuaproject.net/re-sources/articles/how_many_people_groups_are_there), accessed on August 25, 2017. See also a list of ethnic groups by nation in the CIA's "The World Factbook" (at: https://www .cia.gov/library/publications/the-world-factbook/fields/2075.html), accessed on August 25, 2017.

17. See the United Nations "Statement on race," July 1950 (at: http://unesdoc.unesco.org/ images/0012/001229/122962eo.pdf).

18. "How many major races are there in the world?" *World-Mysteries*, February 18, 2011 (at: http://blog.world-mysteries.com/science/how-many-major-races-are-there-in-the-world/); see also Roger Highfield, "DNA survey finds all humans are 99.9pc the same," *The Tele-graph*, December 20, 2002 (at: http://www.telegraph.co.uk/news/worldnews/northamerica/ usa/1416706/DNA-survey-finds-all-humans-are-99.9pc-the-same.html).

19. Taken from an email sent from David Roever to David Barton on August 23, 2017. Also available at www.daveroever.org.

20. When the Matthew Shepard and James Byrd, Jr. Hate Crimes Prevention Act of 2009 was being marked up in the Judiciary Committee, Rep. Louis Gohmert introduced an amend-ment that the law also include the military and seniors under its protections, but it was voted down. Special protection was thus expanded to victims of crimes based on sexual orientation but not victims of crimes from other groups. See, for example, Louie Gohm-ert, "Hate Crimes Bill Infringes First Amendment Rights," *Texas Insider*, April 27, 2009 (at: http://www.texasinsider.org/hate-crimes-bill-infringes-first-amendment-rights/); "H.R. 1913: All Actions," *Library of Congress: THOMAS*, 2009 (at: https://www.congress.gov/ bill/111th-congress/house-bill/01913/all-actions-without-amendments).

21. See examples such as Thornton Stringfellow's "The Bible Argument: or, Slavery in the Light of Divine Revelation," and "An Examination of Elder Galusha's Reply to Dr. Richard Fuller of South Carolina," in *Cotton is King and Pro-Slavery Arguments* (Augusta, GA: Pritchard, Ab-bott & Loomis, 1860), pp. 461, 492. Or more recently see Bob Jones, Sr.'s 1960 radio address, *Is Segregation Scriptural?*, transcript available at "Is Segregation Scriptural? A Radio Address from Bob Jones on Easter of 1960," *The Gospel Coalition*, July 26, 2016 (at: https://www .thegospelcoalition.org/blogs/evangelical-history/is-segregation-scriptural-a-radio-address-from-bob-jones-on-easter-of-1960/).

22. *Scott v. Sandford*, 60 U.S. 393 (1856), 407.

23. *The Constitution of the United States with the Acts of Congress Relating to Slavery* (Roch-ester: D. M. Dewey, 1854), pp. 22–23, "Fugitive Slave Law of 1850," September 18, 1850.

24. *Congressional Globe, 36th Congress, 2nd Session* (Washington, DC: Congressional Globe Office, 1861), pp. 268–270, January 7, 1861.

25. *A Declaration of the causes which impel the State of Texas to secede from the Federal Union* (1861), p. 4.

26. "Henry Walton Age 84," *Mississippi Slave Narratives from the WPA Records*, 2008 (at: http://msgw.org/slaves/walton-xslave.htm).

27. *Slave Narratives: A Folk History of Slavery in the United States from Interviews with Former Slaves* (Washington, DC: Library of Congress, 1941), Volume XI: North Carolina Narratives, Part 2, p. 229, "Hattie Rogers."

28. Frederick Douglas, *Narrative of the Life of Frederick Douglas, an American Slave* (Dublin: Webb and Chapman, 1845), p. 79.

29. Sojourner Truth, *Narrative of Sojourner Truth; A Bondswoman of Olden Time*, Olive Gilbert, editor (Boston: 1875), pp. 26-27.

30. Harriet Ann Jacobs, *Incidents in the Life of A Slave Girl*, L. Maria Child, editor (Boston: Thayer and Eldridge, 1861), p. 76.

31. T.H. Breen, Stephen Innes, *"Myne Owne Ground": Race and Freedom on Virginia's Eastern Shore, 1640-1676* (New York: Oxford University Press, 2004), pp. 13–15; Peter Wood, *Strange New Land, Africans in Colonial America* (New York: Oxford University Press, 2003), pp. 28–29; "Johnson, Anthony (?–1670)," *blackpast.org* (at: http://www.blackpast .org/aah/johnson-anthony-1670), accessed on August 25, 2017; "The Blurred Racial Lines of Famous Families: Johnson," *PBS* (at: http://www.pbs.org/wgbh/pages/frontline/shows/ secret/famous/johnson.html), accessed on August 25, 2017.

32. See this book by Carter Woodson in which he lists each free black slave-owner and the numbers of slaves they owned: Carter G. Woodson, *Free Negro Owners of Slaves in the United States in 1830* (Washington, DC: The Association for the Study of Negro Life and History, 1924), *passim*. This information was used to form statistical tables in *The Journal of African American History* (Winter, 2006), Vol. 91, No. 1, pp. 81–87, Thomas J. Pressly, "'The Known World" of Free Black Slaveholders: A Research Note on the Scholarship of Carter G. Woodson."

33. *The Journal of African American History* (Winter, 2006), Vol. 91, No. 1, pp. 81–87, Thomas J. Pressly, "'The Known World'" of Free Black Slaveholders: A Research Note on the Scholarship of Carter G. Woodson."

34. See 1830 United States Census Statistical Information, compiled from Steven Manson, Jonathan Schroeder, David Van Riper, and Steven Ruggles. "IPUMS National Historical Geographic Information System: Version 12.0 [Database]," (Minneapolis: University of Minnesota, 2017), at: http://doi.org/10.18128/D050.V12.0; *The Journal of African American History* (Winter, 2006), Vol. 91, No. 1, pp. 81–87, Thomas J. Pressly, "'The Known World'" of Free Black Slaveholders: A Research Note on the Scholarship of Carter G. Woodson."

35. Thomas Donaldson, *Extra Census Bulletin. Indians. The Five Civilized Tribes of Indian Territory* (Washington, DC: Government Printing Office, 1893), p. 41, citing the census of 1860 (at: https://books.google.com/books?id=I1pAAQAAMAAJ&pg=PA41#v=onepage& q&f=false).

36. Alan Gallay, "Indian Slavery in the Americas," *The Gilder Lehrman Institute of American History* (at: https://www.gilderlehrman.org/history-by-era/origins-slavery/essays/indian-slavery-americas), accessed on August 25, 2017.

37. See, for example, John Donoghue, Professor of History at Loyola University, "'Out of the Land of Bondage': The English Revolution and the Atlantic Origins of Abolition," *American Historical Review* (October, 2010), p. 950; "Slavery and Indentured Servants," *Law Library of Congress* (at: https://memory.loc.gov/ammem/awhhtml/awlaw3/slavery.html), accessed on September 1, 2017; "Slavery and the Law in Virginia," *Colonial Williamsburg* (at: http://www.history.org/history/teaching/slavelaw.cfm), accessed on September 1, 2017.

38. Alan Gallay, "Indian Slavery in the Americas," *The Gilder Lehrman Institute of American History* (at: https://www.gilderlehrman.org/history-by-era/origins-slavery/essays/indian-slavery-americas), accessed on August 25, 2017.

39. Alan Gallay, "Indian Slavery in the Americas," *The Gilder Lehrman Institute of American History* (at: https://www.gilderlehrman.org/history-by-era/origins-slavery/essays/indian-slavery-americas), accessed on August 25, 2017.

40. John Donoghue, Professor of History at Loyola University, "'Out of the Land of Bondage': The English Revolution and the Atlantic Origins of Abolition," *American Historical Review* (October 2010), p. 952.

41. Janet Levy, "Christian Slaves, Muslim Masters," *American Thinker*, September 14, 2016 (at: http://www.americanthinker.com/articles/2016/09/christian_slaves_muslim_masters.html) and Jeff Grabmeier, "When Europeans Were Slaves: Research Suggests White Slavery Was Much More Common Than Previously Believed," *The Ohio State University*, March 8, 2004 (at: https://news.osu.edu/news/2004/03/08/whtslav/), providing information from Robert Davis, *Christian Slaves Muslim Masters* (Palgrave Macmillan, 2003); Charles Hansford Adams, *The Narrative of Robert Adams: A Barbary Captive* (New York: Cambridge University Press, 2005), pp. xlv–xlvi.

42. "Results from the 1860 Census" (at: http://www.civil-war.net/pages/1860_census.html), accessed on August 25, 2017; for original numbers see, Joseph C.G. Kennedy, *Agriculture of the United States in 1860* (Washington, DC: Government Printing Office, 1864), pp. 223–248.

43. Richard Allen, *The Life, Experience and Gospel Labors of the Rt. Rev. Richard Allen* (Philadelphia: F. Ford and M.A. Riply, 1880), p. 55, "To the People of Color."

44. John Wise, *A Vindication of the Government of New-England Churches* (Boston: I. Allen, 1717), p 39.

45. John Woolman, *A Journal of the Life and Travels of John Woolman in the Service of the Gospel* (Lindfield: 1838), pp. 80–81, 88–92; John Woolman, *The Journal and Essays of John Woolman* (New York: The MacMillan Company, 1922), pp. xix–xx for a list of works by John Woolman.

46. See, for example, *The Living Age*, Eliakim Littell, editor (Boston: Littell, Son, and Company, 1865), Vol. 86, p. 200, "The Anti-Slavery Revolution in America"; Samuel J. May, *Some Recollections of Our Antislavery Conflict* (Boston: Fields, Osgood, & Co., 1869), p. 335; etc.

47. See for an example of such claims "How many of the signers of the Declaration of Independence owned slaves? 41," *Mr. Heintz*, 2014 (at: http://www.mrheintz.com/how-many-signers-of-the-declaration-of-independence-owned-slaves.html).

48. Thomas Jefferson, *A Summary View of the Rights of British America, set forth in some Resolutions Intended for the Inspection of the Present Delegates of the People in Virginia, Now in Convention* (London: G. Kearsly, 1774), pp. 28–29.

49. For early examples see *Vermont State Papers: Being a Collection of Records and Documents* (Middlebury: J.W. Copeland, 1823), p. 244, 1777 Constitution, Ch. 1, Art. 1; *The Constitution of the Pennsylvania Society, for Promoting the Abolition of Slavery, and the Relief of Free Negroes, Unlawfully Held in Bondage* (Philadelphia: Francis Bailey, 1788), p. 8, "An Act for the Gradual Abolition of Slavery," March 1, 1780.

50. See, for example, "The Founding Fathers and Slavery," *WallBuilders*, December 29, 2016 (at: https://wallbuilders.com/founding-fathers-slavery/); "The Bible, Slavery, and America's Founders," *WallBuilders*, December 31, 2016 (at: https://wallbuilders.com/bible-slavery-americas-founders/); "George Washington, Thomas Jefferson & Slavery in Virginia," *WallBuilders*, December 31, 2016 (at: https://wallbuilders.com/george-washington-thomas-jefferson-slavery-virginia/).

51. John Hancock, *The Great Question for the People! Essays on the Elective Franchise; or, Who has the Right to Vote?* (Philadelphia: Merrihew & Son, 1865), pp. 22–23, 27; see also William D. Kelley, Wendell Phillips, and Frederick Douglass, *The Equality of All Men Before the Law Claimed and Defended* (Boston: Rand & Avery, 1865), pp. 9–11, 15, and passim.

52. *Congressional Record of The Proceedings and Debates of the Forty-Third Congress, First Session* (Washington, DC: Government Printing Office, 1874), Vol. II, p. 409, Speech on the 1875 Civil Rights Bill by African American Rep. Robert Brown Elliott, January 6, 1874.

53. "An international Look at the Single-Parent Family," *Education Next*, Spring 2015 Vol. 15, No. 2 (at: http://educationnext.org/international-look-single-parent-family/); Mark Barajas, "Academic Achievement of Children in Single Parent Homes: A Critical Review," *The Hilltop Review*, Fall 2011 Vol. 5, Art. 4 (at: http://scholarworks.wmich.edu/cgi/viewcontent.cgi?article=1044&context=hilltopreview); "Family and Faith: The Roots of Prosperity, Stability, and Freedom," *Heritage Foundation*, 2001, "Education and School Performance: Chart 20" (at: https://www.heritage.org/marriage-and-family/report/family-and-faith-the-

roots-prosperity-stability-and-freedom) based on statistics from the National Longitudinal Survey of Adolescent Health, 1995, by the National Institute of Health.

54. Nicholas Zill, 1994. "Understanding Why Children in Stepfamilies Have More Learning and Behavior Problems than Children in Nuclear Families" in Alan Booth and Judy Dunn (eds.) *Stepfamilies: Who Benefits, Who Does Not?* (Hillsdale, NJ: Lawrence Erlbaum Associates): 97–106 as referenced in "The Marriage Movement: A Statement of Principles," *Institute for American Values*, p. 12; January 2000 (at: http://americanvalues.org/catalog/pdfs/marriagemovement.pdf).

55. "Father Absence and Youth Incarceration," *Journal of Research on Adolescence*, September 14, 2004, pp. 369–397 (at: http://onlinelibrary.wiley.com/wol1/doi/10.1111/j.1532-7795.2004.00079.x/full); "Boys with Absentee Dads Twice as Likely to be Jailed," *The Washington Post*, August 21, 1998 (at: https://www.washingtonpost.com/archive/politics/1998/08/21/boys-with-absentee-dads-twice-as-likely-to-be-jailed/40bc3e3c-2e37-40d8-ab5c-55837e0c77a2/?utm_term=.a563eb61f652).

56. Reported by John Leo, "All in the Family," September 26, 2005, p. 2, 2000 study by Todd Michael Franke, cited in "Can Married Parents Prevent Crime?" *Institute for Marriage and Public Policy*, September 21, 2005, p. 2.

57. Reported by John Leo, "All in the Family," September 26, 2005, p. 3, 2002 study by Cesar J. Rebellon, cited in "Can Married Parents Prevent Crime?" *Institute for Marriage and Public Policy*, September 21, 2005, p. 3.

58. "Children of divorce: Crime statistics," *divorceforum.org* (at: http://www.divorcereform.org/crime.html), citing a study published in *Los Angeles Times*, 19 September, 1988.

59. Wade C. Mackey and Nancy S. Coney, "The enigma of Father Presence in Relationship to Sons' Violence and Daughters' Mating Strategies: Empiricism in Search of a Theory," *Journal of Men's Studies* 8 (2000): pp. 349–373, as quoted in iMAPP, "Can Married Parents Prevent Crime?" Reported by John Leo, "All in the Family," September 26, 2005, p. 3, 2000 study by Wade Mackey and Nancy Coney.

60. Reported by John Leo, "All in the Family," September 26, 2005, p. 3, 2003 study by Robert M. O'Brien and Jean Stockard.

61. "Youth Risk Behavior Surveillance – United States, 2015," *Center for Disease Control and Prevention*, June 10, 2016, pp. 63–64 (at: https://www.cdc.gov/mmwr/volumes/65/ss/pdfs/ss6506.pdf).

62. "Illiteracy Statistics," *Statistics Brain*, August 22, 2016 (at: http://www.statisticbrain.com/number-of-american-adults-who-cant-read/).

63. "Use of selected substances in the past month among persons aged 12 and over, by age, sex, race, and Hispanic origin: United States, selected years 2002-2015," *Center of Disease Control*, 2016 (at: www.cdc.gov/nchs/data/hus/2016/050.pdf).

64. "Pregnancies, Births and Abortions Among Adolescents and Young Women in the United States, 2013: National and State Trends by Age, Race and Ethnicity," *Guttmacher Institute*, August 2017 (at: https://www.guttmacher.org/sites/default/files/report_pdf/us-adolescent-pregnancy-trends-2013.pdf), pp. 11–13, 34. See also "U.S. Teenage Pregnancies, Births and Abortions, 2010: National and state Trends by Age, Race and Ethnicity," *Guttmacher Institute*, 2014, pp. 3, 9 (at: https://www.guttmacher.org/sites/default/files/report_pdf/ustp-trends10.pdf).

65. "Nonmarital Births: An Overview," *Congressional Research Service*, July 30, 2014, p 13 (at: https://fas.org/sgp/crs/misc/R43667.pdf).

66. Gertrude Shaffner Goldberg, "Revisiting the Feminization of Poverty in Cross-National Perspective," *The Feminization of Poverty in Rich Nations* (Oxford: Oxford University Press, 2010), pp. 3–6, 12.

67. "Characteristics of U.S. Abortion Patients in 2014 and Changes Since 2008" *Guttmacher Institute* (2016), p. 1, 5, 6 (at: https://www.guttmacher.org/sites/default/files/report_pdf/characteristics-us-abortion-patients-2014.pdf).

68. "United States: Races and Hispanic Origin," *United States Census Bureau* (at: https://www.census.gov/quickfacts/fact/table/US/PST045216), accessed on August 24, 2017.

69. "HIV Among African Americans," *Centers for Disease Control and Prevention* (at:https://www.cdc.gov/hiv/group/racialethnic/africanamericans/index.html), accessed on April 27, 2018.

70. "HIV Among African Americans," *Centers for Disease Control and Prevention* (at:https://www.cdc.gov/hiv/group/racialethnic/africanamericans/index.html), accessed on April 27, 2018.

71. "Criminal Victimization, 2015," *Bureau of Justice Statistics*, October, 2016 (at: https://www.bjs.gov/content/pub/pdf/cv15.pdf); "Black Victims of Violent Crime," *Bureau of Justice and Statistics*, 2007 (at: https://www.bjs.gov/content/pub/pdf/bvvc.pdf).

72. "Crime in the United States 2013: Murder–Race, Ethnicity, and Sex of Victim, by Race, Ethnicity, and Sex of Offender," *FBI Criminal Justice Information Services Division* (at: https://ucr.fbi.gov/crime-in-the-u.s/2013/crime-in-the-u.s.-2013/offenses-known-to-law-enforcement/expanded-homicide/expanded_homicide_data_table_6_murder_race_and_sex_of_vicitm_by_race_and_sex_of_offender_2013.xls), accessed on August 24, 2017.

73. "Crime in the United States 2010: Murder—Race, Ethnicity, and Sex of Victim, by Race, Ethnicity, and Sex of Offender," *FBI Criminal Justice Information Services Division* (at: https://ucr.fbi.gov/crime-in-the-u.s/2010/crime-in-the-u.s.-2010/tables/10shrtbl06.xls), accessed on August 24, 2017; "Crime in the United States 2011: Murder—Race, Ethnicity, and Sex of Victim, by Race, Ethnicity, and Sex of Offender," *FBI Criminal Justice Information Services Division* (at: https://ucr.fbi.gov/crime-in-the-u.s/2011/crime-in-the-u.s.-2011/tables/expanded-homicide-data-table-6), accessed on August 24, 2017; "Lynching, Whites and Negroes, 1882-1968," *Tuskegee University* (at: http://archive.tuskegee.edu/archive/bitstream/handle/123456789/511/Lyching%201882%201968.pdf?sequence=1&isAllowed=y), accessed on August 24, 2017.

74. Dawne Mouzon, "Why Has Marriage Declined Among Black Americans?" *Scholars Strategy Network*, October 2013 (at: http://www.scholarsstrategynetwork.org/brief/why-has-marriage-declined-among-black-americans).

75. John Blosser, "Number of Unmarried Americans Now Over 50 Percent," *Newsmax*, September 12, 2014 (at: http://www.newsmax.com/Newsfront/marriage-unmarried-adults-percentage/2014/09/12/id/594414/); D'Vera Cohn, "Barely Half of U.S. Adults are Married—A Record Low," *Pew Research Center*, December 14, 2011 (at: http://www.pewsocialtrends.org/2011/12/14/barely-half-of-u-s-adults-are-married-a-record-low/).

76. Wendy Wang, "Record Share of Americans Have Never Married," *Pew Research Center*, September 24, 2014 (at: http://www.pewsocialtrends.org/2014/09/24/record-share-of-americans-have-never-married/).

77. "Percent of Single-Parent Families by Race/Ethnicity, 2011-15," *Center for Governmental Research* (at: http://www.actrochester.org/children-youth/family-support/single-parent-families/single-parent-families-by-race-ethnicity/data-tables), accessed on August 25, 2017.

78. "Poverty in Black America," *BlackDemographics.com* (at: http://blackdemographics.com/households/poverty/), accessed on August 25, 2017.

79. Patrick F. Fagan, Andrew J. Kidd, and Henry Potrykus, "Marriage and Economic Well-Being: The Economy of the Family Rises or Falls with Marriage," *Marriage & Religion Research Institute*, May 4, 2011 (at: http://downloads.frc.org/EF/EF11E70.pdf).

80. Dawn Lee, "Single Mother Statistics," *Single Mother Guide*, August (at: https://singlemotherguide.com/single-mother-statistics/).

81. "Closing the Wage Gap is Crucial for Women of Color and Their Families," *National Women's Law Center*, November 2013 (at: https://nwlc.org/wp-content/uploads/2015/08/2013.11.13_closing_the_wage_gap_is_crucial_for_woc_and_their_families_1.pdf).

82. Lecture by George Fooshee, author of "You Can Be Financially Free," attended by Jim Garlow in Bartlesville, OK, in 1978.

83. Adapted from the Loren Eiseley story "The Star Thrower" in *The Unexpected Universe* (San Diego: Harcourt Brace & Company, 1994).

84. "Senators Lankford and Scott: Americans Should Dine With Families of Other Races" *Time Magazine*, July 28, 2016 (at: http://time.com/4428490/america-race-relations/).

85. "Population estimates, July 1, 2017," *United States Census Bureau* (at: https://www.census.gov/quickfacts/fact/table/US).

86. "Inmate Race," *Federal Bureau of Prisons*, November 25, 2017 (at: https://www.bop.gov/about/statistics/statistics_inmate_race.jsp).

87. "Statements of Principles," *Right on Crime* (at: http://rightoncrime.com/the-conservative-case-for-reform/statement-of-principles/), accessed on December 29, 2017.

88. "Time on Death Row," *Death Penalty Information Center* (at: https://deathpenaltyinfo.org/time-death-row), accessed on May 4, 2018, chart shows 190 months, which is just under 16 years.

89. "3 in 4 Former Prisoners in 30 States Arrested Within 5 Years of Release," *Bureau of Justice Statistics*, April 22, 2014 (at: https://www.bjs.gov/content/pub/press/rprts05p0510pr.cfm).

90. Chuck Colson, "Give me that old-time religion – or else," *Townhall.com*, January 14, 2005 (at: http://www.townhall.com/columnists/ChuckColson/2005/01/14/give_me_that_old-time_religionor_else).

91. "Sesame Street reaches out to 2.7 million American children with an incarcerated parent," *Pew Research Center*, June 21, 2013 (at: http://www.pewresearch.org/fact-tank/2013/06/21/sesame-street-reaches-out-to-2-7-million-american-children-with-an-incarcerated-parent/).

92. "Incarcerated—Children of Parents in Prison Impacted," *Texas Department of Criminal Justice*, July 12, 2008 (at: https://www.tdcj.state.tx.us/gokids/gokids_articles_children_impacted.html).

93. "Top voting issues in 2016 election," *Pew Research Center*, July 7, 2016 (at: http://www.people-press.org/2016/07/07/4-top-voting-issues-in-2016-election/).

94. Jeffrey Anderson, "Trump Won on the Issues," *Real Clear Politics*, November 18, 2016 (at: https://www.realclearpolitics.com/articles/2016/11/18/trump_won_on_the_issues_132383.html).

95. Jeffrey Anderson, "Trump Won on the Issues," *Real Clear Politics*, November 18, 2016 (at: https://www.realclearpolitics.com/articles/2016/11/18/trump_won_on_the_issues_132383.html).

96. "Immigration," *Gallup* (at: http://news.gallup.com/poll/1660/immigration.aspx), accessed on January 8, 2018.

97. Dave Levinthal, "Journalists shower Hillary Clinton with campaign cash," *The Center for Public Integrity*, October 17, 2016 (at: https://www.publicintegrity.org/2016/10/17/20330/journalists-shower-hillary-clinton-campaign-cash).

98. Antonia Blumberg, "Thousands Of Religious Leaders Speak Out Against Trump's 'Extreme Vetting' Proposal," *Huffington Post*, January 27, 2017 (at: https://www.huffingtonpost.com/entry/thousands-of-religious-leaders-speak-out-against-trumps-extreme-vetting-proposal_us_588bb5a1e4b0b065cbbbeea5).

99. Laurie Goodstein, "Christian Leaders Denounce Trump's Plan to Favor Christian Refugees," *The New York Times*, January 29, 2017 (at: https://www.nytimes.com/2017/01/29/us/christian-leaders-denounce-trumps-plan-to-favor-christian-immigrants.html).

100. Daniel Burke, "Religious leaders condemn Trump's immigration order. But who's listening?" *CNN Politics*, January 31, 2017 (at: http://www.cnn.com/2017/01/30/politics/trump-immigration-religion/index.html).

101. Kimberly Winston, "Refugee ban, border wall: Religious leaders respond," *Religion News Service*, January 25, 2017 (at: http://religionnews.com/2017/01/25/refugee-ban-border-wall-religious-leaders-respond/).

102. Maya Rhodan, "Evangelicals Battle Over 'Biblical' Immigration," *Time*, October 23, 2013 (at: http://swampland.time.com/2013/10/22/evangelicals-battle-over-biblical-immigration/).

103. Daniel Burke, "Religious leaders condemn Trump's immigration order. But who's listening?" *CNN Politics*, January 31, 2017 (at: http://www.cnn.com/2017/01/30/politics/trump-immigration-religion/index.html).

104. Jerald Stinson, "Why I Don't Believe in Borders," *United Church of Christ*, November 28, 1993 (at: http://www.ucc.org/justice/immigration/worship/JStinsonSermon.html).

105. "See, for example, *Blue Letter Bible* where a search for "love" in the New Testament NKJV lists 214 occurrences (at: https://www.blueletterbible.org/search/search.cfm?Criteria=love&t=NKJV&csr=9#s=s_primary_0_1); similar numbers are reported for the same search in other versions.

106. See C. S. Lewis' *The Four Loves* for a further breakdown and explanation of the four different Greek ideas of love.

107. Kimberly Winston, "Refugee ban, border wall: Religious leaders respond," *Religion News Service*, January 25, 2017 (at: http://religionnews.com/2017/01/25/refugee-ban-border-wall-religious-leaders-respond/).

108. Kimberly Winston, "Refugee ban, border wall: Religious leaders respond," *Religion News Service*, January 25, 2017 (at: http://religionnews.com/2017/01/25/refugee-ban-border-wall-religious-leaders-respond/).

109. Israel Zangwill, *The Melting Pot* (New York: The MacMillan Company, 1909), Act 1, p. 37.

110. Theodore Roosevelt, *Fear God and Take Your Own Part* (New York: George H. Doran Company, 1916), pp. 361–362, "Address delivered before the Knights of Columbus, Carnegie Hall, New York," October 12, 1915.

111. Herbert M. Beck, *Aliens' Text Book on Citizenship: Laws of Naturalization of the United States* (Camden, NJ: Sinnickson Chew & Sons Co., 1919), p. 7.

112. See, for example, "Which European countries offer the most social benefits to migrants?," *EuroNews*, September 16, 2015 (at: http://www.euronews.com/2015/09/16/which-european-countries-offer-the-most-social-benefits-to-migrants).

113. See, for example, "Migrants refuse to claim asylum in Denmark – because they don't get enough benefits," *The Express*, September 17, 2015 (at: https://www.express.co.uk/news/world/605252/Migrants-Denmark-Finland-Sweden-Marwen-el-Mohammed-TV2-News-Immigration-Refugee); "Migrants housed in Latvia moan their benefits are not enough and 'this is not Britain,'" *The Express*, December 23, 2015 (at: https://www.express.co.uk/news/world/623131/Migrant-crisis-Latvia-refugees-Europe-cold-welfare-system-not-generous); and others.

114. Justin Huggler, "Migrant Crime in Germany rises by 50 per cent, new figures show," *The Telegraph*, April 25, 2017 (at: http://www.telegraph.co.uk/news/2017/04/25/migrant-crime-germany-rises-50-per-cent-new-figures-show/); and "Migrants linked to 69,000 would-be or actual crimes in Germany in first three months of 2016: police," *Reuters*, June 7, 2016 (at: https://www.reuters.com/article/us-europe-migrants-germany-crime/migrants-linked-to-69000-would-be-or-actual-crimes-in-germany-in-first-three-months-of-2016-police-idUSKCN0YT28V); and others.

115. Joe Alton, "Sweden Is In A Welfare State Of Delusion," *The Daily Caller*, February 22, 2017 (at: http://dailycaller.com/2017/02/22/sweden-is-in-a-welfare-state-of-delusion/).

116. Joe Alton, "Sweden Is In A Welfare State Of Delusion," *The Daily Caller*, February 22, 2017 (at: http://dailycaller.com/2017/02/22/sweden-is-in-a-welfare-state-of-delusion/).

117. "EU takes action against eastern states for refusing to take refugees," *The Guardian*, June 13, 2017 (at: https://www.theguardian.com/world/2017/jun/13/eu-takes-action-against-eastern-states-for-refusing-to-take-refugees).

118. Lizzie Dearden, "Poland's Prime Minister says country will accept no refugees as EU threatens legal action over quotas," *Independent*, May 17, 2017 (at: http://www.independent.co.uk/news/world/europe/poland-no-refugees-eu-legal-action-infringement-quotas-resettlement-beata-szydlo-commission-a7741236.html).

119. Information conveyed to Mr. David Barton by a Polish cabinet member involved in the nation's domestic policy in meeting on September 20, 2017.

120. "Crime and Criminal Justice: Statistics Illustrated," *Eurostat*, 2015 (at: http://ec.europa.eu/eurostat/web/crime/statistics-illustrated).

121. Liam Clancy, "No Refugees, No Terror for Poland, Hungary," *WND*, July 5, 2017 (at: http://www.wnd.com/2017/06/no-refugees-no-terror-for-poland-hungary/).

122. Dorota Bartyzel, "Poland Can't Get Enough of Ukrainian Migrants," *Bloomberg Markets*, March 6, 2017 (at: https://www.bloomberg.com/news/articles/2017-03-06/million-migrants-fleeing-putin-score-a-policy-jackpot-for-poland).

123. Dorota Bartyzel, "Poland Can't Get Enough of Ukrainian Migrants," *Bloomberg Markets*, March 6, 2017 (at: https://www.bloomberg.com/news/articles/2017-03-06/million-migrants-fleeing-putin-score-a-policy-jackpot-for-poland).

124. "Declaration of Independence: A Transcription," *National Archives* (at: https://www.archives.gov/founding-docs/declaration-transcript) (accessed on January 8, 2018).

125. Patrick Young, "The Immigrants Among the Founding Fathers," *Long Island Wins*, July 3, 2014 (at: https://longislandwins.com/news/national/the-immigrants-among-the-founding-fathers/).

126. Benjamin Franklin, *The Complete Works of Benjamin Franklin* (New York: G. P. Putnam's Sons, 1887), Vol. II, pp. 297–298, to Peter Collison, May 9, 1753.

127. Benjamin Franklin, *The Complete Works of Benjamin Franklin* (New York: G. P. Putnam's Sons, 1887), Vol. II, pp. 299, to Peter Collison, May 9, 1753.

128. Thomas Jefferson, *Notes on the State of Virginia* (Boston: David Carlisle, 1801), pp. 129–130, Query VIII.

129. Thomas Jefferson, *Notes on the State of Virginia* (Boston: David Carlisle, 1801), p. 129, Query VIII.

130. Thomas Jefferson, *The Writings of Thomas Jefferson* (Washington, DC: The Thomas Jefferson Memorial Association, 1907), Vol. XV, p. 140, to George Flower, September 12, 1817.
131. Alexander Hamilton, *The Works of Alexander Hamilton* (New York: G. P. Putnam's Sons, 1904), Vol. VIII, p. 289, "Examination of Jefferson's Message to Congress of December 7, 1801, No. VIII."
132. Alexander Hamilton, *The Works of Alexander Hamilton* (New York: G. P. Putnam's Sons, 1904), Vol. VIII, p. 291, "Examination of Jefferson's Message to Congress of December 7, 1801, No. VIII."
133. James Madison, *The Writings of James Madison* (New York: G. P. Putnam's Sons, 1903), Vol. IV, p. 147, "Thursday, August 9, in Convention, 1787."
134. James Madison, *The Writings of James Madison* (New York: G. P. Putnam's Sons, 1903), Vol. IV, p. 147, "Thursday, August 9, in Convention, 1787."
135. Fisher Ames, *The Works of Fisher Ames* (Boston: Little, Brown and Company, 1854), Vol. I, p. 247, to Christopher Gore, December 18, 1798.
136. Rufus King, *The Life and Correspondence of Rufus King* (New York: G. P. Putnam's Sons, 1895), Vol. II, p. 348, to the Secretary of State, June 14, 1798.
137. Rufus King, *The Life and Correspondence of Rufus King* (New York: G. P. Putnam's Sons, 1895), Vol. II, p. 371, to Col. Pickering, June 19, 1798.
138. Cf. "making proof to the satisfaction of such Court that he is a person of good character"; "An act to establish an uniform Rule of Naturalization" (March 26, 1790), Text retrieved from: http://www.indiana.edu/~kdhist/H105-documents-web/week08/ naturalization1790.html; and Cf. "Thirdly. . . . he has behaved as a man of a good moral character, attached to the principles of the constitution of the United States, and well-disposed to the good order and happiness of the same"; "An act to establish an uniform rule of Naturalization; and to repeal the act heretofore passed on that subject" (January 29, 1795), Text retrieved from: http://www.indiana .edu/~kdhist/H105-documents-web/week08/naturalization1790.html
139. Cf. "taking the oath or affirmation prescribed by law to support the Constitution of the United States"; "An act to establish an uniform Rule of Naturalization" (March 26, 1790), Text retrieved from: http://www.indiana.edu/~kdhist/H105-documents-web/week08/natu- ralization1790.html
140. Cf. "First. He shall have declared . . . his intention to become a citizen of the United States, and to renounce forever all allegiance and fidelity to any foreign prince, potentate, state, or sovereignty whatever, and particularly, by name, the prince, potentate, state or sovereignty whereof such alien may, at that time, be a citizen or subject"; "An act to establish an uni- form rule of Naturalization; and to repeal the act heretofore passed on that subject" (Janu- ary 29, 1795), Text retrieved from: http://www.indiana.edu/~kdhist/H105-documents-web/ week08/naturalization1790.html
141. Cf. "Secondly. . . . that he will support the constitution of the United States; and that he does absolutely and entirely renounce and abjure all allegiance and fidelity to any foreign prince, potentate, state, or sovereignty"; "An act to establish an uniform rule of Natural- ization; and to repeal the act heretofore passed on that subject" (January 29, 1795), Text retrieved from: http://www.indiana.edu/~kdhist/H105-documents-web/week08/naturaliza- tion1790.html
142. Cf. "Fourthly. In case the alien applying to be admitted to citizenship shall have borne any hereditary title, or been of any of the orders of nobility . . . [shall] make an express renunciation of his title or order of nobility . . . ."; "An act to establish an uniform rule of Naturalization; and to repeal the act heretofore passed on that subject" (January 29, 1795), Text retrieved from: http://www.indiana.edu/~kdhist/H105-documents-web/week08/natu- ralization1790.html
143. Cf. "Secondly. . . . he has resided within the United States, five years at least, and within the state or territory, where such court is at the time held, one year at least"; "An act to establish an uniform rule of Naturalization; and to repeal the act heretofore passed on that subject" (January 29, 1795), Text retrieved from: http://www.indiana.edu/~kdhist/H105- documents-web/week08/naturalization1790.html
144. Cf. "And the children of such person so naturalized, dwelling within the United States, being under the age of twenty one years at the time of such naturalization, shall also be

considered as citizens of the United States."; "An act to establish an uniform Rule of Naturalization" (March 26, 1790), Text retrieved from: http://www.indiana.edu/~kdhist/H105-documents-web/week08/naturalization1790.html

145. Cf. "Provided, that the right of citizenship shall not descend to persons whose fathers have never been resident in the United States"; "An act to establish an uniform Rule of Naturalization" (March 26, 1790), Text retrieved from: http://www.indiana.edu/~kdhist/H105-documents-web/week08/naturalization1790.html; and Cf. "SEC. 3. And be it further enacted, that the children of persons duly naturalized, dwelling within the United States, and being under the age of twenty-one years, at the time of such naturalization, and the children of citizens of the United States, born out of the limits and jurisdiction of the United States, shall be considered as citizens of the United States: Provided, That the right of citizenship shall not descend to persons, whose fathers have never been resident of the United States"; "An act to establish an uniform rule of Naturalization; and to repeal the act heretofore passed on that subject" (January 29, 1795), Text retrieved from: http://www.indiana.edu/~kdhist/H105-documents-web/week08/naturalization1790.html

146. Cf. "SECTION 1 . . . it shall be lawful for the President of the United States at any time during the continuance of this act, to order all such aliens as he shall judge dangerous to the peace and safety of the United States, or shall have reasonable grounds to suspect are concerned in any treasonable or secret machinations against the government thereof, to depart out of the territory of the United States . . . and shall never after be admitted to become a citizen of the United States . . . "; "An Act Concerning Aliens" (June 25, 1798), Text retrieved from: https://www.ourdocuments.gov/doc.php?flash=false&doc=16&page=transcript.

147. Cf. "SEC. 3. And be it further enacted, That every master or commander of any ship or vessel which shall come into any port of the United States after the first day of July next, shall immediately on his arrival make report in writing to the collector or other chief officer of the customs of such port, of all aliens, if any, on board his vessel, specifying their names, age, the place of nativity, the country from which they shall have come, the nation to which they belong and owe allegiance, their occupation and a description of their persons, as far as he shall be informed thereof, and on failure, every such master and commander shall forfeit and pay three hundred dollars, for the payment whereof on default of such master or commander, such vessel shall also be holden, and may by such collector or other officer of the customs be detained. And it shall be the duty of such collector or other officer of the customs, forthwith to transmit to the office of the department of state true copies of all such returns."; "An Act Concerning Aliens" (June 25, 1798), Text retrieved from: https://www.ourdocuments.gov/doc.php?flash=false&doc=16&page=transcript.

148. Cf. "Provided also, that no person heretofore proscribed by any States, shall be admitted a citizen as aforesaid, except by an Act of the Legislature of the State in which such person was proscribed"; "An act to establish an uniform Rule of Naturalization" (March 26, 1790), Text retrieved from: http://www.indiana.edu/~kdhist/H105-documents-web/week08/naturalization1790.html

149. *Time* (October 13, 1952), Dwight Eisenhower, "Eisenhower on Communism."

150. Matthew Spalding, "From Pluribus to Unum: Immigration and the Founding Fathers," *Policy Review* (Winter, 1994) (at: https://www.thefreelibrary.com/From+pluribus+to+unum%3A+immigration+and+the+Founding+Fathers.-a015028217).

151. *Henderson v. Mayor of City of New York*, 92 U.S. 259 (1875) and *Chy Lung v. Freeman*, 92 U.S. 275 (1876).

152. Cf. "SEC. 7. That the office of superintendent of immigration is hereby created [1891] and established, and the President, by and with the advice and consent of the Senate, is authorized and directed to appoint such officer"; "An act in amendment to the various acts relative to immigration and the importation of aliens under contract or agreement to perform labor," *Statutes at Large*, Fifty-First Congress, Session II, Chapter 551 (March 3, 1891), 1085.

153. Cf. Sections 1 and 3 of "An act supplementary to the acts in relation to immigration," *Statutes at Large*, Forty-Third Congress, Sessions II, Chapter 141 (March 3, 1875), 477.

154. Cf. Section 5 of "An act supplementary to the acts in relation to immigration," *Statutes at Large*, Forty-Third Congress, Sessions II, Chapter 141 (March 3, 1875), 477.

155. Cf. Section 1, "All idiots, insane persons, paupers or persons likely to become a public charge, persons suffering from a loathsome or a dangerous contagious disease, persons who have been convicted of a felony or other infamous crime or misdemeanor involving moral turpitude, polygamists, and also any person whose ticket or passage is paid for with the money of another or who is assisted by others to come"; "An act in amendment to the various acts relative to immigration and the importation of aliens under contract or agreement to perform labor," *Statutes at Large* (March 3, 1891), 1084.

156. Cf. "SEC. 3. That it shall be deemed a violation of said act of February twenty-sixth, eighteen hundred and eighty-five, to assist or encourage the importation or migration of any alien by promise of employment through advertisements printed and published in any foreign country" and Section 8, "It shall be the duty of the aforesaid officers and agents of such vessel to adopt due precautions to prevent the landing of any alien immigrant at anyplace or time other than that designated by the inspection officers"; "An act in amendment to the various acts relative to immigration and the importation of aliens under contract or agreement to perform labor," *Statutes at Large* (March 3, 1891), 1084–1086.

157. Cf. "SEC. 10. That all aliens who may unlawfully come to the United States shall, if practicable, be immediately sent back on the vessel by which they were brought in" and "SEC. 11. That any alien who shall come into the United States in violation of law may be returned as by law provided, at any time within one year thereafter, at the expense of the person or persons, vessel, transportation company, or corporation bringing such alien into the United States, and if that cannot be done, then at the expense of the United States" and "any alien who becomes a public charge within one year after his arrival in the United States from causes existing prior to his landing therein shall be deemed to have come in violation of law and shall be returned as aforesaid."; "An act in amendment to the various acts relative to immigration and the importation of aliens under contract or agreement to perform labor," *Statutes at Large* (March 3, 1891), 1086.

158. Cf. Section 8, "That the Secretary of the Treasury may prescribe rules for inspection along the borders of Canada, British Columbia, and. Mexico so as not to obstruct or unnecessarily delay, impede, or annoy passengers in ordinary travel between said countries"; "An act in amendment to the various acts relative to immigration and the importation of aliens under contract or agreement to perform labor," *Statutes at Large* (March 3, 1891), 1086.

159. Cf. *Babylonian Talmud: Tractate Yebamoth*, Folio 24b, "Our Rabbis learnt: No proselytes will be accepted in the days of the Messiah. In the same manner no proselytes were accepted in the days of David nor in the days of Solomon. Said R. Eleazar: 'What Scriptural [support is there for this view]? — Behold he shall be a proselyte who is converted for my own sake,' he who lives with you shall be settled among you, he only who 'lives with you' in your poverty shall be settled among you; but no other."; and the footnote that explains that such times were when Israel was, "Prosperous and Prospective proselytes will be attracted by worldly considerations"; Retrieved at: http://www.come-and-hear.com/yebamoth/yebamoth_24.html#24b_25.

160. Calvin Coolidge, "Remarks to a Delegation of Foreign Born Citizens at the White House," *The American Presidency Project*, October 16, 1924 (at: http://www.presidency.ucsb.edu/ws/index.php?pid=24181).

161. Bruce Thornton, "Melting Pots and Salad Bowls," *Hoover Digest*, October 26, 2012 (at: https://www.hoover.org/research/melting-pots-and-salad-bowls).

162. Benjamin Harrison, "March 4, 1889: Inaugural Address, *Miller Center* (at: https://miller-center.org/the-presidency/presidential-speeches/march-4-1889-inaugural-address).

163. Jens Manuel Korgstad, Jeffrey S. Passell, D'Vera Cohn, "5 facts about illegal immigration in the U.S." *Pew Research Center*, April 27, 2017 (at: http://www.pewresearch.org/fact-tank/2017/04/27/5-facts-about-illegal-immigration-in-the-u-s/); "The U.S. Immigration Debate," *Council for Foreign Relations*, September 6, 2017 (at: https://www.cfr.org/backgrounder/us-immigration-debate-0?gclid=EAIaIQobChMIuKfdwOyZ2AIVDpl-Ch3NAQ7xEAAYASAAEgImIvD_BwE).

164. Jens Manuel Korgstad, Jeffrey S. Passell, D'Vera Cohn, "5 facts about illegal immigration in the U.S." *Pew Research Center*, April 27, 2017 (at: http://www.pewresearch.org/fact-tank/2017/04/27/5-facts-about-illegal-immigration-in-the-u-s/).

165. Jeffrey s. Passel, D'Vera Cohn, "2. State unauthorized immigrant populations," *Pew Research Center*, September 20, 2016 (at: http://www.pewhispanic.org/2016/09/20/2-state-unauthorized-immigrant-populations).

166. Jens Manuel Korgstad, Jeffrey S. Passell, D'Vera Cohn, "5 facts about illegal immigration in the U.S." *Pew Research Center*, April 27, 2017 (at: http://www.pew research.org/fact-tank/2017/04/27/5-facts-about-illegal-immigration-in-the-u-s/).

167. Jens Manuel Korgstad, Jeffrey S. Passell, D'Vera Cohn, "5 facts about illegal immigration in the U.S." *Pew Research Center*, April 27, 2017 (at: http://www.pew research.org/fact-tank/2017/04/27/5-facts-about-illegal-immigration-in-the-u-s/).

168. Jens Manuel Korgstad, Jeffrey S. Passell, D'Vera Cohn, "5 facts about illegal immigration in the U.S." *Pew Research Center*, April 27, 2017 (at: http://www.pew research.org/fact-tank/2017/04/27/5-facts-about-illegal-immigration-in-the-u-s/).

169. Jens Manuel Korgstad, Jeffrey S. Passell, D'Vera Cohn, "5 facts about illegal immigration in the U.S." *Pew Research Center*, April 27, 2017 (at: http://www.pew research.org/fact-tank/2017/04/27/5-facts-about-illegal-immigration-in-the-u-s/).

170. See, for example, "Nearly 1 million Christians reportedly martyred for their faith in the last decade," *FoxNews*, January 17, 2017 (at: http://www.foxnews.com/world/2017/01/17/nearly-1-million-christians-reportedly-martyred-for-their-faith-in-last-decade.html); "'90,000 Christian martyrs annually' claim disputed," *World Watch Monitor*, January 20, 2017 (at: https://www .worldwatchmonitor.org/2017/01/90000-christian-martyrs-annually-claim-disputed/); "Persecution of Christians in 2016," *Center for the Study of Global Christianity* (at: https://us11. campaign-archive.com/?e=[UNIQID]&u=060e80f6eebfc8804f8049bad&id=c0d75f13c6).

171. Walter Russell Mead, "The Plight of the Middle East's Christians," *Wall Street Journal*, May 15, 2015 (at: https://www.wsj.com/articles/the-plight-of-the-middle-easts-christians-1431700075).

172. "Christians in the Middle East: And then there were none," *The Economist*, January 2, 2016 (at: https://www.economist.com/news/middle-east-and-africa/21684795-fed-up-and-fearful-christians-are-leaving-middle-east-and-then-there-were).

173. Phillip Connor, "U.S. admits record number of Muslim refugees in 2016," *Pew Research Center*, October 5, 2016 (at: http://www.pewresearch.org/fact-tank/2016/10/05/u-s-admits-record-number-of-muslim-refugees-in-2016/).

174. Phillip Connor, "U.S. admits record number of Muslim refugees in 2016," *Pew Research Center*, October 5, 2016 (at: http://www.pewresearch.org/fact-tank/2016/10/05/u-s-admits-record-number-of-muslim-refugees-in-2016/).

175. David Brody, "Brody File Exclusive: President Trump Says Persecuted Christians Will Be Given Priority as Refugees," *CBN News*, January 27, 2017 (at: https://www1.cbn.com/the-brodyfile/archive/2017/01/27/brody-file-exclusive-president-trump-says-persecuted-christians-will-be-given-priority-as-refugees); Max Greenwood, "Trump: Persecuted Christian refugees will get priority," *The Hill*, January 27, 2017 (at: http://thehill.com/homenews/administration/316586-trump-persecuted-christian-refugees-are-priority).

176. Daniel Burke, "Trump says US will prioritize Christian refugees," *CNN*, January 30, 2017 (at: http://www.cnn.com/2017/01/27/politics/trump-christian-refugees/index.html). See also, Hazel Torres, "Trump Vows To Prioritize Persecuted Christians' Entry to U.S. As Refugees: 'They've Been Horribly Treated,'" *Christian Today*, February 1, 2017 (at: https://www .christiantoday.com/article/trump-vows-to-prioritise-persecuted-christians-entry-to-u-s-as-refugees-theyve-been-horribly-treated/104320.htm).

177. Nicholas Kulish and Fernanda Santos, "Illegal Border Crossings Appear to Drop Under Trump," *New York Times*, March 8, 2017 (at: https://www.nytimes.com/2017/03/08/us/trump-immigration-border.html).

178. Emily Badger, "What happened to the millions of immigrants granted legal status under Ronald Reagan?" *The Washington Post*, November 26, 2014 (at: https://www.washingtonpost.com/news/wonk/wp/2014/11/26/what-happened-to-the-millions-of-immigrants-granted-legal-status-under-ronald-reagan/). See also Brad Plumer, "Congress tried to fix immigration back in 1986. Why did it fail?" *The Washington Post*, January 30, 2013 (at: https://www.washingtonpost.com/news/wonk/wp/2013/01/30/in-1986-congress-tried-to-solve-immigration-why-didnt-it-work/); "A Regan Legacy: Amnesty for Illegal Immigrants," *NPR*, July 4, 2010 (at: https://www.npr.org/templates/story/story.php?storyId=128303672).

179. Daniel Burke, "Pope suggests Trump 'is not Christian,'" *CNN*, February 18, 2016 (at: http://www.cnn.com/2016/02/18/politics/pope-francis-trump-christian-wall/index.html).

180. Elizabeth Roberts, "Report: Mexico was second deadliest country in 2016," *CNN*, May 10, 2017 (at: http://www.cnn.com/2017/05/09/americas/mexico-second-deadliest-conflict-2016/index.html).

181. Matthew Bell, "Christian leaders are coming out against Trump's travel ban," *Public Radio International*, February 10, 2017 (at: https://www.pri.org/stories/2017-02-10/christian-leaders-are-coming-out-against-trump-s-travel-ban).

182. "Political Apologies: Chronological List," *upenn.edu*, January 23, 2003 (at: http://www.upenn.edu/pnc/politicalapologies.html).

183. Stuart Taylor, "U.S. Says Army Shielded Barbie; Offers Its 'Regrets' to the French," *The New York Times*, August 17, 1983 (at: http://www.nytimes.com/1983/08/17/world/us-says-army-shielded-barbie-offers-its-regrets-to-the-french.html). See also, Danny Lewis, "Five Times the United States Officially Apologized," *Smithsonian.com*, May 27, 2016 (at: https://www.smithsonianmag.com/smart-news/five-times-united-states-officially-apologized-180959254/).

184. Danny Lewis, "Five Times the United States Officially Apologized," *Smithsonian.com*, May 27, 2016 (at: https://www.smithsonianmag.com/smart-news/five-times-united-states-officially-apologized-180959254/).

185. Danny Lewis, "Five Times the United States Officially Apologized," *Smithsonian.com*, May 27, 2016 (at: https://www.smithsonianmag.com/smart-news/five-times-united-states-officially-apologized-180959254/).

186. "S.Res. 39 (109th): Lynching Victims Senate Apology resolution," 2005 (at: https://www.govtrack.us/congress/bills/109/sres39/text).

187. Danny Lewis, "Five Times the United States Officially Apologized," *Smithsonian.com*, May 27, 2016 (at: https://www.smithsonianmag.com/smart-news/five-times-united-states-officially-apologized-180959254/).

188. "Competing Worldviews Influence Today's Christians," *Barna* (May 9, 2017) (at: https://www.barna.com/research/competing-worldviews-influence-todays-christians/).

189. "What is BDS?," *BDS Movement*, accessed on January 5, 2018 (at: https://bdsmovement.net/).

190. Among the things developed by Israelis are driver-assistance systems that avoid collisions, GPS based navigation, the USB flash drive, laser keyboards, instant messaging, voice-over-internet protocol, drugs for the treatment of Parkinson's and multiple sclerosis, biological pest control, robotic spinal surgery, and dozens of other major inventions and discoveries.

191. "Poll: Arabs Prefer to Live in Israel, Not 'Palestine,'" *United With Israel* (December 22, 2014) (at: https://unitedwithisrael.org/palestinians-want-to-live-in-israel-not-under-the-pa/).

192. Cf. Mordechai Nisan, "The Two State Delusion," *Middle East Quarterly*, Volume 21: Number 1 (Winter 2014) (at: http://www.meforum.org/3679/two-state-delusion); Liora Chartouni, "70 Years after UN Resolution 181: An Assessment," *Jerusalem Center for Public Affairs,* November 26, 2017 (at: http://jcpa.org/article/70-years-un-resolution-181-assessment/); "The Palestinians Want Peace—Just Not With a Jewish State," *The Dennis Prager Show*, September 27, 2017 (at: http://www.dennisprager.com/the-palestinians-want-peace-just-not-with-a-jewish-state/).

193. "Foreign Terrorist Organizations," *U.S. Department of State* (at: https://www.state.gov/j/ct/rls/other/des/123085.htm), accessed on January 5, 2018; "Major Palestinian Terror Attacks Since Oslo," *Jewish Virtual Library* (at: http://www.jewishvirtuallibrary.org/major-palestinian-terror-attacks-since-oslo), accessed on January 5, 2018.

194. "3379. Elimination of all forms of racial discrimination," *General Assembly—Thirtieth Session: Resolutions adopted on the reports of the Third Committee* (November 10, 1975) (at: https://documents-dds-ny.un.org/doc/RESOLUTION/GEN/NR0/000/92/IMG/NR000092.pdf?OpenElement).

195. "Full text of May 2017 UNESCO resolution on 'Occupied Palestine,'" *The Times of Israel*, May 1, 2017, (at: https://www.timesofisrael.com/full-text-of-may-2017-unesco-resolution-on-occupied-palestine/); "On Independence Day, UNESCO okays resolution denying Israeli claims to Jerusalem," *The Times of Israel*, May 2, 2017 (at: https://www.timesofisrael.com/on-independence-day-unesco-okays-resolution-ignoring-jewish-links-to-jerusalem/).

196. Jerusalem Embassy Act of 1995, Public Law 104–45, Section 1322 (retrieved from: https://www.congress.gov/104/plaws/publ45/PLAW-104publ45.pdf).

197. "Statement by President Trump on Jerusalem," *The White House,* December 6, 2017 (at: https://www.whitehouse.gov/briefings-statements/statement-president-trump-jerusalem/).

198. "Fall 2014 Campus Activity Report," *Israel on Campus Coalition* (2014), p. 2 (at: https://israelcc.org/wp-content/uploads/2017/01/ICC-Fall-2014-Activity-Report.pdf).

199. Mitchell Bard, "West Bank Security Fence," *Jewish Virtual Library,* 2017 (at: http://www.jewishvirtuallibrary.org/background-and-overview-of-israel-s-security-fence).

200. Judah Ari Gross, "Masters of disaster, IDF field hospital may be recognized as world's best," *The Times of Israel,* October 18, 2016 (at: https://www.timesofisrael.com/masters-of-disaster-idf-field-hospital-may-be-recognized-as-worlds-best/).

201. Judah Ari Gross, "UN ranks IDF emergency medical team as 'No. 1 in the world,'" *The Times of Israel,* November 13, 2016 (at: https://www.timesofisrael.com/un-ranks-idf-emergency-medical-team-as-no-1-in-the-world/).

202. "Profile: Arab League," *British Broadcasting Corporation,* August 24, 2017 (at: http://www.bbc.com/news/world-middle-east-15747941).

203. See, Joshua Keating and Chris Kirk, "The Middle East Friendship Chart," *Slate,* July 17, 2014 (at: http://www.slate.com/blogs/the_world_/2014/07/17/the_middle_east_friendship_chart.html); Michael Broning, "The End of the Arab League?" *Foreign Affairs,* March 30, 2014 (at: https://www.foreignaffairs.com/articles/persian-gulf/2014-03-30/end-arab-league).

204. See the Edict of Thessalonica in Clyde Pharr's *The Theodosian Code and Novels, and the Sirmondian Constitutions* (Union, NJ: Law Book Exchange, 2001), 16.1.2.

205. For an overview see, "Jews in America: President John Adams Embraces A Jewish Homeland," *Jewish Virtual Library* (2018), at: http://www.jewishvirtuallibrary.org/president-john-adams-embraces-a-jewish-homeland-1819-2.

206. For biographical sketch see, "Mordecai Manuel Noah," *Jewish Virtual Library* (1996), at: http://www.jewishvirtuallibrary.org/mordecai-manuel-noah.

207. Charles D Smith, *Palestine and the Arab-Israeli Conflict: A History with Documents* (Bedford-St. Martins, 2000), p 80.

208. Shelomo Alfassa, *Reference Guide to the Nazia and Arabs During the Holocaust* (New York: International Sephardic Leadership Council, 2006), p. 25.

209. "Hitler book bestseller in Turkey," *British Broadcasting Corporation,* March 18, 2005) (at: http://news.bbc.co.uk/2/hi/europe/4361733.stm).

210. "Full official record: What the mufti said to Hitler," *The Times of Israel,* October 21, 2015 (at: https://www.timesofisrael.com/full-official-record-what-the-mufti-said-to-hitler/); "Italy," *The Holocaust Encyclopedia* (New Haven: Yale University Press, 2001), p. 330.

211. Robert Wistrich, *From Ambivalence to Betrayal: The Left, The Jews, and Israel* (Lincoln University of Nebraska Press, 2012), p. 541.

212. See, "Franklin Roosevelt Administration: Letter to King of Saudi Arabia Regarding Palestine," *Jewish Virtual Library,* April 5, 1945 (at: http://www.jewishvirtuallibrary.org/president-roosevelt-letter-to-king-of-saudi-arabia-regarding-palestine-april-1945); Rabbi Benjamin Blech, "Israel & FDR's Secret Correspondence with the Saudi King," *Aish,* April 19, 2015 (at: http://www.aish.com/h/iid/Israel--FDRs-Secret-Correspondence-with-the-Saudi-King.html); Rafael Medoff, "What FDR said about Jews in private," *Los Angeles Times,* April 7, 2013 (at: http://articles.latimes.com/2013/apr/07/opinion/la-oe-medoff-roosevelt-holocaust-20130407).

213. "President Truman's Decision to Recognize Israel," *Jerusalem Center for Public Affaris,* May 1, 2008 (at: http://jcpa.org/article/president-truman's-decision-to-recognize-israel/).

214. Haj Amin al-Husseini quoted in Michael D. Evans, *Jerusalem Betrayed* (Dallas: World Publishing, 1997), Chapter 10: The Struggle for Autonomy."

215. "Palestine Liberation Organization: The Original Palestine National Charter," *Jewish Virtual Library,* 1964 (at: http://www.jewishvirtuallibrary.org/the-original-palestine-national-charter-1964).

216. "Israel-Arab Peace Process: The Khartoum Resolutions," *Jewish Virtual Library,* September 1, 1967 (at: http://www.jewishvirtuallibrary.org/the-khartoum-resolutions).

217. "Israel-Arab Peace Process: The Khartoum Resolutions," *Jewish Virtual Library,* September 1, 1967 (at: http://www.jewishvirtuallibrary.org/the-khartoum-resolutions).

218. "UNSC Resolutions on Israel: Resolution 242," *Jewish Virtual Library,* November 22, 1967 (at: http://www.jewishvirtuallibrary.org/un-security-council-resolution-242).

219. Justin Martyr, *The Dialogue with Trypho* (London: Society for Promoting Christian Knowledge, 1930), CXXXIII.6. 275.

220. John Chrysostom, "Against the Jews: Homily 1," *Tertullian.org* (2011), at: http://www
.tertullian.org/fathers/chrysostom_adversus_judaeos_01_homily1.htm.

221. John Chrysostom, "Against the Jews: Homily 1," *Tertullian.org* (2011), at: http://www
.tertullian.org/fathers/chrysostom_adversus_judaeos_01_homily1.htm.

222. John Chrysostom, "Against the Jews: Homily 6," *Tertullian.org* (2011), at: http://www
.tertullian.org/fathers/chrysostom_adversus_judaeos_06_homily6.htm.

223. *A Select Library of Nicene and Post-Nicene Fathers of the Christian Church* (New York:
Charles Scribner's Sons, 1900), Vol. XIV, p. 54, "From the Letter of the Emperor to all
those no present at the Council."

224. Jacob Rader, *The Jew in the Medieval World, a Source Book, 315-1791* (Cincinnati: The
Sinai Press, 1937), 1. I. 4.

225. Eusebius Pamphilus, *The Life of the Blessed Emperor Constantine* (Boston: Samuel Bagster
and Sons, 1845) Book III, Chapter XVIII, 129.

226. Jacob Rader, *The Jew in the Medieval World, a Source Book, 315-1791* (Cincinnati: The Sinai
Press, 1937), 1. II. 4.

227. Jacob Rader, *The Jew in the Medieval World, a Source Book, 315-1791* (Cincinnati: The Sinai
Press, 1937), 1. III. 5.

228. Jacob Rader, *The Jew in the Medieval World, a Source Book, 315-1791* (Cincinnati: The Sinai
Press, 1937), 1. IV. 6–7.

229. Jacob Rader, *The Jew in the Medieval World, a Source Book, 315-1791* (Cincinnati: The Sinai
Press, 1937), 4. I. 20–22.

230. Jacob Rader, *The Jew in the Medieval World, a Source Book, 315-1791* (Cincinnati: The Sinai
Press, 1937), 4. II. 22.

231. "Encyclopedia Judaica: Forced Baptism," *The Jewish Virtual Library,* 2008 (at: http://www
.jewishvirtuallibrary.org/forced-baptism).

232. Jacob Rader, *The Jew in the Medieval World, a Source Book, 315-1791* (Cincinnati: The Sinai
Press, 1937), 7. Title XXIV. Law XI. 39.

233. Jacob Rader, *The Jew in the Medieval World, a Source Book, 315-1791* (Cincinnati: The Sinai
Press, 1937), 7. Title XXIV. Law III. 35–36.

234. "The Crusades (1095 - 1291)," Jewish Virtual Library, 2008 (at: http://www.jewishvirtual-
library.org/the-crusades).

235. Jacob Rader, *The Jew in the Medieval World, a Source Book, 315-1791* (Cincinnati: The
Sinai Press, 1937), 5, 24-27.

236. Jacob Rader, *The Jew in the Medieval World, a Source Book, 315-1791* (Cincinnati: The
Sinai Press, 1937), 11.51.

237. Emily McFarlan Miller, "Berlin exhibit highlights how the Nazis exploited Martin Luther's
legacy," *Religion News Service*, October 19, 2017 (at: http://religionnews.com/2017/10/19/
berlin-exhibition-highlights-how-the-nazis-exploited-martin-luthers-legacy/); "Nazi Propaganda Depicting Martin Luther," *Facing History*, 2017 (at: https://www.facinghistory.org/
resource-library/image/nazi-propaganda-depicting-martin-luther).

238. Jacob Rader, *The Jew in the Medieval World, a Source Book, 315-1791* (Cincinnati: The
Sinai Press, 1937), 33.II.167–168.

239. Raul Hilberg as quoted by Michelle Brown and Nicole Rafter in "Genocide Films, Public Criminology, Collective Memory," *The British Journal of Criminology*, Volume 53,
Issue 6, 1 November 2013, pp. 1017–1032 (at: https://academic.oup.com/bjc/article/53/6/
1017/416127).

240. "Antisemitism in History: From the Early Church to 1400" Jewish Virtual Library, accessed
January 8, 2018, (at: https://www.jewishvirtuallibrary.org/the-catholic-church), "*Antisemitism:
A Historical Survey*," Simon Wiesenthal Center Multimedia Learning Center Online, accessed
January 8, 2018 (at: http://motlc.wiesenthal.com/site/pp.asp?c=gvKVLcMVIuG&b=394713).

241. "Immigration to Israel: British Restrictions on Jewish Immigration to Palestine (1919 -
1942)," *Jewish Virtual Library*, accessed January 8, 2018 (at: http://www.jewishvirtual-
library.org/british-restrictions-on-jewish-immigration-to-palestine).

242. "Holocaust Encyclopedia: Voyage of the St. Louis," *United States Holocaust Memorial Museum,* accessed: January 8, 2018 (at: https://www.ushmm.org/wlc/en/article.php?
ModuleId=10005267).

243. Benjamin Netanyahu quoted in "What People are Saying," *Christians United for Israel*, accessed January 8, 2018 (at: https://www.cufi.org/impact/about-us/what-people-are-saying/).

244. This quote has been historically attributed to St. Francis of Assisi, but recently this has been disputed. Regardless of the original authenticity, the axiom's truth remains unalterably true.

245. See, for example, "Who are the Millennials?" *Life Science*, September 8, 2017 (at: https://www .livescience.com/38061-millennials-generation-y.html); "Millennials: Finances, Investing & Retirement," *Investopedia* (at: https://www.investopedia.com/terms/m/millennial.asp) (accessed on December 12, 2017); "Millennials overtake Baby Boomers as America's largest generation," *Pew Research Center*, April 25, 2016 (at: http://www.pewresearch.org/fact-tank/2016/04/25/millennials-overtake-baby-boomers/).

246. "Millennials," *Wikipedia* (at: https://en.wikipedia.org/wiki/Millennials) (accessed on December 12, 2017).

247. "Poll: Bernie Sanders leads Hillary Clinton among young voters," *US Political News*, January 30, 2016 (at: https://www.uspolitics.news/2016/01/30/news/election-news/poll-bernie-sanders-leads-hillary-clinton-among-young-voters/2491).

248. Reason-Rupe Public Opinion Survey, "Millennials the Politically Unclaimed Generation," Spring 2014, p. 6 (at: http://reason.com/assets/db/14048862817887.pdf).

249. See, for example, Kelly McDonald, "Scandinavia Isn't a Socialist Paradise," *The Federalist*, August 11, 2015 (at: http://thefederalist.com/2015/08/11/scandinavia-isnt-a-socialist-paradise/); Lars Christensen, "European Socialism: Why America Doesn't Want It," *Forbes*, October 25, 2012 (at: https://www.forbes.com/sites/realspin/2012/10/25/european-social-ism-why-america-doesnt-want-it/#1bc5f571ea66); Mark J. Perry, "Why Socialism Failed," *Foundation for Economic Freedom*, May 31, 1995 (at: https://fee.org/articles/why-social-ism-failed/).

250. Emily Ekins, "Millennials like socialism—until they get jobs," *The Washington Post*, March 24, 2016 (at: https://www.washingtonpost.com/news/in-theory/wp/2016/03/24/millennials-like-socialism-until-they-get-jobs/?utm_term=.065439cb5af0).

251. Bradford Richardson, "Millennials would rather live in socialist or communist nation than under capitalism: Poll," *The Washington Times*, November 4, 2017 (at: https://www.wash-ingtontimes.com/news/2017/nov/4/majority-millennials-want-live-socialist-fascist-o/).

252. See, for example, Susan Page and Karina Shedrofsky, "Poll: How Millennials view BLM and the alt-right," *USA Today*, October 31, 2016 (at: https://www.usatoday.com/story/news/politics/onpolitics/2016/10/31/poll-millennials-black-lives-matter-alt-right/92999936/); Israel on Campus Coalition, "2016-2017 Year End Report," pp. 3-5 (at: https://israelcc.org/wp-content/uploads/2017/09/2016-2017-Year-End-Report.pdf).

253. See, for example, Chelsen Vicari, "To My Fellow Millennials: Christian persecution is a Social Justice Issue," *The Christian Post*, May 8, 2014 (at: https://www.christianpost.com/news/to-my-fellow-millennials-christian-persecution-is-a-social-justice-issue-119401/); Jeff Jacoby, "American millennials rethink abortion, for good reasons," *Boston Globe*, June 9, 2015 (at: https://www.bostonglobe.com/opinion/2015/06/09/millennial-americans-rethink-abortion-for-good-reasons/ZCmZNJuCWKVr5brzVfaiuI/story.html).

254. See, for example, Chris Cillizza, "Millennials don't trust anyone. That's a big deal." *The Washington Post*, April 30, 2015 (at: https://www.washingtonpost.com/news/the-fix/wp/2015/04/30/millennials-dont-trust-anyone-what-else-is-new/?utm_term=.52e2efce4185).

255. See, for example, Daniel Bortz, "7 Ways Boomers and Millennials Differ at Work," *The Fiscal Times*, September 4, 2013 (at: http://www.thefiscaltimes.com/Articles/2013/09/04/7-Ways-Boomers-and-Millennials-Differ-Work).

256. See, for example, George Gao, "63% of Republican Millennials favor marijuana legalization," *Pew Research Center*, February 27, 2015 (at: http://www.pewresearch.org/fact-tank/2015/02/27/63-of-republican-millennials-favor-marijuana-legalization/); Elizabeth Nolan Brown, "Poll: Most Americans Reject Criminal Penalties for Prostitution," *reason.com*, June 1, 2016 (at: http://reason.com/blog/2016/06/01/marist-poll-prostitution); Cathy Lynn Grossman, "Millennials are the 'don't judge generation' on sexual morality: Survey," *Religion News Service*, March 27, 2015 (at: http://religionnews.com/2015/03/27/millenni-als-dont-judge-generation-sexual-morality-survey/).

257. Becka A. Alpher, "Millennials are less religious than older Americans, but just as spiritual," *Pew Research Center*, November 23, 2015 (at: http://www.pewresearch.org/fact-tank/2015/11/23/millennials-are-less-religious-than-older-americans-but-just-as-spiritual/).

258. See, for example, "Millennials and the Bible: 3 Surprising Insights," *Barna*, October 21, 2014 (at: https://www.barna.com/research/millennials-and-the-bible-3-surprising-insights/); Sarah Eekhoff Zylstra, "What the Latest Bible Research Reveals About Millennials," *Christianity Today*, May 16, 2016 (at: http://www.christianitytoday.com/news/2016/may/what-latest-bible-research-reveals-about-millennials.html).

259. "Survey Details How the Core Beliefs and Behaviors of Millennials Compare to Those of Other Adults," *American Culture & Faith Institute* (at: https://www.culturefaith.com/survey-details-how-the-core-beliefs-and-behaviors-of-millennials-compare-to-those-of-other-adults/), accessed on December 12, 2017.

260. "Survey Details How the Core Beliefs and Behaviors of Millennials Compare to Those of Other Adults," *American Culture & Faith Institute* (at: https://www.culturefaith.com/survey-details-how-the-core-beliefs-and-behaviors-of-millennials-compare-to-those-of-other-adults/), accessed on December 12, 2017.

261. See, for example, Victor Lipman "Generation Z Is Entering the Workforce – What does This Mean for Management?" *Forbes*, July 10, 2017 (at: https://www.forbes.com/sites/victorlipman/2017/07/10/generation-z-is-entering-the-workforce-what-does-this-mean-for-management/#1a3bafbc4a1d); George Beall, "8 Key Differences between Gen Z and Millennials," *Huffpost*, November 5, 2016 (at: https://www.huffingtonpost.com/george-beall/8-key-differences-between_b_12814200.html); Alex Williams, "Move Over, Millennials, Here Comes Generation Z," *The New York Times*, September 18, 2015 (at: https://www.nytimes.com/2015/09/20/fashion/move-over-millennials-here-comes-generation-z.html).

262. Karen Kaplan, "The paradox of millennial sex: more casual hookups, fewer partners," *Los Angeles Times*, May 9, 2015 (at: http://www.latimes.com/science/sciencenow/la-sci-sn-millennials-sex-attitudes-20150508-story.html); *Archives of Sexual behavior* (November 2015), Vol. 44, Issue 8, pp. 2273–2285, Jean M. Twenge, et. al., "Changes in American Adult's Sexual Behavior and Attitudes, 1972-2012" (at: https://link.springer.com/article/10.1007/s10508-015-0540-2).

263. Charlotte Alter, "Exclusive: Millennials More Tolerant of Premarital Sex, But Have Fewer Partners," *Time*, May 5, 2015 (at: http://time.com/3846289/boomers-generations-millennials-sex-sex-trends-sexual-partners/).

264. "Majority of Americans Now Believe in Cohabitation," *Barna*, June 24, 2016 (at: https://www.barna.com/research/majority-of-americans-now-believe-in-cohabitation/).

265. "Millennials Navigate the Ups and Downs of Cohabitation," *NPR*, November 1, 2014 (at: https://www.npr.org/2014/11/01/358876955/millennials-navigate-the-ups-and-downs-of-cohabitation).

266. Daniel Cox and Robert P. Jones, "How Race and Religion Shape Millennial Attitudes on Sexuality and Reproductive Health," *Public Religion Research Institute*, March 27, 2015, p. 32 (at: https://www.prri.org/wp-content/uploads/2015/03/PRRI-Millennials-Web-FINAL-1.pdf).

267. "STDs in Adolescents and Young Adults" *Centers for Disease Control and Prevention* (at: https://www.cdc.gov/std/stats16/adolescents.htm), accessed on December 12, 2017.

268. Abbie Roth, "HIV in the Millennial World," *Pediatrics Nationwide*, December 1, 2015 (at: http://pediatricsnationwide.org/2015/12/01/hiv-in-the-millennial-world/).

269. "National Youth HIV and AIDS Awareness Day," *American Psychological Association* (at: http://www.apa.org/pi/aids/resources/youth-awareness.aspx) (accessed December 12, 2017).

270. Joy Wilke and Lydia Saad, "Older Americans' Moral Attitudes Changing," *Gallup*, June 3, 2013 (at: http://news.gallup.com/poll/162881/older-americans-moral-attitudes-changing.aspx).

271. "Millennials: Demographics & Facts," *Advocates for Youth* (at: http://www.advocatesforyouth.org/millennials), accessed on December 13, 2017.

272. "What Americans Believe About Sex," *Barna*, January 14, 2016 (at: https://www.barna.com/research/what-americans-believe-about-sex/).

273. "Gallup Analysis: Millennials, Marriage, and Family," *Gallup News*, May 19, 2016 (at: http://news.gallup.com/poll/191462/gallup-analysis-millennials-marriage-family.aspx).

274. "Johns Hopkins: 57 Percent of Children Born to Millennials Are Out of Wedlock," *cnsnews.com*, June 25, 2014 (at: https://www.cnsnews.com/news/article/zoey-dimauro/johns-hopkins-57-percent-children-born-millennials-are-out-wedlock).

275. Wendy Wang, "One-in-Four Millennials in their 30s Are Unmoored from the Institution of Family," *Institute for Family Studies*, September 27, 2017 (at: https://ifstudies.org/blog/one-in-four-millennials-in-their-30s-are-unmoored-from-the-institution-of-family).

276. Lidia Jean Kott, "For These Millennials, Gender Norms Have Gone Out of Style," *NPR*, November 30, 2014 (at: https://www.npr.org/2014/11/30/363345372/for-these-millennials-gender-norms-have-gone-out-of-style).

277. Brynn, "Millennials are the First Generation to Embrace Gender Diversity," *Medium*, November 12, 2015 (at: https://medium.com/the-430th/millennials-are-the-first-generation-to-embrace-gender-diversity-45d044475795).

278. Rhiannon Williams, "Facebook's 71 gender options come to UK users," *The Telegraph*, June 27, 2014 (at: http://www.telegraph.co.uk/technology/facebook/10930654/Facebooks-71-gender-options-come-to-UK-users.html).

279. "Teens & Young Adults Use Porn More Than Anyone Else," *Barna*, January 28, 2016 (at: https://www.barna.com/research/teens-young-adults-use-porn-more-than-anyone-else/).

280. Robert P. Jones, Daniel Cox, Juhem Navarro-Rivera, "A Shifting Landscape," *Public Religion Research Institute*, February 26, 2014, p. 42 (at: https://www.prri.org/wp-content/uploads/2014/02/2014.LGBT_REPORT.pdf).

281. See, for example, "Jennifer Lawrence: Anyone who looked at nude pics 'perpetuating a sexual offense,'" *Fox News*, October 7, 2014 (at: http://www.foxnews.com/entertainment/2014/10/07/jennifer-lawrence-anyone-who-looked-at-nude-pics-perpetuating-sexual-offense.html); "Hundreds of Nude Photos Jolt Colorado School" *The New York Times*, November 6, 2015 (at: https://www.nytimes.com/2015/11/07/us/colorado-students-caught-trading-nude-photos-by-the-hundreds.html); "8 high school boys suspended for nude photos on cellphones," *KOMU*, April 25, 2015 (at: http://www.komu.com/news/8-high-school-boys-suspended-for-nude-photos-on-cellphones/); "School Confiscates Cell Phones After Nude Photos of Junior High Girls Circulate," *Fox News*, May 21, 2008 (at: http://www.foxnews.com/story/2008/05/21/school-confiscates-cell-phones-after-nude-photos-junior-high-girls-circulate.html).

282. "Gallup Analysis: Millennials, Marriage, and Family," *Gallup News*, May 19, 2016 (at: http://news.gallup.com/poll/191462/gallup-analysis-millennials-marriage-family.aspx).

283. "Millennials in Adulthood," *Pew Research Center*, March 7, 2014 (at: http://www.pewsocialtrends.org/2014/03/07/millennials-in-adulthood/).

284. In Jim's extensive pastoral experience, he has come across a number of reasons why Millennials have delayed marriage. Among the anecdotal reasons given him are the following:
    • The high cost of a wedding. Many Millennials have become convinced that a wedding should be as costly as a house down payment or a Broadway show
    • Not being financially stable
    • Prolonged or delayed education. What used to be four years of college now is much longer for many Millennials
    • They don't trust marriage because their parents were divorced, and they didn't like what they saw
    • They have been sexually abused in the past, completely changing their view of sexuality
    • A rise of militant feminism, devaluing men's role in society
    • Immaturity. This is a result of delaying the onset of adulthood (mentioned in the next footnote)
    • Seeking perfection. An instagram culture has allowed Millennials to create fake facades of "perfect" realities
    • Pornography and masturbation replace the need for marital physical intimacy
    • Personal guilt associated with previous sexual activity
    • The hyper-sexualization of women (a result of the scores of highly publicized sexual scandals involving Hollywood moguls and actors, sports stars, broadcast anchors and reporters, national political figures, etc.)
    • Cohabitation is high, and sex is available without marriage, so why get married
    • Timid men afraid to venture out into the dating world
    • In the church world, there appear to be more available Christian women than Christian men.
    All of these are reasons that Jim has personal encountered in his pastoral role.

285. Historically, adulthood has been defined by five standard milestones: (1) completing school (whether high school, college, or graduate school), (2) leaving home, (3) achieving financial independence, (4) marriage, (5) and after marriage, having children. As an anecdotal example of how financial independence has shifted, Jim's grandfather became financially

independent and economically self-sufficient at the age of 12; his father at the age of 16; and Jim at the age of 21. Today, the number is closer to 35 years old (but more on this later in this section).

286. See, for example, Wilson Andrews and Thomas Kaplan, "Where the Candidates Stand on 2016's Biggest Issues," *The New York Times*, December 15, 2015 (at: https://www.nytimes.com/interactive/2016/us/elections/candidates-on-the-issues.html).

287. See, for example, "Fact Check: Which Republican candidates actually cut spending?" *Fox News*, August 28, 2015 (at: http://www.foxnews.com/politics/2015/08/28/fact-check-which-republican-candidates-actually-cut-spending.html).

288. "Watch: Jeb Hits Back After Trump Ad Mocks Him as Boring, Low-Energy," *Fox News Insider*, September 9, 2015 (at: http://insider.foxnews.com/2015/09/09/video-donald-trump-instagram-ad-mocks-jeb-bush-boring-low-energy).

289. Alex Swoyer, "Donald Trump Calls John Kasich 'One for 41,' Mocks Him as a Child, 'I Want It Mommy!,'" *Breitbart*, April 25, 2016 (at: http://www.breitbart.com/2016-presidential-race/2016/04/25/donald-trump-calls-john-kasich-one-41-mocks-child-want-mommy/).

290. "'Little Marco,' 'Lyin' Ted,' 'Crooked Hillary': How Donald Trump makes name calling stick," *The Washington Post*, April 20, 2016 (at: https://www.washingtonpost.com/news/inspired-life/wp/2016/04/20/little-marco-lying-ted-crooked-hillary-donald-trumps-winning-strategy-nouns/?utm_term=.93c0ce340cc2).

291. "'Little Marco,' 'Lyin' Ted,' 'Crooked Hillary': How Donald Trump makes name calling stick," *The Washington Post*, April 20, 2016 (at: https://www.washingtonpost.com/news/inspired-life/wp/2016/04/20/little-marco-lying-ted-crooked-hillary-donald-trumps-winning-strategy-nouns/?utm_term=.93c0ce340cc2).

292. "'Little Marco,' 'Lyin' Ted,' 'Crooked Hillary': How Donald Trump makes name calling stick," *The Washington Post*, April 20, 2016 (at: https://www.washingtonpost.com/news/inspired-life/wp/2016/04/20/little-marco-lying-ted-crooked-hillary-donald-trumps-winning-strategy-nouns/?utm_term=.93c0ce340cc2).

293. See, for example, "Campus Protestors Try to Silence Conservative Speaker, Demand College President's Resignation," *The Daily Signal*, February 26, 2016 (at: http://dailysignal.com/2016/02/26/campus-protestors-try-to-silence-conservative-speaker-demand-college-presidents-resignation/); Chris Perez and Gina Daidone, "Protestors storm NYU over conservative speaker's seminar" *New York Post*, February 2, 2017 (at: https://nypost.com/2017/02/02/protesters-storm-nyu-over-conservative-speakers-seminar/); "College students violently protesting conservative speakers tend to come from wealthy families, study finds," *Fox News*, March 21, 2017 (at: http://www.foxnews.com/us/2017/03/21/college-students-violently-protesting-conservative-speakers-tend-to-come-from-wealthy-families-study-finds.html); Chris Enloe, "Violent mob of angry liberals shut down conservative, pro-police speaker at Calif. College," *TheBlaze*, April 9, 2017 (at: http://www.theblaze.com/news/2017/04/09/violent-mob-of-angry-liberals-shut-down-conservative-pro-police-speaker-at-calif-college-video).

294. See, for example, Dr. Susan Berry, "No, the Constitution is Not Racist, Sexist, or Outdated," *Breitbart*, September 16, 2016 (at: http://www.breitbart.com/big-government/2016/09/16/no-constitution-not-racist-sexist-outdated/).

295. See, for example, Greg Clarke, "The roots of benevolence: Christian ideals and social benefit," *Religion & Ethics*, May 8, 2013 (at: http://www.abc.net.au/religion/articles/2013/05/08/3754498.htm); Edward Kilsdonk "Religious Groups, Benevolent Organizations, and American Pluralism," *The American Religious Experience* (at: http://are.as.wvu.edu/kilsdonk.htm), accessed on December 19, 2017.

296. See, for example, Terrence Moore, "Hating the Constitution 101: The Common Core on the Nation's Founding," *TownHall*, January 6, 2014 (at: https://townhall.com/columnists/terrencemoore/2014/01/06/hating-the-constitution-101-the-common-core-on-the-nations-founding-n1771633).

297. Schuyler Velascro, "Charitable giving sets new record, but why are religious donations waning?" *The Christian Science Monitor*, June 16, 2015 (at: https://www.csmonitor.com/Business/2015/0616/Charitable-giving-sets-new-record-but-why-are-religious-donations-waning).

298. See, for example, "Millennials increasingly are driving growth of 'nones,'" *Pew Research Center*, May 12, 2015 (at: http://www.pewresearch.org/fact-tank/2015/05/12/millennials-increasingly-are-driving-growth-of-nones/).
299. "Postmodern," *Merriam-Webster* (at: https://www.merriam-webster.com/dictionary/post-modern).
300. "The End to Absolutes: America's New Moral Code," *Barna*, May 25, 2016 (at: https://www.barna.com/research/the-end-of-absolutes-americas-new-moral-code/).
301. "2016-2017 Facts and Figures," *Houston Independent School District* (at: http://www.houstonisd.org/site/handlers/filedownload.ashx?moduleinstanceid=48525&dataid=21177 7&FileName=2016-17FactsandFigures.pdf), accessed on December 19, 2017.
302. Jeff Jacoby, "American millennials rethink abortion, for good reasons," *Boston Globe*, June 9, 2015 (at: http://www.bostonglobe.com/opinion/2015/06/09/millennial-americans-rethink-abortion-for-good-reasons/ZCmZNJuCWKVr5brzVfaiuI/story.html).
303. *Life* (April 30, 1965), Vol. 58, No. 17.
304. See, for example, "Marriage and Money: Key Differences Between Millennials and Boomers," *Nasdaq*, August 19, 2016 (at: http://www.nasdaq.com/article/marriage-and-money-key-differences-between-millennials-and-boomers-cm667980); Michele Lerner, "When It Comes to Money, Millennials Bow to Peer Pressure," *AOL.com*, November 4, 2013 (at: https://www.aol.com/article/finance/2013/11/04/money-millennials-peer-pressure/20759276/).
305. See, for example, Martin B. Copenhaver, *Jesus is the Question: The 307 Questions Jesus Asked and the 3 He Answered* (Abingdon Press, 2014); Bob Tiede, *339 Questions Jesus Asked* (2017).
306. See, for example, Michael D. Tanner, "Welfare Reform: Committee on Finance, United States Senate," *CATO Institute*, March 9, 1995 (at: https://www.cato.org/publications/congressional-testimony/welfare-reform). See also Michael Tanner, *The End of Welfare: Fighting Poverty in the Civil Society* (Washington, DC: Cato Institute, 1996), statistics throughout his book.
307. Dr. Susan Berry, "Few Top Colleges Require History Majors to Study American History," *Breitbart*, July 2, 2016 (at: http://www.breitbart.com/big-government/2016/07/02/few-top-colleges-require-history-majors-to-study-american-history/).
308. *American Council of Trustees and Alumni*, "What Will They Learn? 2016-17: A Survey of Core Requirements at Our Nation's Colleges and Universities," p. 16 (available at: https://www.goacta.org/images/download/What_Will_They_Learn_2016-17.pdf).
309. "Characters from 'The Simpsons' More Well Known to Americans Than Their First Amendment Freedoms, Survey Finds," *Robert R. McCormick Foundation*, March 1, 2006 (at: http://documents.mccormickfoundation.org/news/2006/pr030106.aspx).
310. Blake Neff, "Poll: Most Americans Favor Regulating 'Hate Speech' on Campus," *The Daily Caller*, January 6, 2016 (at: http://dailycaller.com/2016/01/06/most-americans-favor-regulating-hate-speech-on-campus/).
311. "Indoctrination," *Oxford Living Dictionaries* (at: https://en.oxforddictionaries.com/definition/indoctrination) (accessed on December 20, 2017).
312. Dr. Martin Luther King, Jr., "The Purpose of Education," *Marron Tiger*, January–February 1947, p. 10, published in *The Papers of Martin Luther King Jr.*, Vol. I and available online at Stanford University (https://kinginstitute.stanford.edu/king-papers/documents/purpose-education).
313. See, for example, Jane C. Timm, "Millennials: We care more about the environment," *MSNBC*, March 22, 2017 (at: http://www.msnbc.com/morning-joe/millennials-environment-climate-change); "Millennials' Strong Views on Climate Change and Other Energy Issues Could Drive Presidential Election Results," *University of Texas*, October 27, 2016 (at: https://news.utexas.edu/2016/10/27/millennials-views-on-climate-change-could-impact-election).
314. See, for example, William F. Jasper "Hiding the Hiatus: Global Warming on Pause," *The New American*, January 6, 2016 (at: https://www.thenewamerican.com/tech/environment/item/22269-hiding-the-hiatus-global-warming-on-pause); Marc Morano, "Global Temperature Update: Still no global warming for 17 years 9 months – Since Sept. 1996," *Climate Depot*, June 4, 2014 (at: http://www.climatedepot.com/2014/06/04/global-

temperature-update-still-no-global-warming-for-17-years-9-months-since-sept-1996/);
Larry Bell, "The New York Times' Global Warming Hysteria Ignores 17 Years of Flat
Global Temperatures," *Forbes*, August 21, 2013 (at: https://www.forbes.com/sites/lar-
rybell/2013/08/21/the-new-york-times-global-warming-hysteria-ignores-17-years-of-flat-
global-temperatures/#6e9fe49b2a4c).

315. See, for example, "Is a mini ICE AGE on the way? Scientists warn the sun will 'go to
sleep' in 2030 and could cause temperatures to plummet," *Daily Mail*, July 10, 2015 (at:
http://www.dailymail.co.uk/sciencetech/article-3156594/Is-mini-ICE-AGE-way-Scientists-
warn-sun-sleep-2020-cause-temperatures-plummet.html); Valerie Richardson, "Mini ice
age likely from 2030 to 2040, European scientists say," *The Washington Times*, July 12,
2015 (at: https://www.washingtontimes.com/news/2015/jul/12/mini-ice-age-likely-from-
2030-to-2040-european-sci/).

316. Brad Plumer, "Only 27 percent of college grads have a job related to their major," *The
Washington Post*, May 20, 2013 (at: https://www.washingtonpost.com/news/wonk/
wp/2013/05/20/only-27-percent-of-college-grads-have-a-job-related-to-their-major/?utm_
term=.983912c2b7a0).

317. "Students & Debt," *debt.org* (at: https://www.debt.org/students), accessed on December
20, 2017.

318. "Students & Debt," *debt.org* (at: https://www.debt.org/students), accessed on December
20, 2017.

319. See, for example, "Adolescence," *Merriam-Webster* (at: https://www.merriam-webster.
com/dictionary/adolescence), accessed on December 20, 2017.

320. See, for example, Phoebe Weston, "Will they ever grow up? Millennials don't consider
themselves adults until they are 30," *Daily Mail*, March 23, 2017 (at: http://www.dai-
lymail.co.uk/sciencetech/article-4341436/Millennials-don-t-consider-adults-30.html);
George Will, "George Will: Extended age of adolescence," *The News-Gazette*, May 14,
2015 (at: http://www.news-gazette.com/opinion/columns/2015-05-14/george-will-extend-
ed-age-adolescence.html); Geraldine Bedell, "Why don't we just grow up?" *The Guardian*,
February 2, 2002 (at: https://www.theguardian.com/theobserver/2002/feb/03/features.re-
view17); Susie Boniface, "How it takes until 35 for most of us to grow up," *Daily Mail* (at:
http://www.dailymail.co.uk/news/article-70052/How-takes-35-grow-up.html), accessed on
December 20, 2017; and others.

321. Susie Boniface, "How it takes until 35 for most of us to grow up," *Daily Mail* (at: http://
www.dailymail.co.uk/news/article-70052/How-takes-35-grow-up.html), accessed on December 20, 2017.

322. George Will, "George Will: Extended age of adolescence," *The News-Gazetee*, May 14,
2015 (at: http://www.news-gazette.com/opinion/columns/2015-05-14/george-will-extend-
ed-age-adolescence.html).

323. Dr. Martin Luther King, Jr., "The Purpose of Education," *Marron Tiger*, January–February
1947, p. 10, published in *The Papers of Martin Luther King Jr.*, Vol. I and available online
at Stanford University (https://kinginstitute.stanford.edu/king-papers/documents/purpose-
education).

324. See, for example, "Testing a Relationship is Probably the Worst Reason to Cohabit," *Institute for Family Studies*, July 19, 2016 (at: https://ifstudies.org/blog/testing-a-relationship-
is-probably-the-worst-reason-to-cohabit); "Majority of Americans Now Believe in Cohabitation," *Barna*, June 24, 2016 (at: https://www.barna.com/research/majority-of-americans-
now-believe-in-cohabitation/#.V-wKM5MrIp8); Gillian B. White, "The Institution of Marriage: Still Going Strong," *The Atlantic*, June 16, 2015 (at: https://www.theatlantic.com/
business/archive/2015/06/millennials-delaying-marriage-money-weddings/395870/).

325. See, for example, Thaddeus M. Baklinski, "Study Confirms Cohabitation Leads to Higher
Chance of Divorce and Lower Relationship Quality," *Life Site*, July 15, 2009 (at: https://
www.lifesitenews.com/news/study-confirms-cohabitation-leads-to-higher-chance-of-di-
vorce-and-lower-rel).

326. See, for example, "Sexually Transmitted Disease Surveillance, 2015," *Centers for Disease
Control and Prevention*, pp. 7, 18, 32, 62–63 (at: https://www.cdc.gov/std/stats15/std-sur-
veillance-2015-print.pdf).

327. "How many STDs are there?" *Chastity Project* (at: https://chastityproject.com/qa/how-
many-stds-are-there/), accessed on December 19, 2017.

328. "How many STIs are there and what are their names?" *Medical Institute for Sexual Health* (at: https://www.medinstitute.org/faqs/how-many-stis-are-there-and-what-are-their-names/), accessed on December 19, 2017.

329. Among these are Hepatitis B, Hepatitis C, Hepatitis D, HIV, AIDS, and HPV. See a more complete list at https://www.std-gov.org/stds/std.htm.

330. "Revenge of the Church Ladies," *Pure Freedom with Dannah Gresh* (at: http://purefreedom.org/revenge-of-the-church-ladies-2/), accessed on December 20, 2017.

331. See, for example, "Hadley Heath Manning, "Yo, Millennials: Marriage Creates Financial Security, Not Vice Versa," *The Federalist*, March 14, 2014 (at: http://thefederalist.com/2014/03/14/yo-millennials-marriage-creates-financial-security-not-vice-versa/).

332. See, for example, Albert Mohler, "The Scandal of Biblical Illiteracy: It's Our Problem," *Christianity.com*, June 29, 2004 (at: https://www.christianity.com/1270946/); Ken Camp, "Most teens lack basic Bible knowledge, survey says," *Baptist News Global*, June 23, 2005 (at: https://baptistnews.com/article/mostteenslackbasicbibleknowledgesurveysays/#.Wjqd2EtG2dY); "U.S. Religious Knowledge Survey," *Pew Research Center*, September 28, 2010 (at: http://www.pewforum.org/2010/09/28/u-s-religious-knowledge-survey/).

333. "Survey Details How the Core Beliefs and Behaviors of Millennials Compare to Those of Other Adults," *American Culture & Faith Institute* (at: https://www.culturefaith.com/survey-details-how-the-core-beliefs-and-behaviors-of-millennials-compare-to-those-of-other-adults/), accessed on December 12, 2017.

334. "Survey Details How the Core Beliefs and Behaviors of Millennials Compare to Those of Other Adults," *American Culture & Faith Institute* (at: https://www.culturefaith.com/survey-details-how-the-core-beliefs-and-behaviors-of-millennials-compare-to-those-of-other-adults/), accessed on December 12, 2017.

335. "Groundbreaking ACFI Survey Reveals How Many Adults Have a Biblical Worldview," *American Culture & Faith Institute* (at: https://www.culturefaith.com/groundbreaking-survey-by-acfi-reveals-how-many-american-adults-have-a-biblical-worldview/), accessed on December 20, 2017.

336. "Groundbreaking ACFI Survey Reveals How Many Adults Have a Biblical Worldview," *American Culture & Faith Institute* (at: https://www.culturefaith.com/groundbreaking-survey-by-acfi-reveals-how-many-american-adults-have-a-biblical-worldview/), accessed on December 20, 2017.

337. Twenge, J. M. (2009), Generational *changes and their impact in the classroom: teaching Generation Me*. Medical Education, 43: 398–405; as referenced on "The Millennial Generation Research Review," *U.S. Chamber of Commerce Foundation*, November 12, 2012 (at: https://www.uschamberfoundation.org/reports/millennial-generation-research-review).

338. *Journal of Business & Psychology* (March 5, 2010), Vol. 25, pp. 225–238, Karen K. Myers and Kamyab Sadaghiani, "Millennials in the Workplace: A Communication Perspective on Millennials' Organizational Relationships and Performance" (at: http://www.ncbi.nlm.nih.gov/pmc/articles/PMC2868990/).

339. See, for example, Rob Asghar, "What Millennials Want in the Workplace (And Why You Should Start Giving It To Them)," *Forbes*, January 13, 2014 (at: https://www.forbes.com/sites/robasghar/2014/01/13/what-millennials-want-in-the-workplace-and-why-you-should-start-giving-it-to-them/#3e9cc5c4c404).

340. "How Millennials Want to Work and Live," *Gallup News*, 2017 (at: http://news.gallup.com/reports/189830/millennials-work-live.aspx?aspnetForm).

341. Jason King, "Q-and-A with Frank Martin," *Yahoo! Sports*, November 22, 2010 (at: https://www.yahoo.com/news/q-frank-martin-151200611--ncaab.html).

342. Frank Martin (@FrankMartin_SC) tweet on March 25, 2017 (at: https://twitter.com/frankmartin_sc/status/845769553326096387).

343. Sam Harris, *Letter to a Christian Nation* (New York: Vintage Books, 2008) and Mark Noll, Nathan Hatch, and George Marsden, *The Search for Christian America* (Colorado Springs: Helmers & Howard, 1989).

344. See, for example, *The Trial of the British Soldiers, of the 29th Regiment of Foot, for the Murder of Crispus Attucks, Samuel Gray, Samuel Maverick, James Caldwell, and Patrick Carr, on Monday Evening, March 5, 1770* (Boston: William Emmons, 1824), p. 117; John

Adams, *The Works of John Adams*, Charles Francis Adams, editor (Boston: Little, Brown and Company, 1854), Vol. IX, p. 470, to Elbridge Gerry, December 6, 1777.

345. John Adams, *The Works of John Adams*, Charles Francis Adams, editor (Boston: Little, Brown and Company, 1856), Vol. X, p. 45, to Thomas Jefferson, June 28, 1813.

346. *The Evangelical Guardian, By An Association of Ministers of the Associate Reformed Synod of the West*, Rev. D. MacDill, editor (Rossville, OH: J. M. Christy, 1845), Vol. II, No. 9, February, 1845, p. 407, Governor Hammond's reply to the Israelites on November 4, 1844. See also *Allegheny v. ACLU*, 492 U. S. 573, fn53 (1989).

347. *The Evangelical Guardian, By An Association of Ministers of the Associate Reformed Synod of the West*, Rev. D. MacDill, editor (Rossville, OH: J. M. Christy, 1845), Vol. II, No. 9, February, 1845, p. 407, Governor Hammond's reply to the Israelites on November 4, 1844. See also *Allegheny v. ACLU*, 492 U. S. 573, fn53 (1989).

348. David Gates and Kenneth Woodward, "How the Bible Made America," *Newsweek* (December 27, 1982), p. 44.

349. Franklin D. Roosevelt, "Statement on the Four Hundredth Anniversary of the Printing of the English Bible," *American Presidency Project*, October 6, 1935 (at: http://www.presidency.ucsb .edu/ws/?pid=14960).

350. Lyndon B. Johnson, "Remarks at a Ceremony Marking 1966 as the 'Year of the Bible,'" *American Presidency Project*, January 19, 1966 (at: http://www.presidency.ucsb.edu/ ws/?pid=27559).

351. *Bible Society Record* (New York: The American Bible Society, 1901), Vol. 46, p. 99, Number 7, "Vice-President Theodore Roosevelt Addresses the Long Island Bible Society."

352. Ronald Reagan, "Proclamation 5018—Year of the Bible, 1983," *American Presidency Project*, February 3, 1983 (at: http://www.presidency.ucsb.edu/ws/?pid=40728). See also George H. W. Bush, "International Year of Bible Reading," *American Presidency Project*, February 22, 1990 (at: http://www.presidency.ucsb.edu/ws/?pid=1816); *The American Missionary* (New York: American Missionary Association, 1876), Vol. XX, No. 8, p. 183, Rev. Addison P. Foster, "America's Experiment with Republican Institutions."

353. William Wirt, *Sketches of the Life and Character of Patrick Henry* (Philadelphia: James Webster, 1817), p. 402.

354. Benjamin Rush, *Essays, Literary, Moral & Philosophical* (Philadelphia: Thomas & Samuel F. Bradford, 1798), p. 93, "A Defence of the Use of the Bible as a School Book."

355. Benjamin Rush, *Letters of Benjamin Rush*, L. H. Butterfield, editor (Princeton, NJ: Princeton University Press, 1951), Vol. I, p. 521, to Jeremy Belknap on July 13, 1789.

356. John Quincy Adams, *Letters to His Son on the Bible and Its Teachings* (New York: Derby, Miller, & Co., 1848), p. 119.

357. B. B. Edwards and W. Cogswell, *The American Quarterly Register* (Boston: Perkins & Marvin, 1840), Vol. XII, p. 86, letter from John Quincy Adams to members of a literary society in Baltimore on June 22, 1838.

358. John Jay, *John Jay: The Winning of the Peace. Unpublished Papers 1780-1784*, Richard B. Morris, editor (New York: Harper & Row Publishers, 1980), Vol. II, p. 709, letter to Peter Augustus Jay on April 8, 1784.

359. John Adams, *The Works of John Adams*, Charles Francis Adams, editor (Boston: Charles Little & James Brow, 1850), Vol. II, pp. 6–7, diary entry for February 22, 1756.

360. Benjamin Rush, *A Memorial Containing Travels Through Life or Sundry Incidents in the Life of Dr. Benjamin Rush* (Lanoraie Quebec, Canada: Louis Alexander Biddle, 1905), p. 127.

361. Samuel Adams, *Life & Public Services of Samuel Adams*, William V. Wells, editor (Boston: Little, Brown and Company, 1865), Vol. III, p. 379, Last Will and Testament of Samuel Adams, attested December 29, 1790.

362. John Witherspoon, *The Absolute Necessity of Salvation Through Christ. A Sermon Preached Before the Society in Scotland for Propagating Christian Knowledge in the High Church of Edinburg, January 2, 1758* (Edinburg: W. Miller, 1758), pp. 19, 44.

363. William Coleman, *A Collection of the Facts and Documents Relative to the Death of Major General Alexander Hamilton* (New York: Hopkins and Seymour, 1804), p. 53, letter from Dr. Mason to the Editor of the Evening Post, July 18, 1804, recounting the last conversation he had with Alexander Hamilton.

364. *Correspondence Between Roger Sherman and Samuel Hopkins* (Worcester, MA: Charles Hamilton, 1889), p. 9, Roger Sherman to Samuel Hopkins on June 28, 1790.

365. *The Constitutions of the Several Independent States of America* (Boston: Norman and Bowen, 1785), pp. 99–100, Delaware, 1776, Article 22.

366. *A Constitution or Frame of Government Agreed Upon by the Delegates of the People of the State of Massachusetts-Bay* (Boston: Benjamin Edes & Sons, 1780), p. 44, Chap. VI, Art. I.

367. See, for example, *The Constitutions of the Several Independent States of America* (Boston: Norman and Bowen, 1785), p. 81, Pennsylvania, 1776, Article II, Section 10; p. 108, Maryland, 1776, Declaration of Rights, Section 35; p. 4, New Hampshire, 1783, Bill of Rights, Article I, Section 6; etc.

368. *The Holy Bible As Printed by Robert Aitken and Approved & Recommended by the Congress of the United States of America in 1782* (New York: Arno Press, 1968), introduction.

369. Memorial of Robert Aitken to Congress, 21 January 1781, obtained from the National Archives, Washington, DC. See also the introduction to the *Holy Bible As Printed by Robert Aitken and Approved & Recommended by the Congress of the United States of America in 1782* (Philadelphia: R. Aitken, 1782) or the New York Arno Press reprint of 1968.

370. *Journals of the Continental Congress* (Washington, DC: Government Printing Office, 1914), Vol. XXIII, p. 572, September 12, 1782.

371. *Journals of the Continental Congress* (Washington, DC: Government Printing Office, 1914), Vol. XXIII, p. 574, September 12, 1782. See also cover page of the "Bible of the Revolution," either the 1782 original or the 1968 reprint by Arno Press.

372. *Journals of The Continental Congress* (Washington, DC: Government Printing Office, 1914), Vol. XXIII, p. 574, September 12, 1782. See also *The Holy Bible* (Philadelphia: Robert Aitken, 1782), introduction.

373. W. P. Strickland, *History of the American Bible Society from its Organization to the Present Time* (New York: Harper and Brothers, 1849), pp. 20–21.

374. *The New Annual Register or General Repository of History, Politics, and Literature for the Year 1783*, (London: G. Robinson, 1784), p. 113, "The Definitive Treaty of Peace and Friendship Between His Brittanic Majesty and the United States of America, signed at Paris the 3rd day of September, 1783."

375. David J. Brewer, *The United States: A Christian Nation* (Philadelphia: John C. Winston Company, 1905), p. 12.

376. David J. Brewer, *The United States: A Christian Nation* (Philadelphia: John C. Winston Company, 1905), p. 57.

377. Stephen Cowell, *The Position of Christianity in the United States in its Relations with our Political Institutions* (Philadelphia: Lippincott, Grambio & Co., 1854), pp. 11–12, Joseph Story, *A Familiar Exposition of the Constitution of the United States* (New York: Harper & Brothers, 1847), p. 260, §442.

378. David J. Brewer, *The United States: A Christian Nation* (Philadelphia: John C. Winston Company, 1905), p. 46.

379. *Vidal v. Girard's Executors*, 43 U. S. 127, 198 (1844).

380. *Church of the Holy Trinity v. U. S.*, 143 U. S. 457, 465, 471 (1892).

381. *United States v. Macintosh*, 283 U. S. 605, 625 (1931).

382. See for example, *Warren v. United States*, 177 F.2d 596 (10th Cir. Ct. of App., 1949); *United States v. Girouard*, 149 F.2d 760 (1st Cir. Ct. of App., 1945); *Steiner v. Darby*, 88 Cal. App. 2d 481 (1948); *Vogel v. County of Los Angeles*, 68 Cal. 2d 18 (Ca. Sup. Ct., 1967); etc.

383. See, for example, *Ross v. McIntyre*, 140 U. S. 453, 463 (1891); *Kinsella v. Krueger*, 351 U. S. 470, 485 (1956); *Reid v. Covert*, 354 U. S. 1 (1957); etc.

384. See, for example, *Beecher v. Wetherby*, 95 U. S. 517, 525 (1877); *Lone Wolf v. Hitchcock*, 187 U. S. 553, 565 (1903); *Yankton Sioux Tribe of Indians v. U. S.*, 272 U. S. 351 (1926); *U. S. v. Choctaw Nation*, 179 U. S. 494 (1900); *Atlantic & P R Co v. Mingus*, 165 U. S. 413 (1897); *Missouri, Kansas & Texas Railway Company v. Roberts*, 152 U. S. 114 (1894); *Buttz v. Northern Pac. R. Co.*, 119 U. S. 55 (1886); *Tee-Hit-Ton Indians v. United States*, 348 U. S. 272 (1955); etc.

385. See, for example, *Davis v. Beason*, 133 U. S. 333, 341-344, 348 n (1890); *The Church of Jesus Christ of Latter-Day Saints v. United States*, 136 U. S. 1, 49 (1890); etc.

386. See, for example, *U. S. v. Macintosh*, 283 U. S. 605, 625 (1931); etc.

387. *Richmond v. Moore*, 107 Ill. 429 (Ill. Sup. Ct.,1883).

388. *Paramount-Richards Theatres v. City of Hattiesburg*, 210 Miss. 271 (Miss. Sup. Ct., 1950).
389. *Town of Pryor v. Williamson*, 374 P.2d 204, 207 (Ok. Sup. Ct. 1959); also cited in *County of Los Angeles v. Hollinger*, 221 Cal.App.2d 154, 165 (Ca. Ct. of Appeals, 2nd Dist., Div. Two,1963).
390. William B. Reed, *Life and Correspondence of Joseph Reed* (Philadelphia: Lindsay and Blakiston, 1847), Vol. II, pp. 36–37n.
391. *The Trial of Samuel Tulley & John Dalton, on an Indictment for Piracy and Murder, Committed January 21st, 1812. Before the Circuit Court of the United States, at Boston, 28th October, 1812. Containing the Evidence at Large, a Sketch of the Arguments of counsel, and the charge of the Hon. Judge Story, on Pronouncing Sentence of Death* (Boston: Joshua Belcher, 1813), p. 25.
392. "The Slave Trade: Sentence of Capt. Gordon of the Silver Erie," *New York Times*, December 2, 1861 (at: http://query.nytimes.com/gst/abstract.html?res=9804EFDD113FEE34BC4 A53DFB467838A679FDE). See also "Why was the Tombs the Execution Site for the Only American Ever Hanged as a Slave Trader?" *New York Correction History Society*, February 2003 (at: http://www.correctionhistory.org/html/chronicl/tombs/gordon/whytombs1. htm).
393. *Debates and Proceedings* (Washington, DC: Gales and Seaton, 1851), Vol. 11, p. 1332, "An Act in Addition to an Act, Entitled, 'An Act in Addition to an Act Regulating the Grants of Land Appropriated for Military Services, and for the Society of the United Brethren for Propagating the Gospel Among the Heathen,'" **April 26, 1802;** *Debates and Proceedings* (1851), Vol. 12, p. 1602, "An Act to Revive and Continue in Force An Act in Addition to an Act, Entitled, 'An Act in Addition to an Act Regulating the Grants of Land Appropriated for Military Services, and for the Society of the United Brethren for Propagating the Gospel Among the Heathen,' and for Other Purposes," **March 3, 1803;** *American State Papers: Documents, Legislative and Executive of the Congress of the United States: Indian Affairs*, Walter Lowrie and Matthew St. Claire Clarke, editors (Washington, DC: Gales and Seaton 1832), Vol. I, p. 687, "The Kaskaskia and Other Tribes," Article 3, **October 31, 1803;** *Debates and Proceedings* (1852), Vol. 12, p. 1279, "An Act Granting Further Time for Locating Military Land Warrants, and for Other Purposes," **March 19, 1804;** *American State Papers: Indian Affairs* (1834), Vol. II, p. 133, "Treaty with the Tyandots, Senecas, Delawares, Shawanees, Pattawatnies, Ottawas and Chippewas," Article 16, **September 29, 1817;** *American State Papers: Indian Affairs* (1834), Vol. II, p. 220, "Treaty with the Osage," Article 10, **June 2, 1825;** *Journal of the House of Representatives of the United States* (Washington, DC: Gales & Seaton, 1828), Vol. 22, p. 16, **December 2, 1828;** *Journal of the Senate of the United States of America* (Washington, DC: Duff Green, 1828), Vol. 18, pp. 12–13, **December 2, 1828;** Article VI; Andrew Jackson, *Society of Christian Indians, Message from the President of the United States to Senate and House of Representatives* (Washington, DC: 1830), 21st Congress, 1st Session, Doc. No. 34 (from an original in the private collection of David Barton); *Public Statutes at Large* (Boston: Little, Brown and Company, 1856), Vol. V, pp. 766, 771, 776–777, 28th Congress, 2nd Session, "An Act Making Appropriations for the Current and Contingent Expenses of the Indian Department and for Fulfilling Treaty Stipulations with the Various Indian Tribes, for the Fiscal Year Commencing on the First Day of July, Eighteen Hundred and Forty-Five and Ending on the Thirtieth Day of June, Eighteen Hundred and Forty Six," **March 3, 1845;** *Statutes at Large and Treaties* (1862), Vol. IX, p. 545, "An Act Making Appropriations for the Current and Contingent Expenses of the Indian Department and for Fulfilling Treaty Stipulations with Various Indian Tribes for the Year Ending June the Thirtieth, One Thousand Eight Hundred and Fifty-One," **September 30, 1850;** *Public Statutes* (1862), Vol. IX, p. 575, "An Act Making Appropriations for the Current and Contingent Expenses of the Indian Department for the Fulfilling Treaty Stipulations with Various Indian Tribes for the Year Ending June the Thirtieth, One Thousand Eight Hundred and Fifty-Two," **February 27, 1851;** *Statutes at Large* (1855), Vol. X, p. 41, "An Act Making Appropriations for the Current and Contingent Expenses of the Indian Department for the Fulfilling Treaty Stipulations with Various Indian Tribes for the Year Ending June Thirtieth, One Thousand Eight Hundred and Fifty-Three," **August 30, 1852;** *Statutes at Large* (1855), Vol. X, p. 226, "An Act Making Appropriations for the Current and Contingent Expenses of the Indian Department for the Fulfilling Treaty Stipulations with Various Indian Tribes for the Year Ending

June Thirtieth, One Thousand Eight Hundred and Fifty-Four," **March 3, 1853**; *Statutes at Large* (1859), Vol. XI, p. 69, "An Act Making Appropriations for the Current and Contingent Expenses of the Indian Department for the Fulfilling Treaty Stipulations with Various Indian Tribes for the Year Ending June Thirtieth, One Thousand Eight Hundred and Fifty-Seven," **August 18, 1856**; *Statutes at Large* (1863), Vol. XII, p. 1194, "Proclamation: Treaty with the Pottawatomies." **November 15, 1861**, Art. VI; *Statutes at Large* (1868), Vol. XIV, p. 650, "Treaty Between the United States of America and the Nez Perce Tribe of Indians," **June 9, 1863**; *Statutes at Large* (1868), Vol. XIV, pp. 309-310, "Chap. CCXCV—An Act for the Relief of the Trustees and Stewards of the Mission Church of the Wyandot Indians," **July 28, 1866**; *Journal of the Senate of the United States of America* (Washington, DC: Government Printing Office, 1871), 41st Cong., 3rd Sess., p. 22, message from the President, **December 5, 1870**; etc.

394. *Reports of Committees of the House of Representatives Made During the First Session of the Thirty-Third Congress* (Washington, DC: A. O. P. Nicholson, 1854), Rep. No. 124, "Chaplains in Congress and in the Army and Navy," pp. 6, 8–9.

395. *The Reports of Committees of the Senate of the United States for the Second Session of the Thirty-Second Congress, 1852-53* (Washington, DC: Robert Armstrong, 1853), Rep. Com. No. 376, p. 3.

396. *Journal of the House of Representatives of the United States: Being the First Session of the Thirty-Fourth Congress* (Washington, DC: Cornelius Wendell, 1855 [sic]), p. 354, January 23, 1856.

397. "Capitol Rotunda," *Architect of the Capitol* (at: https://www.aoc.gov/capitol-buildings/capitol-rotunda) (accessed on December 28, 2017).

398. See descriptions of these scenes from the Architect of the Capitol: "Baptism of Pocahontas" (at: https://www.aoc.gov/art/historic-rotunda-paintings/baptism-pocahontas); "Discovery of the Mississippi by De Soto" (at: https://www.aoc.gov/art/historic-rotunda-paintings/discovery-mississippi-by-de-soto); "Embarkation of the Pilgrims" (at: https://www.aoc.gov/art/historic-rotunda-paintings/embarkation-pilgrims); "Landing of Columbus" (at: https://www.aoc.gov/art/historic-rotunda-paintings/landing-columbus).

399. See a list of statues from the Architect of the Capitol here: https://www.aoc.gov/the-national-statuary-hall-collection.

400. Paul M. Pearson and Philip M. Hicks, *Extemporaneous Speaking* (New York: Hinds, Noble & Eldredge, 1912), p. 177, Woodrow Wilson, "The Bible and Progress," May 7, 1911.

401. Lyndon B. Johnson, "Remarks at the Lighting of the Nation's Christmas Tree," *The American Presidency Project*, December 22, 1963 (at: http://www.presidency.ucsb.edu/ws/?pid=26587).

402. Richard Nixon, "Remarks at the National Prayer Breakfast," *The American Presidency Project*, February 1, 1972 (at: http://www.presidency.ucsb.edu/ws/?pid=3597).

403. Harry S. Truman, "Exchange of Messages With Pope Pius XII," *The American Presidency Project*, August 28, 1947 (at: http://www.presidency.ucsb.edu/ws/?pid=12746).

404. Harry S. Truman, "Address at the Lighting of the National Community Christmas Tree on the White House Grounds," *The American Presidency Project*, December 24, 1946" (at: http://www.presidency.ucsb.edu/ws/?pid=12569).

405. John Adams, *The Works of John Adams, Second President of the United States,* Charles Francis Adams, editor (Boston: Little, Brown and Company, 1856), Vol. X, pp. 45–46, to Thomas Jefferson on June 28, 1813; **Thomas Jefferson,** *The Papers of Thomas Jefferson,* Barbara Oberg, editor (Princeton, NJ: Princeton University Press, 2008), Vol. 35, p. 545, to Gouverneur Morris on November 1, 1801; **John Quincy Adams,** *An Oration Delivered Before the Inhabitants of the Town of Newburyport at Their Request on the Sixty-First Anniversary of the Declaration of Independence, July 4, 1837* (Newburyport, MA: Charles Whipple, 1837), pp. 17–18; **John Tyler,** "Proclamation," *The American Presidency Project,* April 13, 1841 (at: http://www.presidency.ucsb.edu/ws/?pid=67344); **President Benjamin Harrison,** "Executive Order," *The American Presidency Project,* June 7, 1889, quoting Abraham Lincoln's November 1862 Executive Order (at: http://www.presidency.ucsb.edu/ws/?pid=71024); **Zachary Taylor:** *Testimony of Distinguished Laymen to the Value of the Sacred Scriptures, Particularly in their Bearing on Civil and Social Life* (New York: American Bible Society, 1854), p. 24; "The President and the Bible," *New York Semi-Weekly*

Tribune, Wednesday, May 9, 1849, Vol. IV, No. 100, p. 1; **James Buchanan:** *Journal of the Senate of the United States of America* (Washington, DC: George W. Bowman, 1859–1860), 36th Cong., 1st Sess., p. 30, message of the President, December 27, 1859; *A Compilation of the Messages and Papers of the Presidents 1789-1897*, James Richardson, editor (Washington, DC: 1899), Vol. V, p. 468, Message from Buchanan to the Senate on the Arrest of William Walker in Nicaragua, January 7, 1858; **Abraham Lincoln:** General Order of Abraham Lincoln, issued November 15, 1862, from an original in the private collection of David Barton; Abraham Lincoln, *Complete Works of Abraham Lincoln*, John Nicolay and John Hay, editors (Lincoln Memorial University, 1894), Vol. VI, p. 184, First Inaugural Address, March 4, 1861; **Ulysses S. Grant:** *Journal of the Senate of the United States of America* (Washington, DC: Government Printing Office, 1871), 41st Cong., 3rd Sess., p. 10, message from the President, December 5, 1870; *Journal of the Senate of the United States of America* (Washington, DC: Government Printing Office, 1872), 42nd Cong., 2nd Sess., p. 10, message from the President, December 4, 1871; *Journal of the Senate of the United States of America* (Washington, DC: Government Printing Office, 1874), 43rd Cong., 2nd Sess., p. 105, message from the President, January 13, 1875; **William McKinley:** James D. Richardson, *A Compilation of Messages and Papers of the Presidents* (New York: Bureau of National Literature 1897), p. 6292, William McKinley to the Congress of the United States, December, 1897; **Franklin D. Roosevelt,** "Address at Dedication of Great Smoky Mountains National Park," *The American Presidency Project*, September 2, 1940 (at: http://www.presidency.ucsb.edu/ws/?pid=16002); Franklin D. Roosevelt, "Campaign Address at Madison Square Garden, New York City," *The American Presidency Project*, October 28, 1940 (at: http://www.presidency.ucsb.edu/ws/?pid=15885); Franklin D. Roosevelt, "Radio Address of the President Announcing an Unlimited National Emergency," *The American Presidency Project*, May 27, 1941 (at: http://www.presidency.ucsb.edu/ws/?pid=16120); Franklin D. Roosevelt, "Message on Christmas Eve," *The American Presidency Project*, December 24, 1942 (at: http://www.presidency.ucsb.edu/ws/?pid=16213); Franklin D. Roosevelt, "Fireside Chat," *The American Presidency Project*, April 28, 1942 (at: http://www.presidency.ucsb.edu/ws/?pid=16252); etc.; **Dwight D. Eisenhower,** "Address Before the Council of the Organization of American States," *The American Presidency Project*, April 12, 1953 (at: http://www.presidency.ucsb.edu/ws/?pid=9816); and so forth.

406. *A General View of the Rise, Progress, and Brilliant Achievements of the American Navy, Down to the Present Time* (Brooklyn, 1828), pp. 70–71.

407. Thomas Jefferson, *The Writings of Thomas Jefferson*, Andrew A. Lipscomb, editor (Washington, DC: The Thomas Jefferson Memorial Association, 1903), Vol. V, p. 195, to William Carmichael on November 4, 1785.

408. Thomas Jefferson, *The Papers of Thomas Jefferson*, Julian P. Boyd, editor (Princeton, NJ: Princeton University Press, 1954), Vol. 9, p. 358, Report of Thomas Jefferson and John Adams to John Jay, March 28, 1786.

409. President Washington selected Col. David Humphreys in 1793 as sole commissioner of Algerian affairs to negotiate treaties with Algeria, Tripoli, and Tunis. He also appointed Joseph Donaldson, Jr., as Consul to Tunis and Tripoli. In February of 1796, Humphreys delegated power to Donaldson and/or Joel Barlow to form treaties. James Simpson, US Consul to Gibraltar, was dispatched to renew the treaty with Morocco in 1795. On October 8, 1796, Barlow commissioned Richard O'Brien to negotiate the treaty of peace with Tripoli. See, for example, Gardner W. Allen, *Our Navy and the Barbary Corsairs* (Boston: Houghton, Mifflin and Company, 1905), pp. 46, 52–56; Ray W. Irwin, *The Diplomatic Relations of the United States with the Barbary Powers* (Chapel Hill: The University of North Carolina Press, 1931), p. 84.

410. See, for example, the treaty with **Morocco:** ratified by the United States on July 18, 1787 (*Treaties and Other International Agreements of the United States of America: 1776-1949*, Charles I. Bevans, editor (Washington, DC: Department of State, 1976), Vol. IX, pp. 1278–1285); **Algiers:** concluded September 5, 1795; ratified by the U. S. Senate March 2, 1796; see also, "Treaty of Peace and Amity" concluded June 30 and July 6, 1815; proclaimed December 26, 1815 (*Treaties and Conventions Concluded Between the United States of America and Other Powers Since July 4, 1776* (Washington, DC: Government Printing Office,

1889), pp. 1–15); **Tripoli:** concluded November 4, 1796; ratified June 10, 1797; see also, "Treaty of Peace and Amity" concluded June 4, 1805; ratification advised by the U. S. Senate April 12, 1806 (*Treaties, Conventions, International Acts, Protocols and Agreements between the United States of America and Other Powers: 1776-1909,* William M. Malloy, editor (Washington, DC: Government Printing Office, 1910), Vol. II, pp. 1785–1793); **Tunis:** concluded August 1797; ratification advised by the Senate, with amendments, March 6, 1798; alterations concluded March 26, 1799; ratification again advised by the Senate December 24, 1799 (*Treaties, Conventions, International Acts, Protocols and Agreements between the United States of America and Other Powers: 1776-1909,* William M. Malloy, editor (Washington, DC: Government Printing Office, 1910), Vol. II, pp. 1794–1799).

411. *The American Diplomatic Code, Embracing A Collection of Treaties and Conventions Between the United States and Foreign Powers from 1778 to 1834,* Jonathan Elliot, editor (Washington, DC: Jonathan Elliot, 1834), Vol. I, pp. 473–479, "Treaty with Morocco," signed in January, 1787, Articles 6, 11, & 21; Vol. I, pp. 479–489, "Treaties with Algiers," signed on November 28, 1795, Articles 16 & 17; and "Treaties with Algiers," signed on July 3, 1815; Vol. I, pp. 492–493, "Treaties with Algiers," signed on December 23, 1816), Articles 14 & 15; pp. 498–501, "Treaties with Tripoli," signed on January 3, 1797, Article 11; pp. 501–506, "Treaties with Tripoli," signed on June 4, 1805, Article 14; and so forth.

412. (See general bibliographic information from footnote 71 for each of these references) **Morocco:** see Articles 10, 11, 17, and 24; **Algiers:** See Treaty of 1795, Article 17, and Treaty of 1815, Article 17; **Tripoli:** See Treaty of 1796, Article 11, and Treaty of 1805, Article 14; **Tunis:** See forward to Treaty.

413. *Acts Passed at the First Session of the Fifth Congress of the United States of America* (Philadelphia: William Ross, 1797), pp. 43–44, "Treaty of Peace and Friendship Between the United States of America and the Bey and Subjects of Tripoli of Barbary," signed November 4, 1796.

414. J. Fenimore Cooper, *The History of the Navy of the United States of America* (Philadelphia: Thomas, Cowperthwait & Co., 1847), pp. 147–151. See also *A Compilation of the Messages and Papers of the Presidents: 1789-1897,* James D. Richardson, editor (Washington, DC: Published by Authority of Congress, 1899), Vol. I, p. 193, from Washington's "Eighth Annual Address," December 7, 1796.

415. *Dictionary of American Naval Fighting Ships* (1968), Vol. III, pp. 521–523, shown at "John Adams," Hazegrey.org (at: http://www.hazegray.org/danfs/frigates/j_adams.htm) (accessed on December 29, 2017).

416. Charles Prentiss, *The Life of the Late Gen. William Eaton: Several Years an Officer in the United States' Army, Consul at the Regency of Tunis on the Coast of Barbary, and Commander of the Christian and Other Forces that Marched From Egypt Through the Desert of Barca, in 1805, and Conquered the City of Derne, Which Led to the Treaty of Peace Between the United States and the Regency of Tripoli* (Brookfield, MA: E. Merriam & Co., 1813), p. 150, from General Eaton to Timothy Pickering on July 4, 1800.

417. Prentiss, pp. 92–93, from General Eaton to Timothy Pickering on June 15, 1799.

418. Prentiss, p. 146, from General Eaton to Mr. Smith on June 27, 1800.

419. Prentiss, p. 185, from General Eaton to General John Marshall on September 2, 1800.

420. *Naval Documents Related to the United States Wars with the Barbary Powers,* Claude A. Swanson, editor (Washington, DC: Government Printing Office, 1939), Vol. I, pp. 451, "To Secretary of State from Richard O'Brien, U. S. Consul General, Algiers," May 12, 1801, 453–454, "To Nicholas C. Nissen, Danish Consul General, Tripoli, from James L. Cathcart, U. S. Consul, Tripoli," May 15, 1801. See also Glen Tucker, *Dawn Like Thunder: The Barbary Wars and the Birth of the U. S. Navy* (Indianapolis: Bobbs-Merrill Company, 1963), p. 127.

421. Thomas Jefferson, *The Papers of Thomas Jefferson,* Barbara Oberg, editor (Princeton, NJ: Princeton University Press, 2008), Vol. 35, p. 545, to Gouverneur Morris on November 1, 1801.

422. See, for example, Prentiss, p. 325, from Eaton's journal, April 8, 1805; and Prentiss, p. 334, from Eaton's journal, May 23, 1805.

423. Charles Prentiss, *The Life of the Late Gen. William Eaton; Several Years an Officer in the United States' Army, Consul at the Regency of Tunis on the Coast of Barbary, and Com-*

mander of the Christian and Other Forces That Marched from Egypt Through the Desert of Barca, in 1805, and Conquered the City of Derne, Which Led to the Treaty of Peace Between the United States and the Regency of Tripoli; Principally Collected from His Correspondence and Other Manuscripts (Brookfield, MA: E. Merriam & Co., 1813).

424. Jeff Jacoby, "The freedom not to say 'amen,'" *Jewish World Review*, February 1, 2001 (at: http://www.jewishworldreview.com/jeff/jacoby020101.asp).

425. Aaron Zelman, "An open letter to my Christian friends," *Jews for the Preservation of Firearms Ownership* (at: http://www.jpfo.org/filegen-a-m/christian-selfdefense.htm).

426. Dennis Prager, "Books, Arts & Manners: God & His Enemies—Review," *BNet*, March 22, 1999.

427. Don Feder, *A Jewish Conservative Looks at Pagan America* (Lafayette, LA: Huntington House Publishers, 1993), pp. 59–60.

428. Don Feder, "Yes—Once and For All—American is a Christian Nation," February 16, 2005 (at: http://www.catholicleague.org/yes-once-and-for-all-america-is-a-christian-nation/).

429. Don Feder, "The Jewish Case for Merry Christmas," December 8, 2006 (at: http://theroadtoemmaus.org/RdLb/31JdXn/Jd/Jews&Xmas.htm).

430. Rabbi Daniel Lapin, "A Rabbi's Warning to U. S. Christians," *World Net Daily* January 13, 2007 (at: http://www.wnd.com/2007/01/39672/).

431. Rabbi Daniel Lapin, "Which Jews does the ADL really represent?" *WorldNetDaily*, August 25, 2006 (at: http://www.wnd.com/2006/08/37614/).

432. *Wallace v. Jaffree*, 472 U. S. 38, 106-107 (1984), Rehnquist, J. (dissenting).

433. Isaac Kramnick and R. Laurence Moore, *The Godless Constitution* (New York: W.W. Nortion & Company, 1996) p. 179.

434. Donald S. Lutz, "The Relative Influence of European Writers on Late Eighteenth Century American Political Thought," *American Political Science Review*, Vol. 78, Issue 1, March 1984, p. 191.

435. Lutz, "Relative Influence," pp. 191–193; see also Lutz, *The Origins of American Constitutionalism* (Baton Rouge, LA: Louisiana State University Press, 1988), pp. 141–142.

436. *Ex parte Newman*, 9 Cal. 502, 509 (1858).

437. *City Council of Charleston v. S. A. Benjamin*, 2 Strob. 508, 518-521 (Sup. Ct. S.C. 1846)

438. See, for example, *Holy Trinity Church v. U. S.*, 143 U.S. 457 (1892); *City Council of Charleston v. S.A. Benjamin*, 2 Strob. 508, 518-520 (Sup. Ct. S.C. 1846); *State v. Ambs*, 1854 WL 453 (Sup.Ct.Mo. 1854); *John Neal v. William F. Crew*, 1852 WL 1390 (Sup. Ct. Ga. 1852); *Doremus v. Bd. Of Ed. Of the Borough of Hawthorne*, 71 A.2d 732, 7 N.J. Super. 442 (1950); *State v. Chicago, B. & Q. R. Co.*, 143 S.W. 785, 803 (Mo. 1912); and many others.

439. James Madison, *The Writings of James Madison*, Gaillard Hunt, editor (New York: G. P. Putnam's Sons, 1904), Vol. V, p. 30, to Thomas Jefferson on October 24, 1787.

440. *Reports of the Proceedings and Debates of the Convention of 1821, Assembled for the Purpose of Amending The Constitution of the State of New York* (Albany, NY: E. and E. Hosford, 1821), p. 575, Rufus King, October 30, 1821.

441. John Adams, *The Works of John Adams*, Charles Francis Adams, editor (Boston: Little, Brown and company, 1854), Vol. IX, p. 229, to the Officers of the First Brigade of the Third Division of the Militia of Massachusetts on October 11, 1798.

442. John Witherspoon, *Lectures on Moral Philosophy* (Princeton, NJ: Princeton University Press, 1912), p. 130, "Lecture XVI: Of Oaths and Vows."

443. George Washington, *Address of George Washington, President of the United States, and Late Commander in Chief of the American Army, to the People of the United States, Preparatory to His Declination* (Baltimore: George and Henry S. Keatinge, 1796), p. 23.

444. Noah Webster, *Letters to a Young Gentleman Commencing His Education* (New Haven: S. Converse, 1823), pp. 18–19, Letter 1; see also a similar comment in Noah Webster, *History of the United States* (New Haven: Durrie & Peck, 1832), pp. 336–337, ¶49, although the Scripture citation in this work is closer to 2 Samuel 23:3 than Exodus 18:21.

445. John Witherspoon, *The Works of John Witherspoon* (Edinburgh: J. Ogle, 1815), Vol. V, pp. 266–267, from "A Sermon Delivered at a Public Thanksgiving after Peace."

446. From a handwritten manuscript of Dr. Benjamin Rush in the private collection of David Barton. In that work, Dr. Rush lists several headings, and under the heading, verses that he

believed pertained to that subject. Under the heading, "Government" in his manuscript, Dr. Rush lists Exodus 18:21 as an applicable verse.

447. For a full explanation of this point, and the use of this verse by the Founders, see *The Founders Bible* (Newbury Park, CA: Shiloh Road Publishers, 2012), the commentary for Jeremiah 17:9. (Cited from John Adams, *A Defense of the Constitutions of Government of the United States of America* (London: John Stockdale, 1794), Vol. III, p. 289, "Letter VI. The Right Constitution of a Commonwealth, examined"; and John Adams, *The Works of John Adams*, Charles Francis Adams, editor (Boston: Charles C. Little and James Brown, 1851), Vol. III, p. 443, "On Private Revenge III," published in the *Boston Gazette*, September 5, 1763.

448. George Washington, *Address of George Washington, President of the United States, and Late Commander in Chief of the American Army, to the People of the United States, Preparatory to His Declination* (Baltimore: George and Henry S. Keating, 1796), p. 22; Alexander Hamilton, James Madison, John Jay, *The Federalist, on the New Constitution Written in the Year 1788* (Washington, DC: Jacob Gideon, Jr., 1818), p. 100, No. XVI by Alexander Hamilton.

449. "Breakfast in Washington," *Time Magazine*, February 15, 1954 (at: http://www.time.com/time/magazine/article/0,9171,936197,00.html).

450. See, for example, *Lilly v. Virginia*, 527 U. S. 116, 141 (1999), Breyer, J., (concurring).

451. Charles Alan Wright, *et al.*, *Federal Practices & Procedure Federal Rules of Evidence* (New York: West Publishing Co., 2010), Vol. 30, sec. 6342, pp. 200–207, 212–214, 234–246.

452. Alexander Hamilton, James Madison, John Jay, *The Federalist, on the New Constitution Written in the Year 1788* (Washington, DC: Jacob Gideon, Jr., 1818), p. 224, James Madison, Federalist No. 37. See also *The Federalist* (1818), p. 14, John Jay, Federalist No. 2; p. 123, James Madison, Federalist No. 20 for other acknowledgments of the blessings of Providence upon America.

453. Alexander Hamilton, John Jay, James Madison and Other Men of Their Time, *The Federalist and Other Contemporary Papers on the Constitution of the United States*, E.H. Scott, editor (New York: Scott, Foresman and Company, 1894), p. 646, Alexander Hamilton to Mr. Childs, October 17, 1787.

454. George Washington, *The Writings of George Washington*, Jared Sparks, editor (Boston: Little, Brown and Company, 1858), Vol. IX, p. 317, to Marquis de Lafayette, February 7, 1788. See also *The Writings of George Washington*, Jared Sparks, editor, (Boston: Ferdinand Andrews, 1840), Vol. XII, p. 145, to the city leadership of Philadelphia, April 20, 1789, in which he said: "When I contemplate the Interposition of Providence, as it was visibly manifested, in guiding us thro' the Revolution in preparing us for the reception of a General Government, and in conciliating the Good will of the people of America, towards one another after its Adoption, I feel myself oppressed and almost overwhelmed with a sense of the Divine Munificence."

455. George Washington, *Writings of George Washington*, Lawrence B. Evans, editor (New York: G. P. Putnam's Sons, 1908, p. 294n, to Marquis de Lafayette, May 28, 1788.

456. Benjamin Franklin, *The Works of Benjamin Franklin*, Jared Sparks, editor (Boston: Hilliard, Gray, and Company, 1840), Vol. V, p. 162, from "A Comparison of the Conduct of the Ancient Jews and of the Anti-Federalists in the United States of America."

457. Benjamin Rush, *Letters of Benjamin Rush*, L. H. Butterfield, editor (Princeton, NJ: American Philosophical Society, 1951), Vol. I, p. 475, to Elias Boudinot on July 9, 1788.

458. Thomas Ginsburg, Zachary Elkins, and James Melton, "The Lifespan of Written Constitutions" *University of Chicago Law School* (at: https://www.law.uchicago.edu/news/lifespan-written-constitutions) (accessed on January 2, 2018).

459. "Les Constitutions de la France" *Conseil Constitutionnel* (at: http://www.conseil-constitutionnel.fr/conseil-constitutionnel/francais/la-constitution/les-constitutions-de-la-france/les-constitutions-de-la-france.5080.html), accessed on January 2, 2018. See also, Bob Corbett, "List of Constitutions and Some Provisions" (at: http://faculty.webster.edu/corbetre/haiti/misctopic/constitution/listof.htm), accessed on January 2, 2018; Robert L. Maddex, *Constitutions of the World* (New York: Congressional Quarterly, 1995) p. 306, "Venezuela" (at: https://books.google.com/books?id=YBcCAwAAQBAJ&lpg=PT461&ots=h3Z9WEMv01&dq=Venezuela%2C%20twenty-five%20constitutions&pg=PT461#v=onepage

&q&f=false); Robert L. Maddex *Constitutions of the World* (Washington, DC: CQ Press, 2008), p. 132, "Ecuador" (at: https://books.google.com/books?id=YaA5DQAAQBAJ&lpg =PA132&ots=bw4uZHNfcI&dq=ecuador%20had%20twenty%20constitutions&pg=PA 132#v=onepage&q&f=false); "Constitutional history of Thailand," *ConstitutionNet* (at: http://www.constitutionnet.org/country/constitutional-history-thailand), accessed January 2, 2018; "Timeline of Constitutions," *Comparative Constitutions Project* (at: http://comparativeconstitutionsproject.org/chronology/), accessed on January 2, 2018.

460. US Patent and Trademark Office, "Extended Year Set - Patent Counts By Country, State, and Year Utility Patents" (at: https://www.uspto.gov/web/offices/ac/ido/oeip/taf/cst_utlh. htm), accessed on January 3, 2018; "U.S. and World Population Clock," *United States Census Bureau* (at: https://www.census.gov/popclock/), accessed on January 2, 2018. See also, "U.S. Population (Live)," *Worldometers* (at http://www.worldometers.info/world-population/us-population/), accessed on January 2, 2018. See also, "Record Year for International Patent Applications in 2016; Strong Demand Also for Trademark and Industrial Design Protection," *World Intellectual Property Organization* (at: http://www.wipo. int/pressroom/en/articles/2017/article_0002.html#designs), March 15, 2017; "Ranking of the 10 countries who filed the most international patent applications in 2016," *Statista* (at: https://www.statista.com/statistics/256845/ranking-of-the-10-countries-who-filed-the-most-international-patent-applications/), accessed on January 2, 2018.

461. "World GDP Ranking 2017," *Knoema* (at: https://knoema.com/nwnfkne/world-gdp-ranking-2017-gdp-by-country-data-and-charts), accessed January 2, 2017. See also, "U.S. GDP as % of World GDP," *YCharts* (at: https://ycharts.com/indicators/us_gdp_as_a_percentage_ of_world_gdp), accessed on January 2, 2018; Robbie Gramer, "Infographic: Here's How the Global GDP Is Divvied Up," *Foreign Policy* (at: http://foreignpolicy.com/2017/02/24/ infographic-heres-how-the-global-gdp-is-divvied-up/), February 24, 2017.

462. Aaron Earls, "Where are all the Megachurches?" *LifeWay: Facts & Trends*, June 5, 2017 (at: https://factsandtrends.net/2017/06/09/where-are-all-the-megachurches/).

463. George Barna and David Barton, *U-Turn* (Lake Mary, FL: Charisma House, 2014), 138.

464. "Religious Congregations in 21st Century America," *National Congregations Study* (December 2015), Table 2: Continuity and Change in American Congregations: Congregations' Perspective, p. 39. (retrieved from http://www.soc.duke.edu/natcong/Docs/NCSIII_ report_final.pdf).

465. Scott Jaschik, "Division in Christian Higher Ed," *Inside Higher Ed*, August 13, 2015 (at: https://www.insidehighered.com/news/2015/08/13/christian-college-group-faces-conflict-over-its-failure-expel-institutions-will-hire).

466. J.C. Derrick, "CCCU adopts new membership policy," *Baptist Press*, October 3, 2016 (at: http://www.bpnews.net/47652/cccu-adopts-new-membership-policy).

467. See, Ann Pietrangelo, "What Are Sexual Norms," *Healthline*, September 29, 2016 (at: https://www.healthline.com/health/what-are-sexual-norms); John Wihbey, "Changes in Americans' a titudes about sex: Reviewing 40 years of data," Journalist's Resource, May 2015 (at: https://journalistsresource.org/studies/society/public-health/changes-americans-attitudes-sex-reviewing-40-years-data); "Bestiality is much, much more common than you think," *Health 24*, February 20, 2015 (at: http://www.health24.com/Sex/Sexual-diversity/ Bestiality-is-much-much-more-common-than-you-think-20150218); "Acceptance of Polygamy Is at a Record High, and TV Might Explain Why," *U.S. News*, July 28, 2017 (at: https://www.usnews.com/news/national-news/articles/2017-07-28/us-acceptance-of-polygamy-at-record-high-and-tv-might-explain-why).

468. J. D. Unwin, "Monogamy as a Condition of Social Energy," *The Hibbert Journal*, Vol. XXV (1927), p. 662.

469. James Kent, *Memoirs and Letters of James Kent*, William Kent, editor (Boston: Little, Brown and Company, 1898), p. 123.

470. In the 366 days of 2016 there were 630 homicides, resulting in a rate of 1.72 per day. See, "2016 Crime in the United States: Table 3, by State, 2016," *FBI: Uniform Crime Reporting* (2016), at: https://ucr.fbi.gov/crime-in-the-u.s/2016/crime-in-the-u.s.-2016/topic-pages/ tables/table-3.

471. In 2016 there were 17,250 murders, making a rate of 47.1 per day. See, "2016 Crime in the United States: Table 1, by Volume and Rate per 100,000 Inhabitants, 1997–2016,"

FBI: *Uniform Crime Reporting* (2016), at: https://ucr.fbi.gov/crime-in-the-u.s/2016/crime-in-the-u.s.-2016/topic-pages/tables/table-1.

472. "Education Expenditures by Country," *National Center for Education Statistics* (May 2017), at: https://nces.ed.gov/programs/coe/indicator_cmd.asp.

473. "Illiteracy Statistics," *Statistic Brain*, July 22, 2017 (at: https://www.statisticbrain.com/number-of-american-adults-who-cant-read/).

474. The estimated total expenditure over the course of Elementary-Secondary education ranges widely from the $254,472 potentially spent in New York to the $78,900 in Utah. See, "Education Spending Per Student by State," *Governing*, December 8, 2017 (at: http://www.governing.com/gov-data/education-data/state-education-spending-per-pupil-data.html).

475. "The latest ranking of top countries in math, reading, and science is out—and the US didn't crack the top 10," *Business Insider*, December 6, 2016 (at: http://www.businessinsider.com/pisa-worldwide-ranking-of-math-science-reading-skills-2016-12), presenting results from the *PISA 2015 Results (Volume 1): Excellence and Equity in Education* (Paris: OECD Publishing, 2016).

476. James D. Agresti and Christopher E. Bohn, "Tax Facts," *Just Facts*, April 29, 2017 (at: www.justfacts.com/taxes.asp).

477. Alex Gray, "This is how much debt your country has per person," *World Economic Forum*, October 4, 2017 (at: https://www.weforum.org/agenda/2017/10/this-is-how-much-debt-your-country-has-per-person/).

478. James D. Agresti and Christopher E. Bohn, "Tax Facts," *Just Facts*, April 29, 2017 (at: www.justfacts.com/taxes.asp).

479. See *Acts and Resolutions of the United States of America Passed at the Second Session of the Forty-First Congress* (Washington, DC: Government Printing Office, 1870), "Public—No. 104." p. 127.

480. David and George recently co-authored the book *U-Turn* (Grand Rapids, MI: Frontline, 2014), and chapter 8 of that book has excellent and extensive information on where the Church was only a generation ago and where it is today.

481. The terminology *"Born Again"* is not the product of jargon introduced by tele-evangelists but rather it is the language of Jesus Himself, who two-thousand years ago announced, *"Very truly I tell you, no one can see the kingdom of God unless they are born again"* John 3:3.

482. "Barna Survey Examines Changes in Worldview Among Christians over the Past 13 Years," *Barna Group* (March 9, 2009), at: https://www.barna.com/research/barna-survey-examines-changes-in-worldview-among-christians-over-the-past-13-years/).

483. "Pastors of Conservative Churches Say They Won't Preach What the Bible Says about the Issues," *American Culture & Faith Institute* (2016), at: https://www.culturefaith.com/pastors-of-conservative-churches-say-they-wont-preach-what-the-bible-says-about-the-issues/.

484. "Pastors of Conservative Churches Say They Won't Preach What the Bible Says about the Issues," *American Culture & Faith Institute* (2016), at: https://www.culturefaith.com/pastors-of-conservative-churches-say-they-wont-preach-what-the-bible-says-about-the-issues/.

485. George Barna, "What God's People Want to Know" *WallBuilders*, March 21, 2017 (at: https://wallbuilders.com/gods-people-want-know/).

486. "Conservative Pastors Don't Always Preach What the Bible Teaches," *American Culture & Faith Institute*, November 12, 2013, (at: https://www.culturefaith.com/conservative-pastors-dont-always-preach-what-the-bible-teaches/).

487. "Pastors of Conservative Churches Say They Won't Preach What the Bible Says about the Issues," *American Culture & Faith Institute*, 2016 (at: https://www.culturefaith.com/pastors-of-conservative-churches-say-they-wont-preach-what-the-bible-says-about-the-issues/).

488. George Barna, "What God's People Want to Know" *WallBuilders*, March 21, 2017 (at: https://wallbuilders.com/gods-people-want-know/).

489. George Barna, "What God's People Want to Know" *WallBuilders*, March 21, 2017 (at: https://wallbuilders.com/gods-people-want-know/).

490. "Pastors of Conservative Churches Say They Won't Preach What the Bible Says about the Issues," *American Culture & Faith Institute* (2016), at: https://www.culturefaith.com/pastors-of-conservative-churches-say-they-wont-preach-what-the-bible-says-about-the-issues/.

491. George Barna and David Barton, *U-Turn* (Lake Mary, FL: Charisma House, 2014), 137.

492. George Barna and David Barton, *U-Turn* (Lake Mary, FL: Charisma House, 2014), 137–138.

493. George Barna and David Barton, *U-Turn* (Lake Mary, Florida: Charisma House, 2014), 136.

494. "State of the Bible 2015," *American Bible Society*, 2015, p.14. (retrieved at: https://www.americanbible.org/uploads/content/State_of_the_Bible_2015_report.pdf).

495. Christine Wicker, "Dumbfounded by divorce. Survey inspires debate over why faith isn't a bigger factor in marriage," *Dallas Morning News*, 2000 (at: http://www.adherents.com/largecom/baptist_divorce.html).

496. George Barna and David Barton, *U-Turn* (Lake Mary, FL: Charisma House, 2014), 146.

497. http://www1.cbn.com/cbnnews/us/2018/march/shocking-51-of-us-christians-have-never-heard-of-the-great-commission.

498. "Barna Survey Reveals Significant Growth in Born Again Population," *Barna Group* (March 27, 2006), at: https://www.barna.com/research/barna-survey-reveals-significant-growth-in-born-again-population/.

499. "Survey: Christians Are Not Spreading the Gospel," *American Culture & Faith Institute*, 2017 (at: https://www.culturefaith.com/survey-christians-are-not-spreading-the-gospel/).

500. "Faith and Lifestyle of Born Again Christians Evaluated in Extensive National Survey," *American Culture & Faith Institute*, 2017 (at: https://www.culturefaith.com/faith-and-lifestyle-of-born-again-christians-evaluated-in-extensive-national-survey/).

501. For full explanation see, James L. Garlow, *Partners in Ministry, Laity and Pastors Working Together* (Kansas City:Beacon Hill Press, 1981).

502. George Barna, "What God's People Want to Know" *WallBuilders*, March 21, 2017 (at: https://wallbuilders.com/gods-people-want-know/).

503. George Barna, "What God's People Want to Know" *WallBuilders*, March 21, 2017 (at: https://wallbuilders.com/gods-people-want-know/).

504. "LifeWay Research Finds Reasons 18- to 22-Year-Olds Drop Out of Church," *LifeWay*, August 7, 2007 (at: http://www.lifeway.com/Article/LifeWay-Research-finds-reasons-18-to-22-year-olds-drop-out-of-church).

505. George Barna and David Barton, *U-Turn* (Lake Mary, FL: Charisma House, 2014), 153.

506. See, Rabbi Daniel Lapin, *Business Secrets from the Bible: Spiritual Success Strategies for Financial Abundance* (Hoboken, NJ: John Wiley & Sons, 2014), "Secret #37: If There Is No Hebrew Word for Something, Then That Thing Does Not Exist."

507. James Wilson, *The Works of the Honorable James Wilson* (Philadelphia: Lorenzo Press, 1804), p. 466.

508. Robert Flood, *The Rebirth of America* (Philadelphia: The Arthur S. DeMoss Foundation, 1986), p. 12.

509. R. W. G. Vail, "A Check List of New England Election Sermons," *Proceedings of the American Antiquarian Society* (October 1935), p. 233.

510. See, William W. Sweet, *The Story of Religion in America* (Grand Rapids, MI: Baker Book House, 1973), Chapter XII: The War of Independence and the American Churches, Section II.

511. For an example see, Daniel Foster, *A Sermon Preached Before His Excellency John Hancock, Esq. Governour; His Honor Samuel Adams, Esq. Lieutenant-Governor; The Honorable The Council, Senate, and house of Representatives of the Commonwealth of Massachusetts, May 26, 1790, Being the Day of General Election* (Boston: Thomas Adams, 1790); William Gordon, *A Sermon Preached before the Honorable house of Representatives On the Day intended for the Choice of Counselors, Agreeable to the Advice of the Continental Congress* (Watertown, MA: Benjamin Edes, 1775); Isaac Beall, *A Sermon Delivered Before His Excellency Jonas Galusha, Esq. Governor; His Honor Paul Brigham, Esq. Lieut. Governor, The Honorable Council, and The House of Representatives, of the State of Vermont, at Montpelier, on the Day of General Election, Oct. 8,1812* (Montpelier, VT: Wright and Sibley, 1812); et al.

512. John Adams, *The Works of John Adams* (Boston: Little, Brown and Company, 1856), Volume X, p. 284. "To H. Niles, Quincy, February 13th, 1818."

513. See, Jonathan Mayhew, *Sermons Upon the following Subjects* (Boston: Richard Draper, 1775); *Christian Sobriety: Being Eight Sermons on Titus II.6. Preached with a Special View to the Benefit of the Young Men Usually Attending the Public Worship at the West Church in Boston* (Boston: Richard and Samuel Draper, 1763); and *Two Discourses Delivered*

October 9th, 1760. Being the Day appointed to be observed As a Day of public Thanksgiving For the Success of His Majesty's Arms, More Especially In the intire Reduction of Canada (Boston: Richard Draper, 1760); et al.

514. Jonathan Mayhew, *A Discourse Concerning Unlimited Submission and Non-Resistance to the Higher Powers; With Some Reflections on the Resistance Made to King Charles I* (Boston: D. Fowle, 1750).

515. Jonathan Mayhew, *A Discourse Concerning Unlimited Submission and Non-Resistance to the Higher Powers; With Some Reflections on the Resistance Made to King Charles I* (Boston: D. Fowle, 1750), pp. 41–44.

516. John Adams, *The Works of John Adams* (Boston: Little, Brown and Company, 1856), Volume X, p. 284. "To H. Niles, Quincy, February 13th, 1818."

517. See, Samuel Cooper, *A Sermon Preached Before His Excellency John Hancock, Esq. Governour, The Honourable The Senate, and The House of Representatives of the Commonwealth of Massachusetts, October 25, 1780. Being the Daye of the Commencement of the Constitution and Inauguration of the New Government* (Commonwealth of Massachusetts: T. and J. Fleet, and J. Gill, 1780); and, *A Sermon Upon Occasion of the Death of Our late Sovereign, george the Second. Preach'd Before His Excellency Francis Bernard, Esq; Captain-General and Governor in Chief, The Honourable His Majesty's Council, and House of Representatives of the Massachusetts-Bay in New-England, January 1, 1761* (Boston: John Draper, 1761).

518. John Adams, *The Works of John Adams* (Boston: Little, Brown and Company, 1856), Volume X, p. 191. "To Dr. J. Morse, Quincy, 5 December, 1815."

519. Charles Chauncy, *A Discourse On "the good News from a far Country." Deliver'd July 24th. A Day of Thanks-giving to Almighty God, throughout the Province of the Massachusetts-Bay in New-England, on Occassion of the Repeal of the Stamp-Act; appointed by his Excellency, the Governor of said Province, at the Desire of it's House of Representatives, with the Advice of his Majesty's Council* (Boston: Kneeland and Adams, 1766).

520. For a survey see Ellis Sandoz, *Political Sermons of the American Founding Era, 1730-1805* (Indianapolis: Liberty Fund, 1998).

521. John Adams, *The Works of John Adams* (Boston: Charles C. Little and James Brown, 1851), Vol. IV, p. 55. "Novanglus: or, A History of the Dispute with America, From its Origin, in 1754, to the Present Time; written in 1774, by John. No. IV."

522. See "Study View: Historical Sermons," *WallBuilders,* 2018 (at: https://wallbuilders.com/study-view/).

523. Charles Finney, "The Decay of Conscience," *The Independent,* December 4, 1873 (retrieved at: https://www.gospeltruth.net/1868_75Independent/731204_conscience.htm).

524. Charles Alan Wright & Kenneth W. Graham, Jr., *Federal Practice and Procedure* (West Group, 1997), Vol. 30, pp. 234–243.

525. There is such information available from many sources, including James Garlow, *Well Versed. Biblical Answers to Today's Tough Issues* (Washington, DC: Regnery Publishing, 2016); Wayne Grudem, *Politics According to the Bible. A Comprehensive Resource for Understanding Modern Political Issues in Light of Scripture* (Grand Rapids, MI: Zondervan, 2010); and *WallBuilders* (at: https://wallbuilders.com/).

526. George Barna, *Maximum Faith. Live Like Jesus* (George Barna, 2011 Kindle Edition), location 2734.

527. John Hancock, "The Boston Massacre," in *Oration of American Orators,* New York: The Co-Operative Publication Society, 1900, Volume I, p. 136.

528. See, Dennis Pollock, "George Whitefield - Evangelist Extraordinaire," *Spirit of Grace Ministries,* accessed January 7, 2018 (at: https://www.spiritofgrace.org/articles/nl_2017/00_whitefield.html); and Arnold Dallimore, *George Whitefield; the Life and Times of the Great Evangelist of the Eighteenth-Century Revival* (Carlisle: Banner of Truth, 1970).

529. Brian Ray, "Research Facts on Homeschooling," *National Facts on Homeschooling,* March 23, 2016 (at: https://www.nheri.org/research-facts-on-homeschooling/).

530. George and Karen Grant, *Just Visiting* (Nashville: Cumberland House Publishers, 1999), n.p., quoted by Roy Maynard, "Traveling by the Book," *World Magazine,* August 14, 1999 (p. 27).